Dred Scott's Advocate

Missouri Biography Series

William E. Foley, Editor

Dred Scott's Advocate

A Biography of

Roswell M. Field

Kenneth C. Kaufman

University of Missouri Press

Columbia and London

Library of Congress Cataloging-in-Publication Data

Kaufman, Kenneth C. (Kenneth Clarence), 1925–
    Dred Scott's advocate : a biography of Roswell M. Field /
  Kenneth C. Kaufman.
        p.   cm.
    Includes bibliographical references and index.
    ISBN 0-8262-1092-9 (alk. paper)
      1. Field, R.M. (Roswell M.), b. 1807.   2. Lawyers—
  Missouri—Saint Louis—Biography.   3. Scott, Dred,
  1809–1858—Trials, litigation, etc.   I. Title.
  KF368.F52K38   1996
  342.73'087—dc20
  [B]
  [347.30287]
  [B]   96-23848
                                                    CIP

Designer: Kristie Lee
Typesetter: BOOKCOMP
Printer and binder: Thomson-Shore, Inc.
Typefaces: Bembo, Runic Condensed, Bellevue

To Ken and John

Abbreviations

Dred Scott's Advocate

Introduction

On Friday, March 6, 1857, Chief Justice Roger B. Taney announced the decision of the United States Supreme Court in the case of *Dred Scott v. John F. Sandford.*[1] Scott, a Missouri slave, had taken his quest for freedom to the nation's highest tribunal after years of unsuccessful litigation in the lower courts.

The court's chamber, located then on the ground floor of the Capitol building in Washington, was filled to overflowing as the spectators anxiously listened to the weak and oftentimes barely audible voice of the aged justice as he read from the fifty-some pages of paper before him. During the two hours the justice spoke, not a person left the courtroom, and after Judge Taney finished there were many who were not certain they knew what exactly he had said.[2] But enough was understood by members of the press who were present in the courtroom to know that what they had heard that day was of great political significance. Dred Scott, the judge ruled, was not entitled to freedom because as a slave of African descent he was not a citizen of the United States and therefore had no right to sue in American courts. The judge then went on to rule that Congress had no authority to declare slavery unlawful in the territories, thus annulling the Missouri Compromise, which Taney said had been unconstitutional from its first enactment by Congress thirty-five years earlier.

The decision had an immediate impact. Within hours, the pronouncement was being reported to Americans throughout the land. The words of Judge Taney

1. Sanford's name was incorrectly spelled on the court records as "Sandford," probably a clerk's error.
2. Spectator reaction based on newspaper accounts. *St. Louis Leader,* March 7, 1857.

burned like fire on the pages of city and rural newspapers, widening the gulf that separated the factions in American political life and inflaming the passions of a nation that stood on the threshold of civil war.

During the almost century and a half that has elapsed since Judge Taney's pronouncement for the court, the Dred Scott case has remained perhaps the most memorable and significant case in the history of the Supreme Court. Few, if any, of the nation's legal controversies have equaled the Dred Scott case in historical interest or impact. In the years since, the decision has been seen by some as a decisive factor that brought about the Civil War.[3] Except for perhaps the famous *Marbury v. Madison* decision of 1803 and *Brown v. The Board of Education of Topeka, Kansas,* rendered in 1954, more has been written about *Dred Scott v. John F. Sandford* than any other case in the judicial history of the United States. And the public interest does not appear to be waning.

Within the past few decades historians such as Walter Ehrlich, Don E. Fehren-bacher, and Vincent C. Hopkins have written extensive works on the subject, building on a long tradition that began with Thomas Hart Benton's famous voluminous study of the decision written only months after Taney delivered it.[4] Historians have dissected the Dred Scott decision paragraph by paragraph and word by word. The ambiguity of the litigation, which covered some ten years from 1846 to 1857, has sent numerous historians back to courthouses and archives to re-cull and recopy the slowly yellowing court documents, seeking to find some scrap of evidence that might clarify some of the perplexing questions in the case. Comparative studies have encompassed not only the extensive legal aspects of the case but also its far-flung political and historic implications.

Almost without exception, historians over the past century and a half have focused their attention on the 1857 Dred Scott Supreme Court decision itself, emphasizing the decision's role in the events leading up to the Civil War. Still other historians have treated the decision's constitutional aspects, evaluating its landmark status in the judicial history of the Supreme Court. And lastly, others have studied the Dred Scott decision against the panorama of racial injustices suffered by African Americans through the centuries.

But long before *Scott v. Sandford* became an event leading up to the Civil War, before it became a landmark Supreme Court decision, and before it became another example of racial injustice, it was first and foremost a common legal action, not unlike hundreds of similar actions brought before the courts in antebellum times. On one side of the case was the plaintiff, and on the other was the defendant. In a judicial adversarial courtroom environment, attorneys for both sides sought and competed for a favorable verdict for the client they represented.

3. Henry A. Forster, "Did the Decision in the Dred Scott Case Lead to the Civil War?" 875.

4. [Thomas Hart Benton], *Historical and Legal Examination of that Part of the Decision of the Supreme Court of the United States in the Dred Scott Case which Declares the Unconstitutionality of the Missouri Compromise Act and the Self-Extension of the Constitution to Territories, carrying Slavery Along With It.*

Furthermore, while historians concentrated on the Dred Scott decision, they ignored and wrote little about the participants in this famous American courtroom drama, most of whom remain rather obscure individuals. With the possible exception of the Supreme Court justices themselves, no biographies have been written about these participants; their names are confined largely to the endnotes and the indexes on the back pages of the Dred Scott books. Even Dred Scott himself, lead player in the drama, remains a shadowy figure. For more than ninety years his grave was unknown and unmarked although it rested within the sight of the gravestones of some of Missouri's most prominent citizens. As for Harriet Scott, whose case for freedom moved almost unnoted through the courts in tandem with that of her husband, no one knows for certain what happened to her. The last history sees of Harriet is in the St. Louis alley hovel where she lived, bent over a washtub, doing laundry for a living.

Then there was fur trader and financier John F. A. Sanford, defendant in the federal case, and his sister, Irene Emerson, defendant in the state case; both nominally, at least, Dred Scott's masters. They fought the slave's efforts to obtain freedom with all the funds and legal talent they could muster, yet their motives—not to mention their characters—remain unclear to this day. As for Dred Scott's friends in Missouri who supported and apparently encouraged him, were they really his friends, or were they simply using him to further their own personal and political aims?

Of course, there were also the attorneys themselves, several on each side of the case. Quite often they played a more dominant role than the clients themselves. When the old court records reported, "Now comes the plaintiff by his attorney" or "Here comes the defendant by his attorney," it is impossible to determine whether the plaintiff or defendant was actually in the courtroom. The court records make clear, however, that the attorneys for the parties were present, even if their clients were not.

Historian Frederick Trevor Hill, in his book *Decisive Battles of the Law,* written almost a century ago, quite correctly observed that "the records of the courts afford the most illuminating foot-notes to history, often revealing the political and human forces at work upon the events in more dramatic and vivid guise than any other medium." But Hill goes on to say that unfortunately "the drama and significance of the court proceeding is lost in the dull official form of a law report." This has certainly been true of the renditions of the Dred Scott story that have been written during the past 140 years. The court reports do not tell us whether a witness became angered during his testimony or the plaintiff broke down in tears when an unfavorable verdict was read, and historians quite understandably are reluctant to fill in these unknown blank spaces. But, suggests Hill, what is needed if the legal case is "to be appreciated in its full historic value," is that the scene "must be vitalized and peopled with the human beings that dominated it."[5]

---

5. Frederick Trevor Hill, *Decisive Battles of the Law,* vii.

What follows, therefore, is a biography of one participant in the Dred Scott drama, a participant who played a major role in the Dred Scott case before the Supreme Court decision and while *Scott v. Sandford* was still only a local court case. He was an attorney for the plaintiff, Dred Scott, and his name was Roswell Martin Field. In the 1850s he was a well-known attorney in St. Louis, and he is remembered today—if he is remembered at all—as the attorney who made the decision to take Dred Scott's bid for freedom from Missouri to the United States Supreme Court. In doing that, he also took it from relative obscurity to national historic significance.

Roswell Field was generally considered "one of the ablest lawyers in the history of Missouri." A fellow lawyer who knew him well said of Field, "He was second to none and he was justly considered as standing in the front rank of the bar in the city and state." His legal reputation seemed to rest primarily on his talents as a "close, logical reasoner," an ability that "was not excelled" by any other attorney in St. Louis or Missouri. When it came to influence, his peers said, there was no one else in the state "whose opinions carried more weight."[6]

Given this reputation and the recognized respect with which he was held by others in his profession, how did it happen that Roswell M. Field became an attorney for an illiterate and penniless slave named Dred Scott? There were in St. Louis at that time more than 150 attorneys, many of whom had far more experience than Field did in handling slave cases. And of these, some had professional credentials, if not more impressive than those of Field, then at least equal to his. Field's reputation as a lawyer resulted from his successful handling of the multitude of land cases that came before the courts in St. Louis in those days. These involved the resolution of conflicts about land ownership and land boundaries growing out of often obscure and contrary land titles that had their roots in the city's early French and Spanish history. For Field and several other St. Louis lawyers who specialized in such land cases, this was a very challenging and lucrative practice, since the plaintiffs and defendants were often some of the more prominent and prosperous citizens of the city. Compared with slave cases, it was also a far more esteemed and reputable field of law, and, in antebellum St. Louis, a far less controversial way of making a living.

What reasons or circumstances prompted Roswell Field to become Dred Scott's attorney? What was it about the case that might have interested him? The answers to these questions remain elusive and obscure, but there are clues.[7] They are to

6. William Hyde and Howard L. Conard, *Encyclopedia of the History of St. Louis,* vol. 2, 740; W. V. N. Bay, *Reminiscences of the Bench and Bar of Missouri,* 236; Melvin L. Gray, "Recollections of Judge Roswell M. Field," 127; *Centennial Proceedings and Other Historical Facts and Incidents Relating to Newfane,* 46.

7. Field left behind no journal or diaries, nor are collections of his correspondence known to exist. After his death, his personal letters to his eldest son were destroyed in a fire. An iron safe in Field's law office, in which he kept "his private papers," mysteriously disappeared following

be found—if found at all—in the character of Roswell Field himself, his interests and beliefs, and the circumstances of the times in which he lived. It was the man himself and the events that shaped his life that drew him to Dred Scott and destined him to be remembered, not for his professional services to prominent St. Louis landowners who paid him well, but to an untutored black slave who paid him nothing at all.

---

his death. A fellow attorney in a deposition dated September 18, 1875, stated that Field "some two years before his death . . . presented me with a large iron safe and letter press, neither of them of much value. I removed them to my office at the northwest corner of 5th and Chestnut Streets . . . Mr. Field reserved the right to keep his private papers in the safe, he having one key and I the other. Just prior to his death he gave me the key he had and further despondent saith not." Estate papers of R. M. Field, Box 8870, St. Louis Probate Court (SLPC).

Prologue

Christmas Eve, 1854

Roswell Field and Dred Scott had some things in common. Both men had good venerable English surnames. Also, they had both been born Americans in the early days of the new Republic when memories of the American Revolution were still vivid. And like many thousands of their fellow countrymen, Dred Scott and Roswell Field had migrated as young men over the mountains and into the fertile Mississippi Valley during the early half of the nineteenth century. Now in the year 1854, both had passed out of their youthful years and into middle-age—Scott in his early fifties, Field in his late forties.

Yet to any American in 1854 who might have seen the two men together in a second-floor room at 36½ Chestnut Street in St. Louis, these similarities would have faded, and it would have been obvious that the two were really quite different. Roswell M. Field was white and free; Dred Scott was black and a slave. This difference alone would have made for a social fissure between the two men as deep and wide as the Mississippi River that flowed past the city's doorstep only a few yards away, a physical barrier separating the free state of Illinois and the slave state of Missouri. Roswell Field could cross the river and migrate to Illinois at a cost of ten cents for ferry fare. For Scott the cost could have been far greater—a good whip lashing being a certainty.[1]

---

1. The address 36½ Chestnut Street was located between Second and Third Streets on the south side of Chestnut. The site today is near the north leg of the Gateway Arch. *The St. Louis Directory for the Years 1854–5*; A captured runaway slave "could be assured of a flogging" at minimum. R. Douglas Hurt, *Agriculture and Slavery in Missouri's Little Dixie*, 254.

The Mississippi represented not only a physical barrier but also a cultural boundary. Whether Field and Scott liked it or not, they were required, as Missouri residents, to live by certain social customs that had been created to differentiate bondage from freedom. It would have been just such a custom that would have required Field to call Scott by his first name, "Dred," and Scott to call Field by his last name, adding for good measure a "mister" before it. The word "mister," according to English tradition, conveys no rank or honorific or professional title, but in St. Louis and other Southern communities of that time, its omission when addressing a white man would have been considered an affront and its application to a man of color a breach of social etiquette.[2]

Scott was frequently in Roswell Field's law office in 1854, and may well have been there just before Christmas that year, for one of Scott's tasks was to clean Field's office.

For well over a year, Roswell Field had been serving as Dred Scott's attorney in the slave's suit for freedom, a role for which Field received no fee. And it had been almost nine years earlier, in April 1846, when Scott had first filed his petition for freedom in the Missouri courts, commencing a prolonged legal litigation that thus far had proved completely fruitless. Roswell Field could well have sympathized with Dred Scott's impatience and frustration. Even Field, who understood far better than Scott the dilatoriness of the judiciary system, probably found the process sometimes vexing. For Field was aware that it was not only Dred Scott who languished in bondage day by day, month by month, and year by year as the litigation crept along, but also Scott's wife, Harriet, and their two daughters, Eliza and Lizzie, who were affected. These three souls would share Dred Scott's fate, to live a life of freedom or slavery, depending on the judgment of the court.[3]

Scott's janitorial duties in Field's legal office on Chestnut Street were probably not arduous. He likely swept the floor, wiped up the tobacco juice that some of Field's less-accurate clients had left on the floor around the brass spittoon, carried the ashes to a barrel in the alley behind, brought in some coal, made sure the hall and the steps leading up from the street were clean, and sometimes, when told, perhaps ran an errand for Field.[4]

But Dred Scott was not Field's slave. The very thought would have been abhorrent to Roswell Field. Neither was he the slave of C. Edmund LaBeaume,

2. In St. Louis and other communities in the South, it was not uncommon to use the diminutive "boy" when speaking to mature male slaves. Hurt, *Agriculture and Slavery,* 257.

3. Slason Thompson, *Life of Eugene Field,* 12; Typescript copy of petitions of Dred and Harriet Scott to the St. Louis Circuit Court, April 6, 1846, Dred Scott Collection, Missouri Historical Society, St. Louis (MHS); On February 12, 1850, it was agreed that since the two suits for freedom, one for Dred Scott and one for Harriet Scott, were "identical," any determination in Dred Scott's suit would apply to Harriet's as well. *Harriet, a woman of color v. Emerson,* record book 19, 339, St. Louis Circuit Court (SLCC).

4. John F. Lee to Mary Louise Dalton, February 10, 1907, Dred Scott Collection, MHS. Description of Field's law office and the furniture and items it contained are listed in an inventory of his estate, SLPC.

a prominent St. Louisan and fellow lawyer who for the past seven years had told Scott what to do. LaBeaume was responsible for Scott's actions and behavior and it was LaBeaume who had made arrangements for Scott to clean Field's office. LaBeaume, as a friend of Scott's, had simply hired the slave for five dollars a month from the sheriff of St. Louis. But the sheriff wasn't Scott's master either. The sheriff, at the court's direction, was simply given custody of Dred Scott while Scott's suit for freedom was in litigation and ordered to hire Scott and his family out until a decision was reached as to their ownership.[5]

Actually, if the truth were known, Dred Scott himself probably did not know who his real master was. More than a decade earlier, he had once been the slave of Dr. John Emerson, an army surgeon, but Dr. Emerson had died in 1843 and Scott and his wife had become through inheritance the slaves of Dr. Emerson's widow, Mrs. Irene Emerson, and her young daughter Henrietta.[6] But Mrs. Emerson was no longer in St. Louis, having moved in 1849 or 1850 to Massachusetts, where she had remarried. In departing St. Louis for a new life back east she had left the slaves behind, to look more or less after themselves. She depended on her brother, John F. A. Sanford, a wealthy financier now living in New York but with frequent business in his home state of Missouri, to handle her St. Louis affairs. This obligation Sanford had assumed, apparently without reluctance, and it was a responsibility that encompassed his sister's estate and included the slaves Dred, Harriet, Eliza, and Lizzie.

This tangled ownership arrangement left Dred Scott to shift for himself in the bustling frontier city of St. Louis, a condition that might have seemed a rather favored position for a slave but which was in reality a far more precarious existence than living in bondage on the master's property. In 1854 St. Louis had a population of 77,860, of whom 4,054 were African Americans. Of these, 2,656 were slaves, while the remaining 1,398 were—to use the then-current expression—free persons of color. It was the mounting number of the latter that those who were white saw as an alarming threat to the peace and welfare of the city and a bad—even dangerous—influence on other blacks still in bondage. Blacks, both slave and free, were therefore well advised to obey the many laws and rules set up by the city to govern their movements and actions: no loitering on the streets, no visiting about the city at night without carrying proper written permission, no unsupervised congregating in large numbers. Added to laws like these were the unwritten codes of conduct that set well-behaved blacks apart from those who by appearance and behavior were seen as being surly, aggressive, and even possibly dangerous.[7]

5. Typescript copies of St. Louis Circuit Court proceedings, Dred Scott Collection, MHS.

6. John Emerson estate papers, 1844, SLPC.

7. Federal census figures for 1850. By 1854 the total population in St. Louis had increased but the number of blacks had decreased. Charles van Ravenswaay, *Saint Louis, An Informal History of the City and Its People, 1764–1865,* 394; In September 1846, a committee of one hundred St. Louis citizens recommended measures that were adopted "for the protection of slave property

Blacks in bondage who lived with their masters could always look to their owners for protection if they should get into trouble or arouse suspicion. As property they had value to their masters, and both the law and neighborly respect for what belonged to others assured a degree of property protection. Free blacks carried with them a slip of paper that declared their status and offered some degree—meager though it often proved—of protection from random abuse. But Dred Scott and his family, living as slaves but with absentee owners and lacking any certificates of freedom, found that life could indeed be precarious and fraught with danger. Scott was a very likely target for abuse from every drunken rabble-rouser, irate shopkeeper, abusive petty official, or zealous policeman in the city.[8]

Thoughts like these could have been on the mind of Roswell Field as Dred Scott went about cleaning his law office. As for Dred Scott, the thought most likely on his mind, and the one he probably often discussed with Field, was, "Am I any closer to freedom?"

As Scott's attorney, what could Field have told his client? He could have told Scott that his suit for freedom was no longer in the Missouri courts but was now in federal court, but would Scott have understood what that meant? Was that good or bad? Field could also have told Scott that his suit for freedom was now before the United States Supreme Court in Washington, D.C.—the highest court in the land. But what did this mean to Scott? Twice the slave's suit had been before the Missouri Supreme Court in Jefferson City, yet Scott was still not free.

There is no way of speculating with any degree of certainty what Roswell Field might have told his client, except that Field most likely tried his best to give the slave some particle of hope that freedom might come about sometime. On occasion, he might well have added, perhaps more for his own assurance than for Scott's, that as Scott's lawyer he was doing his very best and that these things

---

against evil designs of abolitionists and others." These measures were aimed at preventing blacks "from leaving the home of their masters after dark," as well as "Negro preaching," which the committee felt was "dangerous to the happiness, quiet and safety of our slave population." J. Thomas Scharf, *History of St. Louis City and County,* 586; Black codes regulating slave conduct were first introduced into Missouri by French and Spanish authorities. The American code adopted in 1804 was "even more restrictive than the French and Spanish codes." William E. Foley, *A History of Missouri, Volume I, 1673–1820,* 175; "Every contact between the races, casual as well as formal, reminded Negroes of their inferiority. In ordinary conversations they were expected to show deference to all whites. Even the tone of voice or use of words could be offensive. Being 'out of place'—a phrase which covered the whole range of etiquette, might bring a quick reprisal on the spot or a trip to the Mayor's Court." Richard C. Wade, *Slavery in the Cities, The South 1820–1860,* 181.

8. An 1835 act of the Missouri legislature required free blacks to obtain a license from the county court. In addition, a free black had to put up a bond of one hundred to one thousand dollars or find a white person willing to act as security. Lorenzo Greene, Gary R. Kremer, and Antonio F. Holland, *Missouri's Black Heritage,* 64; "There was always the chance that the capricious action of some white would place the Negro before the magistrate on completely trumped-up charges." Wade, *Slavery,* 195.

simply took time. Had Field made such comments, they were probably not very reassuring, but they were probably the best that Field could have offered the poor man with any degree of honesty.

What Field perhaps failed to mention was something that was very much on his mind during the late days of December in 1854. This was the urgent need to find an attorney in Washington, D.C., to argue the case before the United States Supreme Court. Even more challenging, he had to find an attorney willing to handle the case without a fee. More than six months earlier he had written his good friend Montgomery Blair in Washington seeking Blair's assistance, but there had been no reply.[9] Blair, who had practiced law in St. Louis and was considered one of Missouri's ablest lawyers, would be a good attorney to handle the case before the Supreme Court, Field thought, but could Blair be enticed into taking the case?

Field may have noted that day on page one of the *Missouri Democrat* a notice that read:

> Montgomery Blair, attorney & counselor at law, Washington City, D.C. Will practice in the Supreme Court of the United States, and will also attend to cases in the land office at Washington. He will give his attention to licenses in the other departments at Washington requiring professional services.[10]

The notice seemed to indicate that Montgomery Blair was seeking additional clients for his new law practice in Washington—but probably not clients like Dred Scott, a slave without money. Montgomery Blair did not move from St. Louis to Washington and into the impressive mansion on Pennsylvania Avenue across the street from the White House to handle slave suits for freedom. Montgomery was a son of Francis Preston Blair, publisher of the *Washington Globe* and adviser to Presidents Andrew Jackson and Martin Van Buren, and his sights were aimed much higher than that—toward a possible presidential appointment or even a cabinet post. But Dred Scott's case was special, so Field thought. There were some solid legal precedents to support Scott's bid for freedom, and Missouri's highest court had shamelessly ignored them. Field would have to make Blair aware of these arguments. He would have to contact Montgomery Blair again to make another plea for assistance.

Field's Chestnut Street law office was in the heart of the St. Louis business district, and his home was some eight blocks distant, on South Fifth Street, one door north

9. The letter was dated May 25, 1854. William Earnest Smith, *The Francis Preston Blair Family in Politics,* 385.

10. *St. Louis Missouri Democrat,* December 23, 1854; "Montgomery Blair came east from St. Louis in 1853 to live in it [Blair Mansion], and to be near his father while he practiced law in the Supreme Court of the United States." Smith, *Blair Family,* 185.

of Cerré Street. At this time of year, with the Christmas holiday only a day away, the narrow walks on each side of Chestnut would have been crowded with people, and the curbs lined with carriages and wagons. The *Missouri Democrat* had noted in its news columns that "the great event is indicated along our pavements by the crowds of people sauntering slowly by, dressed in fine clothes, with smiles upon their faces and curiosity in their eyes, as they inspect toy shops, candy windows, and show cases of all descriptions."[11]

The weather for December 23 was typical for St. Louis in winter. It had started to rain about midnight the night before and continued all that day. Now in early evening it had stopped, but a gray pall still hung over the city, a heavy mixture of fog and smoke. Down Chestnut Street some two blocks toward the river, barely discernible, was the giant white image of the steamboat *Martha Jewett* moored at the levee; it had arrived from New Orleans the day before laden with sugar, coal, 1,550 sacks of salt, and "a large number of immigrants." Described as an "elegant steamer" on which "passengers will find a pleasant trip," the boat was scheduled to depart again for New Orleans at 10 A.M. on Christmas Day. It was hoped the rain which fell on the city that day would improve the river, which was "at a stand," a condition that to St. Louisans was not only "exceedingly unpleasant," but even worse was "unfavorable to business."[12]

Field's direct route from his office to his home would have taken him up the steep incline of Chestnut from the levee to Fifth Street. Across from his office was Dennison and Richardson's coffeehouse, which would probably have been crowded with customers, all seeking something warm to offset the chill in the evening air.

A block further on at Fourth and Chestnut, diagonally across the street from E. K. Woodward's bookstore and opposite the Planters House, the city's most prestigious hotel, was Jacob Covert's cigar shop, often a meeting place where lawyers and others in the neighborhood stopped by, selected a cigar or some pipe tobacco, and acquainted themselves with the yet-unpublished news of events and happenings in St. Louis.

At Fifth and Chestnut Streets, two blocks from Field's law office and a block west of the cigar shop, was the massive courthouse, which occupied an entire block in the city's center. Its dome—still under construction—dominated the skyline, and from its gallery top on a clear day one could see the entire city spread out on the west bank of the Mississippi as its French founder, Pierre Laclède, had envisioned it some ninety years earlier.

11. Attorneys L. R. Kinsey and Samuel A. Holmes also had offices at the same address as Field's office. Of the 150 or so attorneys in St. Louis in 1854, about half of them had offices on Chestnut Street between Main and Fourth. *The St. Louis Directory for 1854*; The quote is from the *Missouri Democrat,* December 24, 1854.

12. *Missouri Democrat,* December 24, 1854.

There was nothing to distinguish Field's home on the east side of South Fifth Street from the neighboring houses between Poplar and Cerré Streets. It was one of a row of twelve identical red brick houses, each of which abutted the next without any space between. They were all three stories in height with eight identical windows facing the street, two on the first floor and three each on the second and third floors. Each house also had several white stone steps that led up from the brick sidewalk to equally white identical wooden front doors. The cluster of houses, Greek Revival in style, was known as "Walsh's Row," and as city houses they were not very different from hundreds of similar houses built in St. Louis during the mid-1800s.[13] They reflected none of the city's French heritage, being patterned after houses in Philadelphia, Baltimore, and Boston—a reflection of the changing origins of the city's many newly arrived inhabitants.

Here in this house on South Fifth is where Field spent most of his time when he was not at work in his law office, and here is where his growing family resided. On hot St. Louis summer evenings, Field would sit on his white stone steps and play his violin or flute to entertain his wife Frances and his three small sons, along with other neighborhood children who frequently collected around him.[14]

Sometime during that holiday weekend in 1854—for Christmas that year fell on a Monday—Roswell Field had occasion to remember the slave Dred Scott. Perhaps the recollection came in the evening as he sat silently in the parlor of his house, or perhaps it came in the morning as the bells rang out from a nearby church on Walnut Street, or maybe it came as he sat relaxed in his easy chair reading some correspondence or one of his favorite books from the nearby bookcase.

On that Christmas holiday weekend, whatever it was that brought to Roswell Field's mind thoughts about the slave Dred Scott can only be surmised, but it was sufficient to distract Field from the more joyful activities of Christmas Eve, and to move him to take up his pen and write a letter. It was a letter to his friend Montgomery Blair in Washington, and it was one Field had probably intended writing for several weeks. But now on Christmas Eve, he dipped the pen into the ink and on the top of the paper he wrote the date: December 24, 1854.

In the letter, Field reminded Montgomery Blair again, as he had six months earlier, that he had been employed to bring a suit in the federal courts for Dred Scott, whom he described as "a black man held in slavery" and as a man lacking "the means of paying counsel fees." But nonetheless, Field pointed out, the case would be coming before the Supreme Court and an attorney was needed in Washington to argue it.

Field then set forth his plea:

13. The house still stands in downtown St. Louis at 634 S. Broadway and is known today as the Eugene Field House and Toy Museum.
14. Bay, *Reminiscences*, 240.

If you or any professional gentleman at W[ashington] should feel content enough in the case to give it such attention as to bring it to a hearing and decision by the court, the cause of humanity may perhaps be subserved.

Truly your friend and serv't,
R. M. Field.[15]

15. Typescript copy of letter from R. M. Field to Montgomery Blair dated December 24, 1854, Dred Scott Collection, MHS.

Origins

An understanding of Roswell M. Field begins where the man himself began, in the mountains of southern Vermont. Here Field was born and here, for more than three decades, he lived and worked. He was planted and rooted in the hard granite Vermont hills, and throughout his life he never completely severed himself from the nourishment these roots provided. Years later, as death approached, he would speak longingly of Vermont, gazing upon a map of his native state that hung on the wall not far from his bed.[1]

Roswell Field's birthplace was atop a mountain called Newfane Hill, a lofty, conical summit overlooking, far below, the West River, a restless stream of clear cold water that tumbles out of these mountains over giant granite boulders and empties some ten miles farther south into the more placid waters of the Connecticut River. From Newfane village on Newfane Hill, the mountains stretch out in all directions, endlessly repeating themselves until they meet the far horizon.

Roswell Field's birth occurred on February 22, 1807, on what must undoubtedly have been a cold winter day—undoubtedly, because it was always cold on Newfane Hill in winter. The bitter raw winds whistled unimpeded through the boughs of the spruce and hemlock, which along with the rock maples, birch, and beech trees covered the mountain. The frigid northern blasts from Canada met no obstacles on Newfane Hill's summit, racking the settler's dwellings, rattling the windows, and awaking occupants "from their midnight slumbers, clinging to their bed posts."[2]

1. Eugene Field, "The Woman Who Most Influenced Me," 3; Roswell M. Field estate papers, SLPC.

2. Roswell M. Field family record, written in Field's handwriting, and folded and labeled in legal fashion as if they had once been part of a court record. Ludlow-Field-Maury Family

Roswell's father, Martin Field, wrote of these cold Newfane winters in a letter to his brother. "We have," he wrote, "nothing remarkable to tell of here except the severity of the cold which is almost beyond description . . . On the 24th Dec. it commenced with a most terrible cold storm. The thermometer stood all that day at 8 degrees below 0. By the 16th [of] January it was 10 degrees below 0, on the 18th 14 below and yesterday, January 20th, 13 degrees below. What we shall have next God only knows."[3]

But Roswell's father went on to add that the sleighing was excellent—a good thing, because it meant that the winding post road that connected the town of Newfane, where the Field homestead was located, to the outside world was open, and the mail could reach other nearby villages such as Townshend to the north and Brattleboro to the south. This was important to Newfane because it was the shire town, and was not only a trading center for the area but also home to Windham County's courthouse. It was also important to the livelihood of Martin Field, a lawyer and town selectman, and a prominent citizen among Newfane's several hundred inhabitants.[4]

The Field home in which Roswell was born was one of the largest of some twenty residences in Newfane. It was an impressive two-story frame house with a large stone center chimney that rose two stories within the house and exited from the top of a steep-pitched roof. Large windows, each containing eighteen small panes of glass, looked out from the rooms directly onto the town common. This common, located at the intersection of Newfane's most important roads—one going east down the mountain to the river, one south to Williamsville, and another west to Kenny's Pond—contained the courthouse, the jail, and the whipping post. Newfane also boasted a meetinghouse, an academy, two hotels—Townsley's and Jones's—three stores, and a variety of shops.[5] Now in winter, the town common was deep in snow, dissected by numerous trodden paths leading to the various buildings, some dusted with ashes to make them less slippery. But in the warm months, when the snows had melted, the town common was also the setting for most of the major gatherings that took place in Newfane. In contrast to the bleakness of the winter season, the hilltop in warm summer offered a place for

---

Papers, MHS; Field was named for his father's brother, Roswell Field, who was an attorney at Burlington, Vt. *Vermont Special Proceedings,* vol. 43, 87; The quote is from Rev. Hosea Beckley, *The History of Vermont,* 123.

3. Letter from Martin Field to Daniel Kellogg, January 20, 1812, Field Collection, Jones Library (JL).

4. *Directory of Windham County, Vermont, 1724–1884,* 248; Martin Field was Newfane Selectman in 1804, 1811, 1817, and 1818 and town treasurer from 1819 to 1825. Records, Newfane village office, Newfane, Vt.; Martin Field was also state's attorney for Windham County for ten years and "repeatedly represented Newfane in the General Assembly and Constitutional conventions." Frederick Clifton Pierce, *Field Genealogy,* 338.

5. Sketch of house, Field Collection, Windham County Historical Society (WCHS); Hand-drawn map of old Newfane, Collections, WCHS; *Directory of Windham County,* 260.

peaceful relaxation, fanned by the cooling winds from neighboring hills. Here as the July and August suns were declining, and the business of the day finished, the judges and lawyers from neighboring communities joined with the local residents on the green lawn of the common for tea parties, "indulging in social conversation, in glee and merriment," and relating stories of past times with "wit and humor." Here on the common Martin Field, resplendent in his black military uniform adorned with gold braid and epaulets, would also inspect the militia troops, his sword at his side encased in a highly polished and decorated brass scabbard. Field had been appointed by the governor of Vermont as general of the first division of the Vermont State Militia. He obviously esteemed the appointment, for throughout his life he was always addressed and spoken of as General Martin Field, and he had the brass door knocker on the front door of the Field homestead inscribed "General Martin Field."[6]

Martin Field built his house overlooking the town common shortly after he arrived in Newfane in 1800 as a young man of twenty-six, two years after graduating from Williams College. Born on February 12, 1773, in Leverett, Massachusetts, he was invited to settle at Newfane by Luke Knowlton, a Loyalist in the American Revolution and one of the original founders of the town in 1774. Knowlton, who was probably instrumental in having Newfane made a shire town, saw in his friend Martin Field a means of adding to Newfane's judicial stature and strengthening Newfane's claim to shire-town status. Two years later, on February 21, 1802, Martin Field married Esther Smith Kellogg of Amherst, Massachusetts, and brought her, as a twenty-one-year-old bride, to Newfane.[7]

A little more than a year after their marriage, on April 14, 1803, Esther gave birth to a son, Charles Kellogg. As the years unfolded, Charles would develop, as do many first-born children, into the surrogate head of the family, often looking after the younger siblings. Of all the Field children, he alone would remain in Vermont. More than a year later, on September 13, 1804, Martin and Esther had a second child, a daughter, whom they named Mary Hubbard. In the years to come, she would be the one to whom Roswell would turn for help. In doing so, Roswell was not to be disappointed, for Mary would become a strong, intelligent, and capable woman, admired greatly in Amherst, Massachusetts, where she lived. Roswell's birth followed three years after Mary's, and then Martin and Esther Field had their

6. Beckley, *History of Vermont,* 123; Martin Field uniform, Collections, WCHS; Governor's printed appointment, Kellogg Collection, Vermont Historical Society (VHS); Eugene Field, "The Woman Who Most Influenced Me," 4.

7. Charles Kellogg Field III, *A Genealogical And Biographical History of the Field Family of Massachusetts and Vermont and the French-Henry Families of Virginia and Texas,* 38; Luke Knowlton was a Loyalist and "in consequence of the great sacrifices he made in behalf of the British Government in the early part of the Revolutionary War" he received a large and valuable tract of land in Lower Canada. There are no indications that Martin Field shared the same Loyalist sentiments. *Newfane's First Century,* 35; Esther Smith Kellogg was born February 25, 1780. Charles Kellogg Field III, *Field Family,* 38.

last child, a son whom they named John Fisher. He was born on September 15, 1808.[8] Fisher, as he was called, seems to have been from the start a sibling who was destined to be overshadowed by the renown of his older brothers and sister. He, like Roswell, went out into the West; but whereas Roswell left his mark upon the West, Fisher simply disappeared into it.

The Field children undoubtedly had their blemishes and shortcomings, but these have been lost to time. What remains today in family genealogies and correspondence is a portrait of Martin and Esther Field as parents who doted on their children and worried about them. Like many parents, they also made personal sacrifices to assure a fuller life for their children. Esther's brother, Daniel Kellogg, wrote in a letter to a relative that "Esther thinks she has got the finest boys in these parts."[9]

From their New England backgrounds, Martin and Esther each brought to the marriage certain common characteristics that would influence Roswell Field as he matured. Both Esther and Martin evinced a strong self-reliance and a drive for personal achievement, character traits that Roswell was to demonstrate later, especially in his practice of law. Martin and Esther Field also displayed an interest in material wealth, or as they might have expressed it, visible proof of Yankee success in life—a temporal accomplishment that implied, in Puritan New England, a certain degree of divine favor as well. Neighbors were quick to point out, however, that it was Esther Field's "executive ability, combined with energy" that was responsible for the family's financial success. She was, they said, thrifty, industrious, and prudent in financial matters.[10]

Both Martin and Esther Field also shared artistic interests. Martin had a "strong passion" for music and was a "skillful player on the violin," playing that instrument throughout his life until in old age he became too deaf to distinguish musical notes. At an early age, Esther displayed a talent for painting. Before her marriage she decorated the walls of the parlor in her family's Amherst home with large murals of agricultural scenes from the nearby New England countryside, an accomplishment she would cite in later years with great pride.[11]

Both Esther and Martin also shared an avid interest in books and reading. They devoted time and resources to this activity, creating libraries for not only their own enjoyment and edification but also the enlightenment of their children. However, from the subjects and titles of the books each collected it is possible to detect a significant difference in their individual interests. Martin, it would seem, had a great

8. Charles Kellogg Field III, *Field Family*, 46.
9. Daniel Kellogg to Rufus Kellogg, January 25, 1811, Kellogg Collection, VHS.
10. The expression "Yankee proof of success in life" was used by Roswell Field in chiding his friend, Jonathan Bradley, for not evidencing greater wealth after so many years of practicing law. Abby Maria Hemenway, collator, *Vermont Historical Gazetteer*, vol. 5, 137; Pierce, *Field Genealogy*, 339.
11. Pierce, *Field Genealogy*, 14; Esther Field personal note, Field Collection, JL.

interest in the natural world, an interest that increased with age. Among Martin's books were the *Natural History of Birds, Fishes, Reptiles and Insects, Bigland's History of Animals,* and *Elements of Chemistry.* Esther's interests, on the other hand, were focused on religious topics. Among her personal books was a volume called *Solitude Sweetened,* three volumes of *Thadeus of Warsaw,* and *A Compendium of the Bible.* Years later, a grandson would note of Esther's reading, "Grandma was a life member of the American Tract Society, so her library was constantly increasing. . . . There was not in all of grandma's collection, as you can imagine, a book that could not with the utmost propriety be read on Sunday."[12]

The Field children would undoubtedly have noted that the literary interests of their parents differed. They would also probably have observed that their mother and father behaved somewhat differently in their social relations with friends and visitors to the home. They would have seen that Martin Field, as befitting a general in the state militia, was frequently jovial and an excellent storyteller when in the company of others. He was full of anecdotes and could tell a lengthy tale with inimitable grace. At social gatherings Martin Field was genial and friendly, full of humor. By contrast, Esther rarely reflected her husband's jocularity. As Martin joked and slapped his thigh in merriment, she remained quiet and sedate. As if concentrating on matters of a higher nature, she studiously avoided all levity and frivolity, and "never relaxed the gravity of her deportment."[13]

Such differences in Esther and Martin's reading interests and social behavior can perhaps be explained by differences in their family heritages. Martin Field could look back proudly to his fifth-great-grandfather, Sir John Field (1525–1587), an English astronomer, who was the first to introduce the Copernican system to England in 1543. It was primarily through his endeavors that the system's worth was advanced in England. In 1556 he published the first astronomical tables to appear in England. Sir John Field's grandson, Zechariah Field (1596–1666), sailed with his family for America, arriving in Boston in 1629; after withdrawing from the Connecticut churches he came upriver and settled at Hadley, Massachusetts, in 1657.[14]

Esther traced her lineage back to Samuel Smith, who came to Boston from England in 1634. A somber Congregationalist, he strictly conformed "to all the formulas, austerities and self-denying ordinances of the Calvinistic faith." His son and Esther's fourth-great-grandfather, Philip Smith, was a member of the Hampshire County Court that in 1683 accused Mary Webster of Hadley of being a witch. Mary Webster was later acquitted by a Boston jury and returned to

12. Collections, WCHS; Eugene Field, "The Woman Who Most Influenced Me," 3.
13. Pierce, *Field Genealogy,* 17.
14. Charles Kellogg Field III, *Field Family,* 12, 24; Martin Field was the son of Seth and Mary (Hubbard) Field, and a grandson of Capt. Jonathan Field who fought the Indians in the French wars that commenced in 1744. Pierce, *Field Genealogy,* 233.

Hadley, so it was said, to exert her power of enchantment upon Philip, whom she "murder'd with an hideous witchcraft." According to Cotton Mather's *Magnalia Christi Americana,* there in Philip's sickroom "pots of medicines, provided for the sick man, were unaccountably empty'd." About the bed "audible scratchings" were heard even when Philip's hands and feet were held by others. Wrote Mather, " . . . on Monday morning they found the face extreamly tumified and discolour'd. It was black and blue, and fresh blood seem'd running down his cheek upon the hairs. Divers noises were also heard in the room where the corpse lay, as the clattering of chairs and stools, whereof no account could be given. This was the end of so good a man."[15]

Esther Smith Kellogg was thoroughly trained and educated in the discipline and religious faith of her Puritan ancestors, and at the age of fifteen she was admitted into the Congregational Church at Amherst. After marriage, as Esther Field, she would continue to be a devout Congregationalist at Newfane, where she achieved "great prominence and influence in the church" because of her excellent judgment. It was said that she was a "keen and close observer of the human face, and an accurate judge of human character, and when she fixed her dark penetrating eyes upon the face of a stranger she rarely failed to stamp his character at once, and that, too, with marked precision."[16]

However, there was no separate Congregational church at Newfane, only a meetinghouse that served not only the Congregationalists but also the Baptists and the Universalists. The Congregationalists, however, did manage, even while joining in worship with the others on Sunday mornings, to maintain a separate identity, and for many years kept their own church records. These records show that the Congregationalists were "gathered" on June 30, 1774, and the "male members being four in number" they elected Hezekiah Taylor as pastor.[17]

For Esther Field and her family, however, the Sabbath was not merely a Sunday observance at the meetinghouse. Sabbath in the Field house began at 6 P.M. on Saturdays. By then Esther Field had the house swept, the firewood brought in, and the food prepared for the next day, for there could be no work on the Lord's day. Sunday was a day of quiet. For luncheon on Sunday, after the meeting, there would be hard-boiled eggs, bread and butter, cookies, crackers, cheese, gingerbread, and loaf cake. And if the weather was extremely cold, water might be heated in the fireplace for tea.[18]

15. Pierce, *Field Genealogy,* 16; Cotton Mather, *Magnalia Christi Americana,* 454.
16. Pierce, *Field Genealogy,* 339.
17. Records of the Church of Christ in Newfane, Collections, WCHS; At a town meeting on November 19, 1781, the inhabitants of Newfane "voted unanimously that the town approve of and accept the Rev. Mr. Taylor to be minister of the Gospel for said town." They also voted to raise "200 hard dollars" to pay his salary, the money to be assessed annually to the inhabitants of the village. *Brattleboro Vermont Phoenix,* September 3, 1897.
18. Eugene Field, "The Woman Who Most Influenced Me," 2.

The meetinghouse was only a short walk across the common for the Field family. There the family had its own pew that Martin Field had purchased from Luke Knowlton for seventy-seven dollars on April 18, 1807. The pew was number four on the lower floor of the meetinghouse, lying "between the Rev'd Hezekiah Taylor's pew and Phinias A. Pomeroy's pew." Its cost was not cheap, even for Martin Field, for in 1800 the seventy-seven dollars represented a whole year's wages for a farm laborer in Vermont. Even so, there were no frills. The pew was a hard wooden bench with a straight wooden back, and the meetinghouse in which it was located was unheated. Esther Field considered stoves as "abominations of Satan's invention."[19]

But not everything in Newfane was so austere. Simon Fisher's store advertised in 1817 "a very extensive assortment of West India, English and other goods." Specifically mentioned were St. Croix rum, Holland gin, Cognac brandy, and Lisbon wine. There were also silk gloves, Irish linens, fur hats, British shirtings, and various colors of ribbons.[20]

For the Field children, life on Newfane Hill was probably not much different than that of the children of other families. While Martin Field worked as a lawyer, he also had extensive land holdings, and for the Field children there were sheep and cattle to tend, gardens to plant and weed, and water to fetch from nearby springs. For other pastimes there were strawberries and checkerberries to pick and streams to fish for trout. And, of course, providing interest enough to pique any child's curiosity, was the town common and its gaol yard, right next to the Field homestead. Here, just over the fence, prisoners awaited trial, most of them residents of Windham County who had in one fashion or another gotten themselves into trouble. Most were young men like Preston Wellman, a twenty-four-year-old shoemaker from Guilford committed for debt; or Jedediah Jewett, twenty-two, and Joseph Pierce, fourteen, both of Dummerston, committed for theft. Pierce, wearing an "old-ragged, brown suit of clothes," was described by the gaoler as a "down-cast, gallows looking boy." Another prisoner, thirty-two-year-old Joseph Ellis, was in the "habits of intoxication" and was committed for bastardy.[21]

Probably of keenest interest to the Field youngsters was the whipping post, located also on the common, which was last used in 1808 for punishment. Roswell would have been too young to have remembered that final whipping, but his older brother Charles was not, and years later Charles wrote vividly of what took place on that late August afternoon in 1808.

Indicted by the grand jury for "giving in payment certain false, forged and counterfeited bank notes, knowing them to be such," Abigail White, described as

19. Deed book 3, 477, Newfane town office, Newfane, Vt.; A. M. Saunders, "Newfane, the Beautiful," 195; Eugene Field, "The Woman Who Most Influenced Me," 2.

20. *Vermont Phoenix*, June 16, 1817.

21. Descriptions of prisoners by Josiah Willard, deputy gaoler, in an advertisement, *Vermont Phoenix*, February 24, 1817.

"very pleasing in her conversation and manners," was sentenced to "be whipped thirty-nine stripes on the naked back . . . at the public whipping post at Newfane to be applied by the sheriff of Windham County."[22]

Charles wrote, "A great crowd of men and women collected to witness the whipping. The Post was in the form of a cross, with a transverse strip near the top to which her bare arms were bound, and her body was stripped to the waist. The High Sheriff applied a certain number of stripes, and the balance were allotted to his Deputies, some seven in number, and some of whom applied the blows with great vigor. Near the close of the whipping her back became raw, and she suffered excessive pain and she shrieked and screamed terribly in her agony."[23]

The meetinghouse and academy stood but a few rods above the site of the whipping post. From their windows, women and children watched intently as justice was administered.

22. Court records, Windham County Court, Newfane, Vt. (WCC).
23. *Centennial Proceedings,* 33.

Education

By the time of Roswell Field's birth in 1807, Dred Scott had already finished his training for a life of slavery. Scott must have learned, for instance, that as a black child he was set apart from those around him who had white skins. He must have understood that even as a child, naked and barefooted, he was expected to labor during daylight hours alongside other slaves. He must also have learned that he had a master upon whom he and the other slaves were dependent, a master who told them what to do and punished them if they disobeyed. And along with the other slaves with whom he lived, he must have learned to vie for his share of the food allotted from the slaves' common kettle.[1]

Dred was probably about seven or eight years old in 1807; his exact age is uncertain because slave births were usually not recorded, since a slave was considered by law in many respects to be chattel like horses and cows.[2] What history reveals about Dred's early life, therefore, depends largely upon what is known of his master, Peter Blow. Because Blow was living on a farm in Southampton County, Virginia, in 1807 along with his wife, Elizabeth, and three infant children, the slave

1. Thomas C. Parramore, *Southampton County, Virginia,* 69; Laws provided the legal basis for slavery, but convention also required blacks to maintain "social distance." A black was "never allowed to forget his servitude whenever a white man was near." Wade, *Slavery,* 182.

2. Historians give various birth dates for Dred Scott, with the earliest date being 1795 and the latest 1809. A date of about 1795 is given in Dumas Malone, ed., *Dictionary of American Biography,* vol. 16, 488. It is unlikely that the true date of Scott's birth can ever be determined and therefore the birth date on Dred Scott's tombstone of "about 1799" is frequently used in the absence of any other agreed-upon date. The tombstone was placed on Scott's grave by his descendants and friends in 1957.

Dred Scott was probably there also. But this is as uncertain as what name Dred Scott went by in 1807. Working from later probate records, some historians claim Scott was called Sam when he was a slave of Peter Blow; they also say he adopted the name of Dred Scott sometime after he became the slave of a later master.[3]

Southampton County was located along Virginia's southern border in a rural and provincial area of small farms where the land was unsuited for a cotton-and-tobacco plantation economy. However, the county was heavily populated with blacks, and of its six thousand or so residents at that time, some two thousand were black slaves. To work his farm and the other acreage that he owned, Peter Blow probably had about six slaves.[4]

As the only male adult in the household, Peter Blow would have been greatly dependent on his slaves. Their work was required not only to support the needs of the growing Blow family but also to raise additional crops to feed and provide for the slaves themselves. For Peter Blow, it was, at best, a very marginal existence, especially with the Virginia soil beginning to wear out and crop yields declining.[5] Some farmers in the county, also feeling the pinch, were moving west to better lands.

The black slaves in Southampton County, not the families of their white masters, felt these deprivations most acutely. Through the eyes of a young black boy like Dred Scott, slavery "was less a matter of corporate brutality than of acute personal insecurity and squalor." Dred's sleeping place was probably a log structure with a mud floor and thatched roof. His bed would likely have been a couple of wooden planks supported by forked stakes driven into the mud floor and covered with straw or cotton-pickings on which he could lay his naked body, covering it with a worn and dirty blanket. When he reached puberty at age twelve or thirteen, he would by custom have received his first "yearly allotment of two pairs of thin cotton pants and two cotton shirts."[6]

Considering the suffering of its slave population, it was probably no coincidence that Southampton County would give birth to slave Nat Turner, the leader of the South's most famous and terrifying slave rebellion. Turner was a contemporary of

3. John A. Bryan, "The Blow Family and Their Slave Dred Scott," pt. 1, 223; Historian Don E. Fehrenbacher, in *The Dred Scott Case*, 240, notes that the 1830 census for Missouri lists five male slaves for Peter Blow while St. Louis probate records in 1833, after Peter Blow died, list four male slaves by name, a fifth slave named Sam being sold for five hundred dollars. No slave named Scott was listed; Bryan believed that Dred Scott, a "somewhat stupid Negro," took his name while a slave on a military base from U.S. General Winfield Scott, who was often called "Great Scott" by his troops. "Dred," Bryan speculates, was a black dialectical corruption of the word "great." Dred, however, was not an uncommon name among male slaves, and Bryan's speculation does not explain why Scott, as a grown man, would want to change his name. Bryan, "Blow Family," pt. 1, 225.

4. Parramore, *Southampton County*, 30; Estate records of Peter Blow, SLPC.

5. Parramore, *Southampton County*, 30.

6. Ibid., 68, 69.

Dred Scott, born around 1800. The two lived only about eight miles apart but it is unlikely that they ever knew each other.[7]

Just as Dred Scott was trained as a child to the life of a slave, so this formative period also witnessed the molding and development of his personality and character. Of his parents nothing is known, so there is no way of determining what influence they had on the youth. Scott may never have known either of them. It is likely that Dred Scott's adult identity was shaped within the slave family in which he lived and grew up.

Some historians have not been kind in their descriptions of the character and personality of Dred Scott. Trevor Hill, for example, said Scott was a "shiftless, incapable specimen of his race." Stewart H. Holbrook described Scott as "a particularly stupid negro, shiftless, and reliable only at widely spaced and not to be guessed moments." There are other descriptions of similar hue. Unfortunately, few of them were made by the contemporaries who knew Scott best, such as his attorney, Roswell Field. Rather, the roots of these critical descriptions can be traced to one source, Julia Webster Blow, daughter-in-law of Peter Blow, who in 1907, some fifty years after Dred Scott's death, described the slave as a "poor workman, lazy and inefficient." In short, she said, he was "worthless" and "trifling." Mrs. Blow complained that Dred Scott lacked the initiative to compete on his own with other laborers in St. Louis, such as some newly arrived Irish and German immigrants, and bring home sufficient wages to meet the Blow family's expectations.[8]

There is no way to verify the accuracy of Mrs. Blow's memories, nor is there any way now, some 150 years after his death, to recreate the real Dred Scott. Perhaps closer to the truth is the description of Scott as "a good-natured, harmless, faithful negro" made in a newspaper article written at the time of his death.[9]

In any case, all of the descriptions of Scott were written by white people, and historian Kenneth Stampp says anyone trying to evaluate these sources "will always be handicapped by the paucity of first-hand testimony from the slave himself."[10]

---

7. Occasionally, historians will group Dred Scott and Nat Turner together as members of a class of discontented blacks anxious to escape slavery. The comparison is unwarranted. Nat Turner was a "paranoid slave preacher and cunjer man" whose violent action "led his superstition-befuddled followers to kill fifty-five whites of all sexes and ages in an aimless terrorizing of Southampton County." J. C. Furnas, *The Americans, A Social History of the United States,* 408.

8. Hill, *Decisive Battles,* 116; Stewart H. Holbrook, *Lost Men of American History,* 161; Notes taken in an interview between Mrs. William T. Blow and Mary Louise Dalton of the Missouri Historical Society, February 18, 1907. Dred Scott Collection, MHS; Sometime shortly before or after Peter Blow's death in 1832, Dred Scott was hired out to help support the Blow family. Hiring out of slaves "broadened the opportunity for the use of slaves," and usually ran for twelve months. It "generally involved a contract which included the price, length of service, some assurances on treatment, and the nature of the work to be performed." Wade, *Slavery,* 38.

9. *St. Louis Evening News and Intelligencer,* September 20, 1858.

10. Kenneth M. Stampp, *The Imperiled Union,* 45.

By the time Roswell Field was seven years old, he too was being educated for the life he would be expected to lead as the son of General Martin Field.

Common schools existed in Newfane as early as 1784, but on October 31, 1801, residents sought to provide better educational facilities and received approval from the Vermont General Assembly to establish an academy in the town. Martin Field was named one of the eight trustees charged with operating the school.[11]

Roswell Field received his early education in this school. Just how the academy differed from the common school is unclear, but there seems little doubt that the education provided at the academy was seen by Newfane residents as being superior to what they had before. It is not known exactly when Roswell entered the academy, how long he attended, or when he completed his work there. But he undoubtedly did very well in school, for by the year 1816, when he was nine years old, his scholastic attainments equaled those of his brother Charles, who was almost four years older. At that point, Esther and Martin Field decided both boys were ready to be fitted for college. Charles was sent to Brattleboro, some eight miles south of Newfane, and Roswell to Townshend, four miles to the north.[12]

At Townshend, Roswell was placed under the tutelage of the Rev. Luke Whitcomb, the young pastor of the Townshend Congregational Church. There is no indication that the Rev. Whitcomb conducted a school, so it is likely that Roswell Field was instructed privately, perhaps spending the week in the pastor's household and returning to his parents' home on weekends. The selection of the Rev. Whitcomb to fit Roswell for college was undoubtedly a choice that would have pleased Esther Field, and may well have been her decision from the beginning.[13]

In the preparation of Roswell Field for college, the emphasis was on Latin and Greek, and in these two languages the Rev. Whitcomb was probably well qualified to instruct his young pupil. During the two years of preparation, Roswell was made thoroughly familiar with Latin and Greek grammar and mastered the ability to construe and parse selected portions of books such as those of Virgil, the Greek New Testament, Cicero's select orations, and Dalsel's *Collectanea Graeca Majora*.[14] He spent numerous afternoons and mornings translating English into Latin and Latin into English.

By the autumn of 1818, when he was eleven years old, Roswell completed his tutoring with the Rev. Whitcomb and was ready for college. His brother Charles had already finished his tutoring and was attending Amherst College in

11. The academy was called Windham Hall, and here students were "taught the higher branches of English studies, the Mathematics and the elements of the Latin and Greek languages." Zadock Thompson, *History of Vermont*, pt. 2, 143; *Newfane's First Century*, 193.

12. Hemenway, collator, *Vermont Historical Gazetteer*, vol. 5, 187.

13. James H. Phelps, *Collections Relating to the History and Inhabitants of the Town of Townshend, Vermont*, 200.

14. *Catalogue of the Officers and Students of Middlebury College, October, 1821*, 11.

Massachusetts. But it was decided the two brothers would go off to college together and they would attend Middlebury College in Vermont.[15]

The idea of sending his sons to Middlebury College had all the earmarks of a decision that General Martin Field probably made himself. The youths could have gone to Williams College, which Martin Field attended, to Dartmouth College, from which he received an honorary degree, or even to the University of Vermont. But compared with these schools, Martin Field would have found Middlebury College more to his liking because Middlebury placed greater emphasis on science. When Martin Field attended college, science was given very little attention, a deficiency he wished to remedy in the education of his sons. "Science is a treasure of inestimable price," Joshua Bates, the president of Middlebury, told parents and students. "The more the mind is expanded; the more man approximates, in wisdom and understanding . . . the angels of light, who encircle the throne of the Almighty." In this he echoed an earlier president of Middlebury, Henry Davis, who said it was only when religion and science were combined that the condition of man is "ameliorated and society highly improved." Martin would have wholly agreed with both men.[16]

But science, while recognized at Middlebury as important, was far from over-shadowing religion as a crucial element in the growth and development of a young man to meet the challenges of life. From its founding in 1800, all of Middlebury's presidents were trained as Congregationalist ministers, and the majority of the ninety or so students in the college were there to prepare to become ministers of the Gospel. Bates himself had been a Congregationalist pastor for fifteen years before he was named president of Middlebury College. While he saw no conflict between science and religion, he admitted that the study of the sciences "have sometimes produced a spirit of skepticism, and lent their support to the cause of infidelity." He was confident, however, that any student who studied science in depth would see God's hand, "which made and moves the whole . . . impressed on the works of creation."[17]

Such statements by a fellow Congregationalist were probably reassuring to Esther Field, who may have felt some apprehension about sending her eleven-year-old son so far from home. She may also have been reassured by the thought that, in company with so many ministerial students who were giving their lives to the Lord and his church, a certain flame within Roswell might be ignited and propel him in a similar direction. To assist the Lord in this work, and in the hope that her son would not stray too far while away, she presented him with a copy of the Bible as he and Charles departed for Middlebury in the fall of 1819. The

15. *Newfane's First Century,* 46.

16. Charles Kellogg Field III, *Field Family,* 38; Beckley, *History of Vermont,* 275; David M. Stameshkin, *The Town's College: Middlebury College, 1800–1915,* 75; Henry Davis, *Inaugural Oration.*

17. Stameshkin, *Town's College,* 72; *Catalogue of the Officers and Students of Middlebury College, 1901;* Stameshkin, *Town's College,* 75.

leather-bound Bible contained the "Old and New Testaments translated out of the Original Tongues." Roswell, in appreciation, dutifully inscribed the first page, "Roswell M. Field's book, 1819." That fall, there were twenty-seven students in Middlebury's freshman class, almost all from the New England states. Roswell and Charles shared room forty-two in the west college building, for which each was charged $1.50 per quarter. Their meals were taken with a family in town, many of whom boarded students for a weekly fee.[18]

The prescribed curriculum at Middlebury was similar to that of most liberal arts colleges of the time; during the freshman year it was largely a continuation of the preparatory studies in which Roswell had already been tutored by Rev. Whitcomb. Educators felt that Greek and Latin were helpful in disciplining untrained minds, and that an emphasis on the classics helped to control a man's "baser passions and raise his moral and religious consciousness." More beneficial for Roswell Field than Latin and Greek were the studies in modern languages. German was taught as an elective in the senior year, and other modern languages were available in private sessions conducted by Robert B. Patton, professor of languages. It is very likely that Roswell, in addition to Latin and Greek, also learned German, French, and Spanish at Middlebury. By the age of thirty-two, when he began practicing law in St. Louis, he was able to read French and Spanish, and "also mastered the German language, and was able to read and speak it with correctness and fluency." This skill would significantly influence his practice of jurisprudence in the years to come.[19]

During his sophomore year, added to his instructions in the classics, Roswell took classes in mathematics: algebra, trigonometry, and the "Measurement of Superficies and Solids and of Heights and Distances." Like languages, mathematics would become for him a lifelong interest and also "his chief mental recreation."[20] The sciences were not taught until his junior year. These included lectures in chemistry, mineralogy, and geology, frequently accompanied by recitations that tested whether students had memorized their assignments. Such recitations were the bane of students, who much preferred lectures, particularly when they included demonstrations in science. One class that amused the young men greatly while Roswell was a student was taught by Professor Reuben Mussey, who demonstrated the effects of nitrous oxide.

18. Years later the Bible was further inscribed by Roswell Field's son, Roswell, who wrote that the book was given to his father by his grandmother when his father left for college in 1819 and that it was, in turn, given to him upon his father's death in 1869. Field Collection, WCHS; 1821 *Middlebury Catalogue.*

19. During his freshman year, Field would have read Xenophon's *Cyropaedia,* Folson's *Livy,* Homer's *Iliad,* Horace's *Odes,* and Playfair's *Euclid.* Thompson, *History of Vermont,* pt. 2, 154; Stameshkin, *Town's College,* 74; 1821 *Middlebury Catalogue;* Field's proficiency in languages is noted in Gray, "Recollections," 128.

20. 1821 *Middlebury Catalogue; Centennial Proceedings,* 49.

Professor Mussey . . . on having obliged a number of students (who wished it) to exhaust all the atmospheric air from their lungs, gave them this exhilerating [*sic*] gas to breathe and as soon [as] they had breathed a sufficient quantity they were deprived of their reason, their spirits were raised to the highest pitch and they were inspired with a contempt for all around them.[21]

While science was emphasized during the junior and senior years, and the classics during the freshman and sophomore years, it was religion that was woven into the curriculum throughout the full span of a student's life at Middlebury. It was a daily routine in which all participated. There were readings from the Old and New Testaments, lectures on divinity, and courses on Christian ethics and the evidences of Christianity. Twice during the day—at 5 A.M. and at sunset—all students were required to attend prayer services in the chapel. Years later, a relative of Roswell's would tell how on cold winter mornings, Roswell—then just a lad—"was taken out of bed by companions, a cloak thrown about him, and in that costume, was carried into the old chapel to attend morning prayers."[22] One of these companions said of morning chapel:

There was no fire. The chapel was lighted only by a few dim candles. . . . My study hours generally extended far into the night and I kept myself awake by taking strong doses of green tea. On waking up my brain was apt to be overheated, so I usually dipped my head into a basin of cold water before leaving my room. In the chapel my hair soon became a mass of icicles.[23]

While the students sat on hard seats in the cold chapel, President Joshua Bates led the sleepy young men in prayers and singing. The only break in this routine came on Sundays when the students were required to attend church in town, following which they were asked to stay alone in their rooms and to refrain from any indecent noise. There was also to be no unnecessary business and walking about the town.[24]

For Roswell, one of the youngest students on campus, compliance with the rules at Middlebury College was probably not difficult, but for Charles, almost four years older, adherence proved, so it seemed, a real challenge. In the fall of 1819 Charles missed evening prayers and was called before the faculty to confess his wrongdoing:

Whereas having intentionally absented myself last evening from prayers . . . I hereby acknowledge that I was rash and inconsiderate in committing these offences for which I humbly confess. Charles K. Field. Oct. 12, 1819.[25]

21. Stameshkin, *Town's College*, 71.
22. Letter from J. A. E. [Julia A. Eastman] to the editor, *Springfield Republican* (Mass.), July 15, 1869.
23. Stameshkin, *Town's College*, 83.
24. Ibid.
25. *Records of the Judicial Proceedings of the Executive Government of Middlebury College*, Collections, Starr Library, Middlebury, Vt.

Less than a year later, Charles was once again in trouble at the college, this time in company with four of his fellow students. On August 11, 1820, he was called before the executive government to receive his punishment.

> Whereas Charles K. Field, a member of the sophomore class, has been guilty of clandestinely and unlawfully taking fowls; of aggravated falsehood when called before the faculty and of refusing to give information on a subject with which he acknowledged himself acquainted; be it resolved that for these offences he be & hereby is restricted for a period of six weeks. Joshua Bates.[26]

According to testimony taken among the other students involved, the fowls were stolen and afterwards were "cooked and eaten" in the room of one of the students. Several days later the five students appeared as a group before their fellow students and at chapel on the morning of August 15, 1820, offered their "confessions" and pledged "not to be guilty of the like hereafter."[27] Just where Roswell was when the fowls—probably chickens—were consumed by the hungry students is not noted in any of the proceedings.

However, something happened at Middlebury College in the spring of 1822 during the brothers' senior year, this time involving Roswell as well as Charles and this time apparently of a more serious nature. As a result, Charles was expelled from college and Roswell reprimanded. No record of any college proceedings survives, but General Field provides his reaction to the incident in a letter he wrote to his daughter Mary, who at the time was in Troy, New York:

> Yours by Mr. Reed was received, in which I find you allude to the severe and satyrical language of mine in a former letter. That letter was written upon the conduct of my children, which is an important subject to me. If children are disobedient, a parent has a right to be severe with them. If I recollect right, I expressed to you that your two oldest Brothers' conduct was very reprehensible and I then predicted their ruin. But I then little thought that I should so soon witness the sad consequence of their ill conduct. I received a letter from Prest. Bates about two weeks since and another from Charles on the same day that Charles had been turned away and forever dismissed from College the 7th of March, and I wrote on the week after to have him come directly home, but we have heard nothing from him since. Where he is, we can form no conjecture. But probably he is 500 miles distant without money and without friends. I leave you to conjecture the rest—Roswell is left alone at the age 15, to get along, if he is permitted to stay, thro' college—These, Mary! are the consequences of dissipation and bad conduct—And seeing as I do, the temper and disposition of my children, that they are inclined to evil and that continually, can you wonder that I write with severity to them? Our hopes are all blasted, as it related to C. & R. and you cannot conceive the trouble they have given us. Your mother is almost crazy about them: nor are we without fears as to you. I say now, as I said to you in my former letter that I wish my children were all at home at work, for I am convinced that an education will only prove injurious to them. If I had as many sons as had the Patriarch

26. Ibid.
27. Ibid.

Jacob, not one of them should ever again go to college. It is not good calculation to educate children for destruction. The boys' conduct has already brought a disgrace upon our family which we can never outgrow. They undoubtedly possess respectable talents and genius, but what are talents worth when wholly employed in mischief? I have expended almost two thousand dollars in educating the boys, and now just at the close they are sent off in disgrace and infamy. The money is nothing in comparison to the disgrace and ruin that must succeed. Mary, think of these things often, and especially when you feel inclined to be gay and airy. Let your Bros. fate be a striking lesson to you. For you may well suppose that you possess something of the same disposition that he does, but I hope that you will exercise more prudence than he has. You must now return home with a fixed resolution to become a steady, sober and industrious girl. Give up literary pursuits and quietly and patiently follow that calling which I am convinced is most proper for my children. . . . Thus far I have not said much about our affairs at home; but as we have 3 children abroad for whom we have such anxiety, our minds are principally taken up about them. It does appear to me that if children would consider how much anxiety their parents have for them, they would conduct properly, if it was only to gratify their parents. But it is not so. Many of them seem determined not only to wound the feelings of their parents in the most cruel manner, but also to ruin themselves. Remember us respectfully to the Doctor and Mrs. Willard—And I am your affectionate father.
Martin Field.[28]

For all of Martin Field's worry, however, Charles appears to have been able to persuade the college president to readmit him and in August of 1822, both Charles and Roswell Field graduated from Middlebury, having successfully passed the twice-yearly examinations before "the whole Faculty, a committee of the Corporation, and such other literary gentlemen as are disposed to attend."[29] Both returned to Newfane and to the home of their parents.

It is well to take with a grain of salt the words of General Field that not one of his children would ever again go to college. Education was undoubtedly something upon which he placed great importance not only for his children but for himself as well. Among the inhabitants of Newfane at that time, only five had college educations, and three of these were members of the Field family: Martin, Charles, and Roswell. To that list Martin Field was to add still another: his daughter, Mary. Sometime prior to Roswell's final year at Middlebury College and before the incident that almost terminated his student life there, Esther and Martin Field decided to provide an advanced education for their daughter as well. The school they chose was the Emma Willard School—often called the "Female Institution"— at Troy, New York, which was located about seventy-five miles west of Newfane and was reached by some rather tortuous roads over the mountains to Bennington

28. Letter from Martin Field to Mary Field, March 31, 1822, Field Collection, JL.
29. 1821 *Middlebury Catalogue.*

and from there to Troy. At Troy she would meet Theodore Francis French, a merchant, whom she would marry in 1824.[30]

Just as Martin and Esther Field worried about their sons away at Middlebury College, they also had similar concerns about the well-being of their daughter away at her school in Troy. Martin Field wrote:

> You write that your quarter will be out the 17th of April, which I find will be on Wednesday. Of course you cannot set out for home til Friday's stage, the 19th—You must come on to Marlboro that day, and stay over night at Lucius Fields who lives in a house a few rods from Deacon Whitney's in Marlboro, and we shall send over for you on Saturday morning, the 20th. We should be glad to gratify you in your desire of going to Manchester, but there will be insuperable difficulties attending it. There is no stage runs across the mountain to Chester, Rockingham or N.Fane, and the roads are so bad that way that you could better come home from Troy than from Manchester—besides it would be many miles out of your way—We think therefore that you had better come directly home. Your Ma says that you must begin to gather together your clothing and other things immediately and have them well packed before hand; and see to it that you leave nothing behind, except a "good name." We should be glad that you would have company, of your acquaintance, in the stage, but as the stage will not set out from Troy til after day light and will arrive at Marlboro by sunset, we see nothing but that you can come without hazard.[31]

Then, as if recalling his personal commitment to the improvement of his own education, General Field added a footnote. Before Mary left Troy to return home she was to drop by the home of a Dr. Thomas Brown, "the *electrician* at Troy." Her father said, "I expect he will send me by you a small jar, and, if so, you must be very careful to have it so done up that it shall not be injured or broken."[32] This glass jar was needed for General Field's experiments in chemistry. General Field, now with three children educated, was devoting more time to his own education. Of particular appeal to him was the study of the natural sciences, a field in which he had always had an interest, but now in later life he was devoting more time to it than ever. Furthermore, Martin Field was slowly losing his hearing, and as the deafness progressed, he found it increasingly difficult to represent his clients in court.

Equipped with his hammer and picks, and often accompanied by Roswell, who shared his interest, Martin Field walked the hills and valleys about Newfane in search of unusual ores and minerals, and was credited with having "discovered a greater variety of rare minerals than perhaps any other man in Vermont."[33] Later he added two large rooms to his house to contain his increasing collection.

30. *Newfane's First Century,* 193; Charles Kellogg Field III, *Field Family,* 46.
31. Martin Field letter to Mary Field, March 31, 1822, Field Collection, JL.
32. Ibid.
33. Beckley, *History of Vermont,* 275.

New Horizons

When Roswell Field graduated from Middlebury College in August 1822 and returned home to Newfane, he decided, probably with the encouragement of his parents, that he would study law. This idea could have flowered during his four years at college, or more likely, it simply reflected the wish of a young lad to follow in his father's footsteps.

More than two-thirds of the students attending Middlebury College were preparing for either the Christian ministry or the practice of law. While it was possible in the early nineteenth century for young men to become ministers and lawyers without a college education, preparatory college study was encouraged. Educators at Middlebury felt that a knowledge of philosophy, logical induction, and metaphysical reasoning created cultivated men capable of excelling as statesmen and as learned clergymen in the true Calvinistic tradition.[1]

Four years at Middlebury and daily attendance at chapel apparently failed to ignite within Roswell Field a desire to devote his life to the ministry. There is no indication of any personal spiritual awakening, and during the years following his return to Newfane, the Congregational church records do not mention him. This was perhaps emblematic of Roswell's attitude toward religion, for Field tended throughout adulthood to keep a safe distance between himself and established churches of all hues. There is also no indication that he ever displayed any interest in things spiritual, and while he kept throughout his life the Bible his mother gave him when he left for college in 1819, the book showed little evidence of having been overly used. Three other Bibles in his possession, one in French and two in

1. Stameshkin, *Town's College,* 70, 72.

Italian, were probably read to satisfy an interest in languages rather than religion. Perhaps his true sentiments concerning religion were revealed years later when he advised his eldest son, on visiting his grandmother Esther Field, not to be overly influenced by her "superstitions of New England."[2]

His studies at Middlebury therefore did not point the way to the ministry, but provided instead a foundation for the study of law. And since there was no law taught at the college nor lawyers on the faculty, Roswell's interest in law probably stemmed not from any college experience, but from the favorable impressions gained as a youth of his father's profession.

General Field's influence on his son seems to have been strong. Roswell had many opportunities on Newfane Hill to observe his father at work as a lawyer. The one-story, unpainted frame courthouse was only a few steps from Roswell's home, and on days when there was little else for a young boy to do in Newfane, he could spend his idle time watching his father in court. He also would have been acquainted with many of the judges and lawyers who came to the courthouse, and standing alongside his father, he would have overheard their legal discussions. Thus, even though he was only fifteen when he made his decision to become a lawyer, Roswell Field was probably very familiar with what being a lawyer entailed.

The son was patterning himself after the father in other ways, too. It was said of Roswell Field years later that, like his father, he was "very social and entertaining" and "unsurpassed in conversational powers." He also shared his father's interest in science, and it is not difficult to envision this interest growing out of those father-and-son strolls through the hills near Newfane as Martin Field sought out specimens of rocks and wildlife for his science collections. And Roswell shared his father's interest in music as well. In the evenings, when the family gathered in the parlor of the Field homestead, with Esther Field at the piano, both General Field and Roswell would join in with their violins, for Roswell, like his father, was also said to be an accomplished violinist.[3]

Given Roswell Field's wish to become a lawyer, it would have been logical for him to learn the law from Martin Field, as young men through the ages have learned the trades of their fathers. But Roswell's brother Charles, who also went into law after graduation from Middlebury, was already studying with Martin Field, so Roswell was sent to study law under his uncle, Daniel Kellogg.[4]

Daniel Kellogg was a younger brother of Roswell's mother, and when Roswell began the study of law, Kellogg was a young attorney of thirty-one, newly married, with a good practice in the neighboring town of Rockingham, also in Windham County. Daniel Kellogg attended Williams College, and after graduating in 1810,

---

2. Roswell Field estate, SLPC; An 1829 copy of an Italian grammar is among Roswell Field's books, Field Collection, WCHS; Slason Thompson, *Eugene Field,* 7.

3. *Newfane's First Century,* 48; Bay, *Reminiscences,* 240.

4. Hemenway, collator, *Vermont Historical Gazetteer,* 187; *Centennial Proceedings,* 46.

he came to Newfane and studied law under Martin Field. After being admitted
to the bar, Daniel Kellogg, probably at Martin Field's urging, joined the state
militia and was appointed by Governor Jonas Galusha as General Field's personal
aide-de-camp.[5]

Roswell Field had an excellent and knowledgeable teacher in Kellogg, a talented
and respected lawyer who achieved great recognition in the years that followed.
During two administrations he served as secretary to the Governor and Council
of the State of Vermont, and under Presidents Jackson and Van Buren was named
United States District Attorney for Vermont. At the state constitutional convention
of 1843 Kellogg served as president, and climaxed this achievement two years later
in 1845 when he was named associate justice of the Vermont Supreme Court.[6]

Daniel Kellogg was the attorney of record for many cases in the Windham
County Court during the early 1820s, and Roswell Field would have assisted in
at least some of them. He would have helped Kellogg in writing pleadings, taking
depositions, searching out legal precedents, and handling deeds, wills, and other
legal functions expected of an attorney in a small rural community. But generally,
as was often the case for office students learning the law at that time, Roswell Field
was probably left largely to his own devices. Among the law books in Kellogg's
office, he would likely have studied the twenty volumes of the *United States
Reports* that existed in 1822, along with Blackstone and—considering Roswell's
tenacity—perhaps Coke or Littleton. Law books not available in Kellogg's office
were probably available in his father's law office in Newfane, and Roswell may have
received some suggested reading assignments directly from his father. Kellogg, as
a lawyer, had a reputation for order and accuracy and was considered a "practical
and sensible" attorney, traits Kellogg no doubt stressed in working with his
young student.[7]

Sometime during his study of law, Roswell Field became familiar with Joseph
Story, the young associate justice of the United States Supreme Court. Roswell read
and studied Story's legal opinions in detail and apparently with some admiration,
for in many of Field's law cases over the following years, including the Dred Scott
case, Field cited Story's works and correspondence. Story, like Field, was a New
Englander, and like Field had entered the legal profession at a very early age. He was
only thirty-two when he was appointed to the Supreme Court during the tenure
of Chief Justice John Marshall. Story's hallmark was his scholarly or classic approach
to the law and his great respect for English law and tradition. "We should," Story
urged lawyers, "study ancient forms and cases, as we study the old English writers

5. Charles Kellogg Field III, *Field Family*, 140; Esther Field had another brother, Henry
Kellogg, a Yale graduate, who also studied law under Martin Field. Henry Kellogg practiced at
Bennington, Vt. Pierce, *Field Genealogy*, 29; Appointment document, Kellogg Collection, VHS.
6. Pierce, *Field Genealogy*, 27.
7. By 1857 with the publication of the Dred Scott decision in 19 Howard, the number of
volumes of *United States Reports* would increase to sixty; Pierce, *Field Genealogy*, 28.

in general literature; because we may extract from them, not only solid sense, but the best examples of pure and undefiled language." What must have appealed most to Roswell Field about Joseph Story was that Story considered jurisprudence a science. Story wrote that during the reign of King George III, more was done "to give a scientific cast" to the law "than in all the preceding ages."[8]

Roswell Field studied law under his uncle Daniel Kellogg for three years. In the fall of 1825 at age eighteen, having grown to more than six feet in height, he appeared before the county court at Newfane for admittance to the bar. The clerk noted in the court records of September 22, 1825:

"Be it Remembered, that Jonathan D. Bradley, Roswell M. Field and Charles K. Field are duly admitted to practice and sworn as attorneys of the court."[9]

After having been admitted to the bar, Charles Field practiced law in the nearby town of Wilmington and Roswell practiced at Newfane with his father. The third lawyer admitted that day, Jonathan Dorr Bradley, was a graduate of Yale who practiced at Bellows Falls and was one of Roswell's best friends. An acquaintance recalled the time when Bradley, rushing into Roswell Field's office, asked to see Field's copy of Chitty's book on contracts. "What do you wish to know?" Roswell replied. He put one finger on his forehead, said, "I carry my book here." Bradley answered, "I see. And it's bound in calf, too."[10]

Immediately after the admittance of these three young attorneys to the bar, the Windham County Court adjourned for that term. When the court reconvened the next spring, it would not be on Newfane Hill but at a new town site, and the shire town of Newfane was renamed Fayetteville. The old town of Newfane was being abandoned, and during the following years everything in it was moved to the new location some two miles east to a small valley known as Park's Flats. The new site offered greater opportunities for growth and was closer to the geographical center of the county. General Martin Field was the person who suggested the town be renamed Fayetteville after General LaFayette of Revolutionary War fame, a suggestion that was quickly adopted.[11]

8. Typescript of Roswell Field letter to Montgomery Blair, January 7, 1855, in which he mentions Story's *Conflict of Laws*, a work first published in 1834, Dred Scott Collection, MHS; Joseph Story, *Commentaries on the conflict of laws, foreign and domestic, in regard to contracts, rights, and remedies, and especially in regard to marriages, divorces, wills, successions, and judgments*; The quote is from William W. Story, ed., *The Miscellaneous Writings of Joseph Story*, 233, 78.

9. Record book 10, 234, WCC.

10. Mary Roger Cabot, *Annals of Brattleboro*, 537.

11. The official date of transfer of the court was December 3, 1825. Record book 10, 235, WCC; Roswell Field signed a petition to the Vermont General Assembly on October 3, 1829, seeking permission to move the courthouse three hundred feet west. *Vermont Special Proceedings*, vol. 60, 236, Secretary of State Archives; Naming the town Fayetteville may have been prompted by a visit of the Marquis de La Fayette to Vermont in 1824. Beckley, *History of Vermont*, 173; In 1874 the name of the town reverted back to Newfane. Robert L. Crowell, *Historic Newfane Village*, 13.

Along with the courthouse and the jail, the Field homestead was also moved to a new site in Fayetteville, where it again faced, as it did on Newfane Hill, the town common. It also backed up to the Union Church, which was built in 1831 to serve the town's several religious denominations.[12] Eugene Field, Roswell Field's eldest son, described the Field house as he remembered it several decades later:

> It was a long two-story frame house with narrow windows and a green front door. . . . Above the door was an archaic window or transom in the shape of a fan. Three acres of land were around the house, a large front yard and a side yard and an orchard; there were numerous outbuildings, a museum (for my grandfather was an amateur naturalist), a wooden shed, a barn, an ice-house and a carriage house. . . . There was a long gravel walk leading from the front gate to the front door, and on each side of this walk there was a flower-bed, in which, at proper season, prim daffodils bloomed. On the picket fence which divided the front and side yards there was a sun dial, and just to the north of this dial stood a sassafras tree.[13]

But Eugene Field failed to mention perhaps the most unusual feature of the homestead: a small picturesque building to the rear of the house that held Martin Field's law office. Painted white, the small frame building might have been similar to many small outbuildings on the New England countryside except that it was adorned on the front with miniature Greek columns heralding the building's more distinctive role. A sign hanging in front announced in gold lettering, "M. Field's Office."[14]

The small office was strategically located across from the courthouse and therefore was used not only as Martin Field's law office but also as a meeting place for local and visiting lawyers and judges. During the warm summer months, the attorneys and judges could idle away the customary delays in the law by playing quoits on the common under the shade of the elms, but during the bitter cold winter days they took refuge in Martin Field's law office. Here, huddled for warmth around the fire, attorneys and politicians from Windham County and elsewhere discussed the events of the day, exchanged ideas, and planned legal and political strategies. It was Windham County's judicial center, and here in company with lawyers from throughout the county and state Roswell Field first took his place among his peers in the legal profession.[15]

During those early years as a young lawyer beginning his practice in Windham County, Roswell Field, as might be expected, handled no momentous or landmark cases. Neither was he involved in cases that, even by the most generous of definitions, could have been viewed as challenging subjects of litigation. Nor did the cases involve any large amounts of money—no more than one hundred dollars or so, in most instances.

12. *Newfane's First Century,* 206.
13. Slason Thompson, *Eugene Field,* 19.
14. Sign in Field Collection, WCHS.
15. Slason Thompson, *Eugene Field, A Study in Heredity and Contradictions,* 4.

Yet they were probably rather typical of legal actions likely to come before a court in a rural area of Vermont in the early 1800s, which still had a frontier flavor compared with such nearby cities as Boston and New York. And while the cases that Field handled before the Windham County Court lacked the complexity (and certainly the financial stature) of many he would later handle in Missouri, they probably provided a good foundation for a young man starting out in the law.

Typical of such cases was one handled by Field shortly after he was admitted to the bar. Roswell Field was the attorney in a case against Carmi Briggs, a Somerset resident, who in 1825 sold to Artemas Ward, Field's client, a pair of stags for forty-five dollars on the assurance that "said stags were peaceable orderly cattle and not breachy or troublesome to keep"—a claim that Ward found later to be untrue. Briggs replied that "he did not assure and promise in manner and form" as Ward claimed and the case went before a jury of "good and lawful men." The jury decided against Roswell's client, agreeing that Briggs had made no promises. Field's client was ordered to pay $67.78 to cover the legal costs for the defendant.[16]

A number of these early Field cases involved the collection of debts, and frequently the amounts were small, even for that day. In one instance he was successful in collecting debts owed his client by two men who were "safely kept" in the county gaol until they "paid the full sum." Field's client received damages in this case of $53.73, a share of which probably went to Field for handling the case. In a similar case, Field successfully obtained for his client $248.35 of the $400 claimed for "work and labor" performed. Some legal actions to collect debt did not go to court, and in a letter to a Charles Phelps, Roswell Field suggested to Phelps a "clever way" to collect on doubtful notes due him by a debtor in Massachusetts who refused to pay on the notes. Field recommended "endorsing them [the notes] to some friend in Massachusetts" as a means of getting around jurisdictional problems between Vermont and its neighboring state and bringing action for recovery.[17]

However, jurisdictional boundaries between Vermont and Massachusetts were simple issues to settle compared with the sometimes confusing, and often humorous, boundary disputes that arose between brother and brother and even between father and sons as the three Fields—Martin, Roswell, and Charles—practiced law together in Windham County.

Working out of his father's law office, Roswell was often aware early of actions in which his father was retained as counsel, which sometimes provided him an opportunity to seek out defendants and offer them his legal services—sometimes

---

16. *Artemas Ward v. Carmi Briggs,* record book 10, 401, WCC.

17. *Laval Thayer v. Paul Chase,* record book 10, 386, WCC. In the early nineteenth century, Vermonters were sent to jail if they were unable to pay their debts. To get out of jail required a pauper's oath that one's worldly possessions did not exceed twenty dollars. Everything else was auctioned off to pay the debts. *Brattleboro Vermont Reformer,* February 10, 1995; *Edron Higgins v. James Taggart,* record book 10, 465, WCC; Letter of R. M. Field to Charles Phelps, October 27, 1836, Phelps Collection, VHS.

gratis. The result was that Martin Field sometimes found himself facing his own son in court, a son whom he had helped train in the law, and a son who availed himself "of every obsolete technicality, quirk and precedent of the law" to frustrate his aged father, whom he sometimes addressed in court as my "learned but erring brother in the law." Martin Field's indignation and embarrassment were often matched by the admiration he felt for his son's misdirected professional zeal.[18]

Typical of some family confrontations in court was one involving Roswell and Charles in 1829, in which Roswell, representing the plaintiff, won a judgment against a defendant represented by Charles. The court noted, "Charles K. Field personally appearing, acknowledged himself to be indebted to the Plaintiff in the sum of fifty dollars, to be levied of his goods and chattels, lands and tenements, and for want thereof upon his body, if default be made."[19]

In another instance a case involving both Field brothers went all the way to the Vermont Supreme Court. The case involved the constitutionality of an act governing the monetary limitations on cases handled by justices of the peace. Roswell, representing the plaintiff, challenged whether the law, which was passed by the Vermont legislature without the governor's signature, was a lawful act. The court ruled against Roswell's position and agreed with Charles, who represented the defendant. It held that "no person can entertain a doubt that the supreme legislative power of the State is vested in the House of Representatives, and that the exclusive power of preparing bills and enacting them into laws is given to it."[20]

If the justices of the Vermont Supreme Court thought this case involving two brothers as opposing attorneys was a little unusual, they must have been totally nonplused by another case during the same term, this one between a father and a son, with Martin Field representing the plaintiff and Roswell Field representing the defendant.

One of the key issues in the case involved a conflict concerning the time period during which a certain promissory note was pending. The question in this instance was whether the word "month" in Vermont law meant a calendar or a lunar month. Martin Field argued that "whenever the word month or months occur in the Statutes of Vermont, they are considered calendar months" and cited several earlier cases showing that "in New England and most of the other states, a month when mentioned in a statute, generally, has ever been considered a calendar month."

Roswell Field, on the other hand, argued that "a month in law is a lunar month" and that "the word month, when used in a Statute, is, if nothing appear to the contrary, to be understood as a lunar and not a calendar month." He also cited several legal precedents in support of his position, including several English citations.

18. Slason Thompson, *Study in Heredity*, 10.
19. *Phineas White v. Walter Gillet*, record book 11, 64, WCC.
20. *Easterbrook v. Low*, 3 *Vermont Reports*, 133, Vermont Supreme Court (VSC).

The court replied that it was "aware that in all judicial proceedings in England, in the reckoning of time, month or months, if not declared calendar, are taken as lunar" but went on to state that "we are to consider the habits and customs of our citizens, and we are satisfied that in the various intercourse between the inhabitants of this State, where a calculation or computation of time is had, the calendar month is invariably used." Since there were several other issues before the court in this case, the decision in favor of a calendar month was not a total defeat for Roswell, because the court ordered a new trial.[21]

As with any attorney representing his client, Roswell Field was not averse to using a technicality in the law when it proved advantageous to his client. Typical was a case in which Field represented a young man named Elijah Nursel, who was charged by Mary Burnham as the man who "begat said child upon her body and as the father of [her] child." The charge was first examined by the justice of the peace and Elijah Nursel was found guilty, but on appeal to the county court, Field succeeded in having the case quashed since the original complaint of Mary Burnham was not "in writing & signed" and not made under oath.[22]

The only criminal cases that appear to have been handled by Roswell Field were those that came to him while he was serving as state's attorney for Windham County from 1832 through 1835. All of them involved minor legal infractions, although the penalties appear to have been heavy. Typical was the case of William P. Curtis, charged with stealing two pistols worth two dollars from Ezekial Osgood. Curtis was confined to the county jail from which he "did break open and thereby then and there did escape." Curtis pleaded guilty to escaping and was sentenced to two years of "hard labour within the state's prison." Another defendant in a case in which Field was the state prosecutor was Marcus B. Scott, who committed "assault and Battery in and upon Clarissa Scott," and who also escaped from jail. He was sentenced to one year's hard labor at the same state prison.[23]

Since Roswell Field was a young attorney in Windham County during the late 1820s and early 1830s, and considering the cases he handled not only before the county court but also before the Vermont Supreme Court, it might be assumed that, like his father, Field was on his way to becoming a successful and prosperous attorney. But this is an assumption that cannot be supported by the few known facts that survive.

For one thing, it is very likely that Roswell Field did not find the practice of law in the small rural village of Fayetteville all that challenging. As a new and inexperienced lawyer in town, it is unlikely that he represented the more prominent citizens in the county or that he handled the thornier legal suits coming before

21. *Kimball v. Lamson, 3 Vermont Reports,* 136, VSC.

22. *Mary Burnham v. Elijah Nursel,* record book 11, 315, WCC.

23. Judge Frank L. Fish, "Roswell M. Field," 232; *The State of Vermont v. William P. Curtis,* record book 12, 505, WCC; *The State of Vermont v. Marcus B. Scott,* record book 12, 506, WCC.

the Windham County Court. Only a year after being admitted to the bar, Field wrote, somewhat jokingly, to his friend Jonathan Bradley about the law and the cases he was handling. "The law business is as dull as ever," Field told his young friend. "Aunt Lizzy against Uncle Jake, a desperate case—the counterpart of the hog suit."[24]

It is also possible that Field's law practice may not have been as profitable as he wished, although this is difficult to assess. Some attorneys' names appear before the court more frequently than that of Roswell Field—William C. Bradley, John Phelps, and Daniel Kellogg, to mention only a few—but whether this is indicative of success would be difficult to determine.

True, Martin Field had done well as an attorney in Windham County. But in the decades since Martin Field first settled at Newfane in 1800, local economic conditions had changed, and not for the better. During Martin Field's active life as an attorney, between 1800 and 1820, the population of Newfane had increased more than 50 percent. But that was the peak, and in the following decades the population declined significantly, reflecting a shift in population to nearby towns like Rockingham and Brattleboro. There was also a drop in the yields of the county's agricultural products: maple syrup, Indian corn, potatoes, and wool.[25]

The population decline was not limited to Newfane; there was a similar decline throughout most of Vermont. For the first time in the state's history, more young people were leaving than coming in. The attraction was the West, where land was abundantly available and every talent and skill much in need. At the forefront of the migration were the Vermont farmers, but "young doctors, lawyers, preachers and teachers were also on the march."[26] It was, one observer noted, a procession of Vermonters toward the sunset.

When Dred Scott was eighteen years old, about the same age as Roswell Field was when he was admitted to the bar in Vermont, master Peter Blow told his slaves that they and his family were moving west. The year was 1818.[27]

After years of working the soil with meager returns, Blow had finally decided to follow in the tracks of many other Virginians and seek out new and more fertile lands to the west. Here, he hoped, with the work of his slaves and higher crop yields, financial success would follow and his growing family would begin to enjoy the more abundant life that Blow wished for them.

The migration would eventually take them to St. Louis some one thousand miles west, but that was not their intended destination in 1818. Peter Blow's sights were set on Alabama, some four hundred miles west over the mountains, and only

24. Letter dated October 2, 1826, from Roswell M. Field to Jonathan Bradley, Bradley Collection, Arthur and Elizabeth Schlesinger Library on the History of Women in America.

25. *Newfane's First Century*, 28.

26. Lewis D. Stilwell, *Migration from Vermont*, 185.

27. *Missouri Republican*, July 22, 1866.

after meeting failure in Alabama would the family and their slaves pack up once again and migrate farther west to St. Louis in 1830.[28]

Just as the Blows were dependent on their black slaves for farming in Virginia, they were equally dependent on them in the westward trek to Alabama and St. Louis. Peter Blow was the only adult white male in the household, and moving the family and its belongings over the western mountains required great physical effort, much more than Blow could provide by himself. By 1818, Elizabeth Blow had borne her husband six children. Four were girls, of whom the eldest was Mary Anne, age sixteen. The other three daughters were Elizabeth Rebecca, Charlotte, and Martha Ella. The two sons born in Virginia, Peter and Henry, were infants. By the time the Blows reached St. Louis twelve years later, Elizabeth Blow had given birth to two more sons, Taylor and William.[29]

Because of the supportive role the Blow children would later play in the efforts of Dred Scott to obtain freedom, historians have focused much attention and speculation on the relationship between the Blows and Dred Scott. Historian Walter Ehrlich says that Dred Scott was a "companion of the Blows as well as their slave." Don E. Fehrenbacher describes the relationship as one of "personal affection." Trevor Hill says Dred Scott was a "playmate of Taylor Blow."[30]

These comments tend to paint a rather idyllic portrait of Dred Scott's condition as a slave with the Blow family in Virginia. However, not only does this depiction seem to be completely out of keeping with the reported social condition of slaves in Southampton County, but it also overlooks the fact that when the first of the Blow boys was born, Dred Scott was already grown, being about fourteen years old. And if, on the other hand, it was the older Blow daughters who were Dred Scott's childhood playmates, Elizabeth Blow, as a Southern woman, would no doubt have put an end to such activity rather quickly.

However, this is not to dismiss what the historians have correctly detected and to deny the existence of some sort of special bond between the Blow children and Dred Scott. The record is clear that Blow family members willingly came to Dred Scott's aid when he was no longer their slave and did so on numerous occasions. Dred Scott himself added credence to this special relationship when, in later years, he spoke of the sons of Peter Blow as "them boys he was raised with." Just what Scott meant by that is unclear, but most likely—and this is simply speculation— Scott was referring to the special position he enjoyed as a child as a domestic slave in the Blow home. Perhaps, unlike Blow's other slaves who labored in the fields and lived in separate slave quarters, Scott lived and worked in his master's house as a domestic slave. Considering that Dred Scott was reported to have been a very small

28. *St. Louis Daily Evening News,* April 3, 1857.
29. Bryan, "Blow Family," pt. 1, 223.
30. Walter Ehrlich, *They Have No Rights,* 11; Fehrenbacher, *Dred Scott,* 241; Hill, *Decisive Battles,* 116.

man, perhaps only about five-feet six-inches tall, this was a job for which he would have been well suited. In fact, from what is known about him, Scott never worked as a farm laborer for any of his masters. When he was eventually sold by the Blow family, Scott was purchased by his new master to serve as a body servant, indicating Scott was suited and trained for such domestic work. According to one historian, "Slave children were brought into domestic service while still very young. Taught simple tasks and habituated to servitude, they became an important part of the household work force."[31]

The shared experiences on the westward journey of the Blow family from Virginia to Missouri may also have helped forge a close relationship with their slaves. Along the rugged trails leading west, the Blows would have found it difficult, if not impossible, to maintain the same social distinctions that governed relationships with slaves back in Virginia. They would have been forced to share food out of a common kettle, to soothe each others' bruises and cuts, to huddle together for protection from the weather. Such shared hardships could have helped create strong personal attachments.

That the journey west may have been a difficult one can perhaps explain Peter and Elizabeth Blow's premature deaths within a short time after their arrival in St. Louis in 1830. On arriving in St. Louis, Peter Blow was described as being among the town's "slave poor" since he had no land and his slaves represented his primary—and perhaps only—assets. To provide income for the family, Peter Blow rented from Peter Lindell a large house on Pine Street just west of Main and turned it into a boardinghouse called the Jefferson Hotel to serve the growing number of newcomers moving to the frontier town. But the hotel had barely opened when on July 24, 1831, Elizabeth Blow died at age forty-six after a painful illness. A little less than a year later Peter Blow followed her in death.[32]

It was sometime prior to or shortly after Peter Blow's death on June 23, 1832, that Dred Scott was sold to a new master, the date uncertain since no record of the sale has been found. Both Dred Scott and Henry Blow would later say the sale was made by Peter Blow, indicating that it occurred before Blow's death in 1832. The price paid for Dred Scott was probably about five hundred dollars, a fair price at that time for a healthy black male in his prime.[33]

As badly as the Blow family needed funds, the money that Peter Blow received from the sale of Dred Scott probably went to pay bills. It may also have helped defray the costs of Elizabeth Blow's funeral and burial, or perhaps more likely went to

31. *Frank Leslie's Illustrated Newspaper,* June 27, 1857; Wade, *Slavery,* 31.

32. Bryan, "Blow Family," pt. 1, 224, 225; Mrs. W. T. Blow to Mary Louise Dalton in an interview, February 18, 1907, Dred Scott Collection, MHS.

33. Ehrlich, *They Have No Rights,* 12, 13; Speculation that Scott perhaps sold for five hundred dollars, if correct, indicates that he was not a poor worker. In 1829 when Auguste Chouteau of St. Louis had eleven slaves between the ages of sixteen and thirty-five appraised, they averaged $486.35. Harrison Anthony Trexler, *Slavery in Missouri, 1804–1865,* 38.

provide a suitable trousseau for the daughter Charlotte Blow, who on November 8, 1831, at age twenty-one, was married to Joseph Charless Jr. at the First Presbyterian Church in St. Louis. It was a marriage that no well-bred Virginia-born lady would have entered into without a proper and appropriate send-off from her family, a need that in Peter Blow's mind would certainly have justified the selling of one of his slaves. Joseph Charless was not only a member of one of St. Louis's most prominent families but also one of the community's most promising young men. His father, Joseph Charless Sr., had founded the *Missouri Gazette* in 1808, the first newspaper west of the Mississippi. At twenty-seven, the son had graduated from Transylvania University at Lexington, Kentucky, practiced law, and was now in business with his father in a prospering wholesale paint and drug business.[34]

As Joseph Charless was soon to learn, he gained not only a bride in the marriage but also her four brothers and two sisters. For the Blow family was a family closely yoked together, and, as Joseph Charless would further learn, within that harnessed kinship was a slave named Dred Scott.

---

34. Bryan, "Blow Family," pt. 1, 225; Hyde and Conard, *Encyclopedia of the History of St. Louis,* vol. 1, 350.

Roswell's Office

It was a brief note that Roswell Field wrote to his uncle, Henry Kellogg, on Sunday evening, October 20, 1833.

> My Dear Sir. My father expired this evening at 5 o'clock. The funeral service will take place on Tuesday at noon. I can say no more.
>
> Affectionately, R. M. Field.[1]

Martin Field was sixty years old at his death, and whether his death was preceded by a lengthy illness is not known. Even with his impaired hearing, Field had remained active in the affairs of both family and village until his death.

In his will, Martin Field named his wife as executor along with her brother Daniel Kellogg. To Esther he left most of his twelve-thousand-dollar estate including what she may have valued most, the pews numbered one and twenty-eight in the Fayetteville meetinghouse. She had been the vital contributing partner in their marriage, and his will anticipated that after his death she would continue as matron of the Field household. In one paragraph of his will, unable to decide on a fair distribution among his heirs, Martin Field simply delegated the task to Esther, stating his intention to "leave it up to my beloved wife Esther S. Field to see that justice is done to all."[2]

To his son Roswell, the father left his gold watch, several shares of stock in local banks, and half of his 147-volume law library, which he said was "to be divided

---

1. Letter of Roswell Field to Henry Kellogg, October 20, 1833, Field Collection, JL.
2. Will of Martin Field dated December 30, 1830, vol. 13, 442, Marlboro District Probate Court, Brattleboro, Vt.

equally between my two oldest sons." All of the books in his "miscellaneous" library totaling 260 volumes were to go to his daughter Mary upon Esther's death.[3]

Most of the will governed the disposition of Field's science collection, which the befuddled estate appraiser described as including an electrifying machine, a chemical apparatus, maps, and "cabinets of minerals, shells, insects, etc. etc. including the entire collection of whatever kind with cases containing them." No mention was made of an eight-foot-long black snake that Martin Field had acquired four years earlier. Martin's treasured science collection was left to Roswell and Charles along with instructions that the collection was "not to be divided or removed from the Village of Fayetteville so long as any of my family shall continue to reside in said village." Also given to Roswell and Charles were all the books "which treat on scientific subjects, to be equally divided between them, except Gregory's Dictionary of Arts which I give to my beloved wife." Years later, the science collection—said to be the "rarest and most extensive" in Vermont—was given by Esther Field to Middlebury College.[4]

Probably the member of the Field family who felt Martin Field's death most acutely was Roswell. More than the other two sons, he had diligently sought to pattern himself after his father, whether in playing the violin, tramping the Vermont hills in search of minerals, studying to become a lawyer, or practicing his profession in the same town of Fayetteville as his father. Roswell even seems to have tried, as best he could, to carry on after Martin Field's death a correspondence with his father's associates in science. Asked by one of these associates for a specimen of bumblebee that Martin had written about in an article in the *American Journal of Science and Arts,* Roswell sent a wild bee instead. The recipient chided, "Mr. R. M. Field obligingly sent me some insects . . . [but] they proved to be a kind of wild bee . . . at least half as large as the honey bee itself, and were furnished with four wings, in all which respects they differ essentially from . . . [those] described by Gen. Field."[5]

While Roswell Field was unable to achieve the same degree of acceptance that his father had within the New England scientific community, he found it easier to earn the affirmation enjoyed by his father among the attorneys of Windham County. Like his father, Roswell was able to create through friendships and shared interests a professional circle of friends not unlike those who frequently congregated in Martin Field's law office. Roswell's friends—mostly men of his own age—included not only his brother Charles and fellow attorney Jonathan Bradley but also other

3. Martin Field left acreage, cattle, and agricultural items to his youngest son, Fisher Field. Fisher was probably a farmer. Several letters mention Fisher Field's landholdings in Iowa after he migrated west. Kellogg Collection, VHS.

4. Appraiser's inventory of Martin Field's estate. January 1834, vol. 13, Marlboro District Probate Court; "A black snake about 8 feet long was killed by Alvin Boyden on his farm in 1829 and was preserved in the zoology cabinet of Martin Field of Newfane." Charles P. Stickner, "Brookline"; Will of Martin Field; Pierce, *Field Genealogy,* 338.

5. *Green Mountain Democrat* (Vt.), February 27, 1835.

young men of youthful ambition who often gathered in what they called "Roswell's office," a small one-room frame building located on the south side of the Field residence, facing the road. Roswell's office lacked the Greek columns that adorned the front of Martin Field's law office, but those who gathered there probably found Roswell's office equally warm and inviting, especially on cold winter days when a hot tankard of "Flip"—well endowed with rum—would have kept the discussions as heated as the flames that leaped in the fireplace.[6]

Roswell's office served as a forum for those who shared his support of the embryonic Democratic Party, whose membership in Windham County was seen by opponents as comprising "lawyers and nothing but lawyers."[7] Just why Windham County lawyers should have been so heavily attracted to Jacksonian Democracy is uncertain, though, like Field, they perhaps liked the Democrats' "opposition to active governmental interference in society," and resented the tendency of the Whig Party to press for governmental prohibitions in concert with the "aggressive do-goodism" efforts of evangelical New England Protestants. Organizing themselves into *The Friends of Civil and Religious Liberty,* Roswell, his brother Charles, Jonathan Bradley, and perhaps other lawyers focused on issues of conflict arising between, as Field put it, "the orthodox and the liberals." In 1831, the group targeted the efforts of the Whigs and evangelical Christians who wanted to outlaw the movement of mail on the Sabbath. Field saw this as an intrusion of religion into the affairs of government and called for public meetings. He urged the members of *The Friends of Civil and Religious Liberty* to issue a petition memorial "against the passage of a law prohibiting Sunday mails" and asked his friend Bradley to draft the petition, urging it be "grave, sententious, didactick and argumentative with a few touches of the sublime."[8]

Roswell and the friends who congregated in his office constituted, in all likelihood, a group of young freethinkers whose rational approach to the social and political issues of the 1830s kept them out of not only the established Protestant

6. Appraisal of Martin Field estate; "When he [Roswell Field] succeeded to his father's practice he built an office on the street just below the old homestead," *Vermont Phoenix,* November 8, 1895; "Flip" was a favorite drink of Charles and Roswell Field and contained, among its several ingredients, rum, beer, eggs, and sugar and, in addition, "it needs a red hot flip iron plunged in" to make it hot. Field Collection, WCHS.

7. According to the *Vermont Phoenix,* the Democratic Party in Windham County was "Duped and led hither and thither by a few designing lawyers, the mass of the party seem to be mere puppets in the hands of those who stand behind the scene and pull the wires. . . . Now who are the leaders of the self-styled democratic party in this County? Are they farmers, the business men of the County? No, there is scarcely a businessman among them . . . Lawyers and nothing but lawyers are they who pull the wires in the great, or rather little puppet show." The editor then speculated that "lawyer R.M.F., representative from New Fane" has "an eye on a seat in Congress." *Vermont Phoenix,* August 11, 1837.

8. Michael F. Holt, "The Democratic Party 1828–1860," 514; Letter of December 31, 1830, from Roswell Field to Jonathan Bradley, Bradley Collection, The Arthur and Elizabeth Schlesinger Library on the History of Women in America.

churches of the time but also the Whigs, the dominant political party in Vermont. Roswell himself seems to have avoided any affiliation with his mother's Congregational church in Fayetteville, and it appears his friend Jonathan Bradley did likewise. About Bradley, an acquaintance said, "He is a lawyer by profession and his name is J. D. Bradley. If he is a Christian, I think he is not conscious of it, for he belongs to no church, and is rarely in attendance upon religious exercises."[9]

Roswell's office on occasion also served as a refuge for wayfarers passing through the tiny New England village. At least two of these—Zebina Eastman and Oscar Shafter—used Roswell's office as a way station before joining the exodus of other Vermonters migrating to the West.

Zebina Eastman, an orphan lad of eighteen, remembered quite well the first day he arrived in Fayetteville in May 1834.

> I wended my way up the valley of the West River, with a team and wagon loaded with the press and type with which I was to commence the vocation of my life as a printer and editor . . . I soon emerged from the dark wood to Kidder's factory . . . and at the end of the straight road leading up through the heart of the village, I had the whole glory of Fayetteville directly before me, sleeping so quietly amid the hills that surrounded it. And it was to me a pleasant sight. I felt as if I had got to the end of a toilsome journey.[10]

One of Eastman's first visits was to Roswell's office, and here Eastman told Field that having learned the printing trade, he planned to use two thousand dollars left by his father and publish a newspaper and literary journal in Fayetteville. Fayetteville had never had a newspaper, so the idea was probably received with enthusiasm by those gathered in Roswell's office. In the weeks that followed, Eastman and Field became close friends and soon developed what Eastman described as "a very intimate" relationship, in which they shared their thoughts not only on law and politics, but on literature and art as well. Roswell Field had a "splendid genius and intellect," Eastman later recalled, and admitted to friends that Field "had much influence over me in those early days."[11]

On the day Eastman arrived in Roswell's office, another young man was probably also there. Oscar Lovell Shafter also used Roswell's office as a place of sojourn before moving to the West. Shafter, twenty-two years old, was studying law under Roswell Field, having graduated from Wesleyan University in Connecticut.[12] Oscar was the son of William R. Shafter, judge of the Windham County Court.

It took Zebina Eastman a month to get his printing press working, and issue number one came off the press on June 7, 1834. Eastman named his paper the

9. Henry Burnham, Brattleboro, Windham County, Vermont, 137.
10. *Centennial Proceedings,* 113.
11. Paula Glasman, "Zebina Eastman, Chicago Abolitionist," 4; *Centennial Proceedings,* 114.
12. Flora H. Longhead, ed., *Life, Diary and Letters of Oscar Lovell Shafter,* 21.

Vermont Free Press, and told his readers in the first issue, "We intend ours shall be a free press. It shall be bound to no particular political party; the columns shall be open to a fair and candid hearing of the various political parties in our country."[13]

The newspaper was a four-page tabloid with the back page devoted to literary subjects: reviews of books, reprints from New England literary journals, and ads for books that were for sale in a new book shop Eastman opened in town in conjunction with the newspaper. The newspaper also contained comments by the editor, articles and letters written under a variety of pseudonyms, and a large sampling of items borrowed from the columns of newspapers throughout the country, including some as distant as the *Missouri Republican* in St. Louis.[14]

From the start it was a struggle for Eastman to keep his little newspaper going, and Roswell Field and others endeavored to assist him. When Eastman editorially called on the community to hold a Fourth of July celebration and received no reader response, Field volunteered to deliver a patriotic oration to the Democrats of Windham County on that day.[15] Oscar Shafter also assisted and wrote several lengthy articles for the newspaper. The first was entitled "The Legal Profession," and this was followed by a series of three articles headlined, "Is the African Negro a Man?" Shafter's answer to that question was a definite yes, pointing out that if blacks were seen as anything less it was because of prejudice. Shafter wrote:

> Of their sufferings and degradation we are the guilty authors; and let us no more charge the effects of our own injustice as imperfections in the work of the Deity . . . but the time is at hand when the farther progress of this great calumny will be arrested. The present age, with all its defects is treading one hateful prejudice after another into the dust; and the time will soon come, when that moving interrogatory of the poor despised Negro will receive an answer to which no voice will dissent—we are all children of the same family.[16]

Among the friends in Roswell's office, Shafter soon gained a reputation as an abolitionist. This was confirmed later when Shafter organized an antislavery group in the nearby village of Townshend, about four miles north of Fayetteville. Called the Windham County Anti-Slavery Society, the group believed, among other things, that slavery was a sin and that the "prejudice which prevails at the North against people of color is both unnatural and inhuman." Some dozen Windham County residents served as officers of the society but Roswell Field was not one of them, nor were any of his close associates or members of his family. A decade later, it was rumored that the Townshend society became a stop for escaped slaves on

13. *Newfane Vermont Free Press,* June 7, 1834.
14. Ibid., June 14, 1834.
15. Ibid., June 28, 1834.
16. Ibid., December 5, 1834.

the "underground railway that ran up the Connecticut River valley" from Rhode Island to Montpelier.[17]

During the 1830s, abolition was not a popular idea in Vermont; for the most part, it "was widely regarded with contempt and scoffed at by both leading political parties of the day." In Brattleboro, a justice of the peace threatened to tar and feather those who gave lectures on the subject. The feeling among many Vermonters was that since Vermonters had no slaves there was no need to preach to them about the evils of slavery. In 1837, a county convention of abolitionists was held in the courthouse at Fayetteville but "was thinly attended," and "the elite of Brattleboro, Newfane and Townshend did not attend, except for a few curiosity seekers." Even Zebina Eastman, who had at that time very strong antislavery sentiments, avoided using his newspaper for abolitionist pronouncements. It was Eastman's belief that the abolitionist movement was "ill judged and ill timed." He wrote, "No well wisher of his country desires the blacks to be beholden in bondage longer than absolutely necessary. When they and the country are in a state suitable for their liberty, the chain of slavery will be knocked off."[18]

After six months as editor, Eastman had nearly depleted his initial investment of two thousand dollars, and the newspaper was not attracting sufficient readers and advertisers. Perhaps believing that a little controversy might increase interest, Eastman told his readers that "a neutral paper cannot be supported in this place," and announced that henceforth the newspaper would support the Anti-Masonic Party and expose the evils of Freemasonry. Anti-Masonry was at that time a popular cause, and several newspapers in New England had already jumped on the bandwagon. It grew out of a long-simmering suspicion by New Englanders of secret societies, and it was also built on the social and economic unrest of the times. In 1826, the issue developed into a political movement in New York with the murder of a man named William Morgan, who had threatened to publish a book divulging the secrets of Freemasonry. The movement spread throughout New England, and hostility to Freemasonry became so intense in Vermont that many Masons renounced their secret vows.[19] Proclaimed Eastman in the pages of the *Vermont Free Press*:

> The two horrible evils in this country are Freemasonry and Slavery. They are both utterly inconsistent with the theory and the practical enjoyment of freedom.[20]

17. Eastman in later years said Shafter was the first abolitionist he had ever known. *Centennial Proceedings*, 115; the society's officers appear in the *Vermont Phoenix*, March 24, 1837; Wilbert H. Siebert, *Vermont's Anti-Slavery and Underground Railroad Record*, 90.

18. The quotes are from undated newspaper clippings in the Zebina Eastman scrapbook of 1878 in which Eastman describes some of the antislavery activities in Windham County, Chicago Historical Society, and the *Vermont Free Press*, August 9, 1834.

19. *Vermont Free Press*, December 6, 1834; David M. Ludlum, *Social Ferment in Vermont 1791–1850*, 105; James T. Adams, *Dictionary of American History*, 82.

20. *Vermont Free Press*, February 7, 1835.

Roswell Field must have viewed Eastman's writings on Freemasonry—and for that matter the whole Anti-Masonic movement—with mixed feelings. There is no record that Field himself was a member of the order, but his father, Martin Field, certainly had been, and had been a very active Mason at that. In Windham County, the Anti-Masonic movement had strong public support, and in the fall elections of 1834 William A. Palmer, gubernatorial candidate on the Anti-Masonic ticket, received more votes in Fayetteville than either of his Jackson or Whig party opponents.[21]

By November 20, 1834, the Masonic Lodge in Fayetteville voted to "abandon and give up the institution of Freemasonry," and called upon "all Masons throughout our country, especially in the state of Vermont, to abandon the institution." But apparently there was some lingering bitterness, and perhaps even a few die-hard Masons left around still hostile to the movement, for Zebina Eastman announced in February 1835 that the *Vermont Free Press* was ceasing publication, and he blamed the newspaper's demise on the Masons.

> We cast blame for our ill luck upon no person and no thing, but that bloated blood-stained and vicious monster Masonry, that archfiend which we have been warring against unaided, which has itself been crying out 'we are dead let us alone' . . . but we will say this more—Masonry is not more dead now than it was when it murdered William Morgan in cold blood, and we fear that many more Morgans must perish before that institution shall be entombed in oblivion.[22]

It is difficult to determine what Field's opinions were, if any, on these two controversial issues: abolition and Anti-Masonry. Roswell Field seems to have avoided active involvement in either one. The articles written in the *Vermont Free Press* on slavery or Freemasonry were usually written by either Shafter or Eastman, not Field. If Field had wanted to write on these topics for the newspaper, his friend Eastman would likely have published his articles. On abolition and Anti-Masonry, Roswell Field's sentiments may well have matched those of Eastman and Shafter, but if they did, Field apparently did not care to undertake a crusade on their behalf.

However, Field was not completely passive when it came to controversy, and his aggressiveness on behalf of a cause emerged when that cause involved a conflict in law or an issue of judicial significance. In these instances, Field's combative nature moved into action and he turned loose the full force of his legal knowledge and

21. Masonic archives in Missouri and Vermont have no record of a Roswell M. Field during the last century; In 1800 Martin Field delivered "an oration at Walpole, New Hampshire, before the Jerusalem Golden Rule and Olive Branch Lodges of Free and Accepted Masons, at their celebration of the festival of St. John the Baptist, June 14th, Anno Lucis, 5800." Marcus A. McCorison, *Vermont Imprints*, 125; Martin Field's Masonic apron, Field Collection, WCHS; *Vermont Free Press*, September 6, 1834; Anti-Masonic voters not only elected Palmer governor but also voted for the Anti-Masonic presidential candidate in 1832, making Vermont the only state where the candidate received a plurality. Frank M. Bryan, *Yankee Politics in Rural Vermont*, 15.

22. *Vermont Free Press*, February 14, 1835.

skill. On these occasions he became a most zealous crusader for his cause. Such aggressions surfaced several times in Field's life, and each time the cause was judicial in nature, concerning some question of law in which Field obviously felt a deep and personal involvement.

One such instance, and perhaps the earliest in his life, occurred when he was twenty-eight years old and serving in the General Assembly of the State of Vermont. Roswell Field and his brother Charles had been selected as representatives from Windham County, and Roswell was chosen to serve two terms, the first in 1835 and again in 1836. With twenty-three representatives from Windham County alone, the legislature of Vermont, which met at Montpelier, was clearly a large assembly. The legislative roster lists Field's appointment to the claims committee and shows that during the month's session at Montpelier he took his lodgings at Cottrill's Boarding House. According to the proceedings, Field, as a freshman legislator, seems to have introduced no legislation or initiated any actions. Except for his assignment to one special committee involving a judicial question, his presence, except in voting, might have gone unnoticed.[23]

On the morning of October 20, 1835, Roswell Field was named to a select committee to look into the "rights of witnesses" in the Vermont courts. It was obviously a legal question of great interest to Field and one on which he had some strong opinions of his own. Concerning rights of witnesses in the Vermont courts, Field not only prepared an address which he delivered to the assembly but also drafted an act aimed at eliminating the abuses he had found.[24]

On November 9, 1835, only two weeks after being named to the select committee, Roswell Field delivered his report before the assembly. At the same time he also introduced an act that abrogated the rules of common law and prohibited any person from being deemed "incompetent as a witness in any court, matter, or proceeding, on account of his opinions on matters of religious belief." Field told the legislators that his review of the procedures in Vermont courts revealed that "a certain religious faith is necessary to qualify a witness to testify in court" but that Vermont judges had not defined that faith, which varied from court to court. As a result, witnesses were excluded "by reason of the peculiarity of their religious opinions."[25]

23. The Fields' positions in the General Assembly are recorded in *Walton's Vermont Register* and *A List of the Members of the General Assembly for the Year 1835,* manuscript, vol. 76, 34, Vermont Secretary of State archives, Montpelier, Vt.; Roswell Field's freshman record is in *Directory and Rules of the House of Representatives*; On the same day, October 20, a petition was received by the governor and Council of Vermont from Amos Garnsey and others "praying that an act may be passed providing that no person shall be deprived of any civil right, or of giving testimony in a Court of Justice, on account of his religious belief." E. P. Walton, ed., *Records of the Governor and Council of the State of Vermont,* vol. 8, 234.

24. *Journal of the General Assembly of the State of Vermont.*

25. Pierce, *Field Genealogy,* 18; *Acts and Resolves Passed by the General Assembly of the State of Vermont at the October Session,* 1851; *Journal of the General Assembly,* Monday, November 9, 1835, 207.

Field continued, "precisely what a person must believe, to become a competent witness, has not yet been announced by the judges." The result, Field said, is that individual judges "in thus setting up a standard of orthodoxy, and trying the religious faith of witnesses . . . have overstepped the bounds of their jurisdiction, have intermeddled in a matter in which they have no concern, have disregarded the plain injunctions of the Constitution and have violated sacred rights belonging to freemen."[26]

He went on, "It cannot be doubted, that under this Constitution, every citizen is at liberty to adopt or reject any and every religious doctrine, notion, and fancy, which faith has revealed, reason suggested or fanaticism conjured up. He may believe in twenty Gods—in three Gods—or in one God, or in none at all; and he can not, for that cause, be questioned or in any manner put on trial."[27]

Focusing on the judges themselves, Field said they have neither the constitutional right nor the wisdom to "establish a code of theological jurisprudence." He continued, "among the infinite variety of religious doctrines, it is impossible to determine which are right and which wrong. All rests in opinion, and the judges, if they should be able to agree among themselves, are no better qualified to decide upon the hidden mysteries of religion, than the most illiterate person who may be produced as a witness."[28]

Added Field, "The existence of a Supreme Being, first cause, original principle, power or energy, by which the universe is upholden, is an article of faith, received by all mankind; but the essence, nature, and attributes of this being, cause, or principle, are topics of interminable and unavailing dispute and controversy. Can there be, then, in judicial practice, a greater absurdity than a rule requiring belief in a particular existence which no man can define or comprehend?"[29]

Field completed his lengthy address to the legislators by saying, "Experience will attest that whenever topics of religious faith are forced into courts of justice, they obtain there little but scandal and dishonor; and in the fierceness of the controversy, they are likely to be treated with a rudeness calculated to shock the pious and harden the profane."[30]

After Field finished his address, he introduced an act to abolish religious oaths for court witnesses; it was "read and concurred in" and then, after a second reading, was "ordered to lie on the table." The act was never voted on during the two years Field served in the legislature. It would, in fact, remain dormant for sixteen years before the General Assembly of Vermont would once again take it up. On November 19, 1851, long after Roswell Field had left Vermont, the assembly

26. *Journal of the General Assembly,* November 9, 1835, 207.
27. Ibid.
28. Ibid., 208.
29. Ibid.
30. Ibid.

passed the act that Field had first introduced in 1835. It established into Vermont law that "no person [can be deemed] incompetent as a witness on account of his religious belief."[31]

About a year after Roswell Field returned from his second term in the legislature, articles appeared in the newspapers of Vermont relating to an event far to the west, an event that would spur hours of discussion and debate in Roswell's office among Shafter, Eastman, and Field. That event centered on an abolitionist newspaper editor named Elijah P. Lovejoy, who had been run out of St. Louis and into Illinois for his antislavery and anti-Catholic writings.[32] On the banks of the Mississippi River in the town of Alton, across from St. Louis, Lovejoy was attacked on November 7, 1837, by an angry proslavery mob, which mortally wounded the young man by gunfire and destroyed his press. Before the murder, Lovejoy was little known outside of St. Louis, but his murder quickly established him throughout Vermont and the North as a symbol of the evils of slavery and of the dangers to freedom of the press.

Zebina Eastman later recalled that "it was in the office of R. M. Field, while Shafter was there a student, that I first heard of the murder of Lovejoy, at Alton, in defense of freedom of the Press."[33] The subject was, Eastman said, a topic greatly discussed and debated by the three young men. Eastman said that Roswell Field, a "firm believer in the Jacksonian democracy of the hour," used all of "his caustic powers to speak against the abolitionists." Shafter, on the other hand, was "equally embrued with the then new extremes of emancipation" and argued for the abolitionists.[34]

The incident, as might be expected, attracted the attention of newspaper editors throughout Vermont who, like Eastman, identified with Lovejoy and saw the young man as a martyr to the defense of a free American press. Interest in the murder itself had barely waned when trials began in 1838 at Alton of those who had participated in the mob attack. Once again the trials were well publicized in the Vermont press and within months were published in a book that was widely distributed and probably sold in Eastman's bookstore in Fayetteville.[35]

31. Ibid., 209; Fish, "Roswell Field," 232; Whether any politics were involved in the result is unknown. Some idea of party representation can be determined from the vote taken in the assembly for lieutenant governor, where 114 votes were cast for Lebbeus Egerton, Anti-Mason; 69 votes for Samuel Clark, Whig; 28 for Truman Chittenden, Democrat, and three scattered votes. Walton, *Records of Governor and Council,* 165; *Acts and Resolves Passed by the General Assembly.*

32. *An Account Of The Life, Trials And Perils Of Rev. Elijah P. Lovejoy Who Was Killed By A Pro-Slavery Mob At Alton, Illinois The Night of November 7, 1837,* 86–107.

33. *Centennial Proceedings,* 114.

34. Eastman Scrapbook of 1878, Chicago Historical Society.

35. [John Towler Trow], *Alton Trials: of Winthrop S. Gilman, Enoch Long, Amos B. Roff, George H. Walworth, George H. Whitney, William Harned, John S. Noble, James Morris Jr., Henry Tanner, Royal Weller, Reuben Gerry, and Thaddeus B. Hurlbutt; For The Crime Of Riot.*

The prosecutor in the trials was the young city attorney for Alton named Francis B. Murdoch, born in Maryland and educated for the law in Pennsylvania.[36] In a few years, as unlikely as it might have seemed in 1838 to those gathered in Roswell's office, Francis Murdoch and Roswell Field would share in a common cause as attorneys for two Missouri slaves named Dred and Harriet Scott.

The Lovejoy trials, for there were actually two, were held in January 1838, only two months after the murder, and some two dozen men were charged in the riot. Locally, everyone knew that it would be difficult to get convictions, but Francis Murdoch and two other attorneys for the state made a notable effort. Murdoch carefully avoided the touchy question of abolition, concentrating instead on the issue of freedom of the press. Murdoch told the jury:

> If there is one privilege more dear to us than another, it is the right of free discussion; the liberty of the press; the freedom of conscience. These have civilized and elevated a world; and better, far better, that all the evils which it is predicted abolition will bring on the country, should be actually fulfilled, than that these dearest rights of freedom should be surrendered, and the Constitution of your country brought with the blood of freemen, and sanctified by the memory of our fathers, should be nugatory. Then, indeed, will we be slaves. Yes, gentlemen, the liberty of the press is inseparably connected with our freedom, and the day that high prerogative of a free people is given up, will be the birthday of a nation of slaves.[37]

Attorney Francis Murdoch's plea failed to sway the Alton jury, however, and the men charged with destroying the printing press and killing Elijah Lovejoy were never convicted.[38] The editor of the *Vermont Phoenix* in nearby Brattleboro wrote:

> The murdered Lovejoy died, a MARTYR to the FREEDOM OF THE PRESS. It was a noble cause. Looking upon him as a freeman, bravely labouring for the right; as a patriot, taking his own life in his hands, as of less consequence that the establishment of one of the dearest and most precious blessings of our free constitution, we would embalm his memory, and plant the emblem of immortality to grow upon his grave.[39]

The editor of the *Vermont Watchman* wrote:

> Slaveholders, or their emissaries, invaded the limits, disturbed the peace, and violated the laws of a free state; and we fear these assassins have also succeeded in making their escape, and found sanctuary in the slave state of Missouri. It would only be carrying out the spirit of this atrocious act, should the government of Missouri refuse any aid in arresting the perpetrators. But we shall see.[40]

36. Ehrlich, *They Have No Rights,* 37.
37. Trow, *Alton Trials,* 123.
38. *History of Madison County, Illinois,* 188.
39. Joseph C. Lovejoy and Owen Lovejoy, *Memoir Of The Rev. Elijah P. Lovejoy,* 326.
40. Ibid., 328.

For Zebina Eastman the events in Alton and the martyrdom of Elijah Lovejoy had a lasting impact. Years later he recalled that in 1838 he told his friends in Roswell's office, "I would go to Illinois and print an abolition paper, or something like it, if I died for it." These words proved prophetic for Eastman. Within a year he had migrated to Chicago, where for thirteen years he edited the *Western Citizen,* an abolitionist publication that circulated widely throughout the Midwest. In influence, the newspaper was said by some to have equaled William Lloyd Garrison's *Liberator* in swaying public opinion against slavery. In the years preceding the Civil War, Eastman became a leading abolitionist, organizing groups throughout the North. Active in Republican Party politics, he was named by President Abraham Lincoln as consul at Bristol, England, during the Civil War.[41]

As for Oscar Shafter, whom Eastman considered a "young man of handsome talents," he, too, would soon leave Fayetteville for the West.[42] After attending Harvard Law School, where he studied under Joseph Story, Shafter ran unsuccessfully as the Free Soil candidate for governor of Vermont in 1848 and then, like Eastman, headed west, eventually reaching San Francisco. A distinguished legal career followed, and in 1864 Shafter was named associate justice of the Supreme Court of California, a position he held for ten years.[43]

For months after the trial, the editors in Vermont continued their attacks not only on those involved in Lovejoy's death but also on the proslavery communities and press in the South. One newspaper, the *Vermont Caledonian,* described St. Louis as a theater of murder and warned readers to stay away.

> Let this place be forever remembered—let its name be written in the catalogue of all that is execrable—let the emigrant avoid it as he values his liberty—let him pass by on the other side of this Sodom of the West, lest, if he should tarry in it, the wrath of insulted heaven in fire and water, should descend and destroy this place, with its wicked, pusillanimous, and shameless inhabitants who, like base cowards, permitted the murder of one of their fellow-citizens.[44]

41. *Centennial Proceedings,* 115; Glasman, "Zebina Eastman," 8; Roughly two-thirds of the circulation of the *Western Citizen* was in Illinois, with most of the remaining circulation in Wisconsin, Iowa, Michigan, and Indiana. Among the few subscribers in New England was "Mrs. E. S. Field, Fayetteville, Windham County, Vermont." Roswell Field's name could not be found on the subscription list, perhaps because the newspaper was not mailed into slave states, or was prohibited from entering. *Western Citizen* Mail Book for 1846–1847, Zebina Eastman Collection, Chicago Historical Society; Glasman, "Zebina Eastman," 2; Zebina Eastman Civil War correspondence from England to America, Eastman Collection, Chicago Historical Society.

42. *Centennial Proceedings,* 114; *Vermont Free Press,* August 23, 1834.

43. Longhead, *Oscar Shafter,* 23–26.

44. Lovejoy, *Memoir,* 326.

The "Unhappy Incident"

Roswell Field remembered clearly that he first met Mary Almira Phelps on the afternoon of August 30, 1832. It was one of those beautiful late summer days in Vermont, and Mary Almira, accompanied by Roswell's sister, Mary, along with Susan Bradley, the wife of Roswell's good friend Jonathan Door Bradley of Brattleboro, pulled up in a chaise at the entrance gate to the Field homestead.[1] The three ladies had arrived in Fayetteville after a leisurely ten-mile ride from Brattleboro along the banks of the West River.

In testimony presented before the Chancery Court and later the Vermont Supreme Court, it was reported that when the ladies' chaise came to a stop before the Field house, "Roswell advanced to hand them out, and then for the first time saw and was introduced to . . . Mary Almira, who received him with a nod and a broad good-humored laugh."[2] Roswell's gesture that afternoon was, at most, nothing more than the polite offering of a gentleman's hand to assist three ladies out of a carriage. And the incident itself, trivial as it was, would today not be remembered—much less recorded for posterity in the published annals of the Vermont Supreme Court—had not subsequent events ordained otherwise. In the months and years that followed, this casual first meeting with Mary Almira Phelps would develop into a bitter and turbulent dispute, and before it played itself out in the courtrooms and newspapers of Vermont, it would completely change the

1. Roswell M. Field pleading, *Jeremiah H. Clark et al. v. Roswell M. Field,* Windsor County Superior Court, February term, 1835 (6 *Vermont Reports,* 460–76). Court records in the Vermont State Archives, Middlesex, Vt.

2. Ibid.

course of Roswell Field's life, leading him eventually not only to St. Louis, but also to a slave named Dred Scott.

Roswell related to the court that "some conversation of a general nature" passed between him and Mary Almira at that first meeting, and that she was by his judgment "a young lady of very pleasing face and form and agreeable manners." But he added that after this brief visit and her return to Brattleboro where she was staying with the Bradley family, he "did not then expect ever to see her more."[3]

It is likely, however, that he was impressed enough by her beauty to ask questions of his sister following the young lady's departure. From Mary, his sister, Roswell Field would have learned that Mary Almira was eighteen years old, having celebrated her birthday only a month earlier, and that she was the daughter of a widow, Susanna Phelps, who had recently remarried and was now known as Susanna Torrey. Along with her mother, stepfather, brothers, and sisters, Mary Almira lived in the town of Windsor some thirty miles north. Her father, Dr. Elisha Phelps, had been prominent in the county, and after his death he had left Susanna and the children with a comfortable inheritance. Roswell's sister might also have added that Mary Almira had attended the academy at Leicester, Massachusetts. At about this point in his sister's account of the young lady's life, Roswell Field's interest probably waned, for his sister must have further related that as a student at the academy, Mary Almira had met a young man named Jeremiah Clark to whom she formed "a natural and virtuous attachment" and to whom she was now engaged to be married.[4]

It must have been a very surprised Roswell Field who, twelve days later on September 11, 1832, found Mary Almira again seated in a carriage at the gate of his home, this time in company with Roswell's fellow attorney, Jonathan Bradley, whose "professional business called him to Fayetteville during the sitting of the court." Mary Almira, the court was later told, had decided to accompany him on the trip and to spend eight days visiting her new friend, Roswell's sister Mary, who had earlier graciously extended an invitation for Mary Almira to visit at any time.[5]

During these eight days when Mary Almira was a guest in the Field household, young love took its natural course, a full description of which is meticulously related in volume six of the Vermont Supreme Court records, and is one of three cases involving Field and Mary Almira that would reach Vermont's high court. That Roswell Field was not at all pleased at having his private and personal affairs aired in public is evident in his pleading, for not only did he plainly state his reluctance, but he also wrote his pleading in the vernacular of a skillfully applied legal vocabulary with a reticence and remoteness designed to obscure his deep personal feelings. He protested, for example, "against the indelicacy of calling him

3. Ibid.
4. Jeremiah Clark pleading, *Clark v. Field*.
5. Roswell Field pleading, *Clark v. Field*.

before this august and honorable court to render an account of his attentions and addresses to a Lady."[6]

According to Roswell Field, Mary Almira had been a guest in his home for two days, when on the evening of September 13, he first passed, by his own judgment, "beyond the boundaries of formal civility in his relations with the young woman." He told the court that on that evening, "when bidding the said Mary Almira good-night in the sitting room as he was about to retire to his lodgings, Roswell plucked a leaf from the rosebush in the room, kissed it, and presented it to her; on the next day when he saw the said Mary Almira she took from her bosom a paper, unfolded it, and showed Roswell a leaf (the same, he supposes, that was presented the evening before), neatly stitched on the paper, and which she again carefully folded and replaced in her bosom."[7]

A day or so later, as Mary Almira and Roswell played chess, he asked her permission to name the queen "Miss Phelps," and he bent all his energies and talent toward capturing that particular piece. Field told the court that when, after sacrificing every point of the game, he triumphantly captured the queen, "he took note of the pleasure and delight manifested by said Mary Almira at the ardor with which he pursued his object and kissed his prize." In another game of chess he recalled that "Jeremiah was introduced into the game as a black bishop, and very soon was exchanged for a pawn."[8]

After Mary Almira had spent four days at the Field home, Jonathan Bradley stopped by to say that he was called to the nearby town of Westminster; he asked Mary Almira if she wished to accompany him on the ride. At this, Mary Almira turned to Roswell and "inquired with a smile if it was not likely to rain?" To this Roswell "told her that it would be very imprudent for her to set out." That same afternoon, after Mary Almira declined Bradley's invitation to visit Westminster, she "graciously pleased to make, with her own fair hand, a pocket pin-cushion of blue silk and to put the same into Roswell's hands, at the same time remarking that blue was the emblem of love and constancy," and Roswell reported that "he received the same with a profound bow." Roswell then complimented "the beauty of said Almira's hair, whereupon she graciously consented to present him with a lock of the same, and he humbly accepted, kissed, and pressed it to his heart."[9]

The next morning, as they stood side by side, with Roswell holding her hand "and carelessly turning over the leaves of a Bible," his eye accidentally rested on

6. Three cases involving Roswell Field and Mary Almira Phelps reached the Vermont Supreme Court: *Mary Almira Clark, survivor of Jeremiah Clark v. Roswell M. Field, 6 Vermont Reports, Susanna Torrey v. Roswell M. Field, 5 Vermont Reports,* and *Roswell M. Field, and Mary A. Field, his wife, v. Susannah Torrey, 4 Vermont Reports,* VSC; In the court records, there is some confusion in the spelling of the names Clark and Clarke, and Susanna and Susannah; The quote is from Slason Thompson, *Study in Heredity,* 69.

7. Field pleading, *Clark v. Field.*

8. Ibid.

9. Ibid.

the passage in the book of Jeremiah which read, "As for me, behold, I am in your hand: do with me as seemeth good and meet unto you." Roswell further stated "that with the kind permission of said Mary Almira he did at various times press the hand of said Mary Almira and with her like gracious permission did kiss her hand, her cheek and her lips."[10]

Field believed that "his attentions and addresses were from the first agreeable to Mary's feelings and welcome to her heart" and he said "that they were always permitted and received with great kindness and sweetness of manner." So when Mary Almira left the Field residence in the company of Jonathan Bradley on Wednesday, September 19, for the return to Brattleboro, Roswell Field promised to call on her the following Wednesday at the Bradley home. He kept this appointment faithfully, then he called again a week later on Thursday afternoon, September 27, and then again on Monday evening, October 1, and the next day in the afternoon and evening and again the following day, October 3, in the afternoon and evening.[11]

Roswell reported to the court that on all visits with Mary Almira he sat in the parlor of the Bradley home and that Jonathan Bradley and his wife usually sat with them unless "Mr. Bradley was engaged in business at his office and Mistress Bradley employed about her domestic concerns in the house."[12]

However, Roswell Field told the court that he "well remembers that on Wednesday evening the 3rd of October, he sat in Mister Bradley's parlour with the said Mary Almira, that Mister and Mistress Bradley both came into the parlour and a general conversation took place, that, about the hour of nine in the evening, the defendant, perceiving a reserve in the manner of Mister and Mistress Bradley, was on the point of withdrawing to his lodgings, and took his hat in hand for that purpose, when the said Mary Almira wrote something on a bit of paper with a pencil, and handed the same to the defendant . . . the Defendant took the paper and found written thereon the words 'Don't go yet'—and the Defendant confesses that he obeyed the precept and remained until after said Bradley and wife had retired."[13]

Roswell returned home to Fayetteville for a few days but returned to Brattleboro to visit Mary Almira on Wednesday, October 10 and again on October 12, 13, and 14. The visits might have continued had not word of them reached Mary Almira's mother, Susanna Torrey, in Windsor, who immediately dispatched a note calling for the daughter's prompt return home. The news brought Mary Almira to Roswell's bosom, to which, according to court testimony, she clung "with all the ardor of youthful, passionate love." Roswell and Mary Almira, according to Field's pleading, resolved to wed immediately, and asked Justice Jonathan Bradley

10. Ibid.
11. Ibid.
12. Ibid.
13. Ibid.

to perform the ceremony then and there in his home but he declined, saying he did not wish to do so without the consent of Mary Almira's mother. It was then decided that the marriage would take place at Putney, a small town on the post road to Windsor, by a justice of the peace.[14]

On October 15, Mary Almira, with Jonathan Bradley driving the carriage, left Brattleboro for Windsor, and when they reached Putney, Roswell was there waiting. The wedding ceremony followed, described in court testimony as being "in a solemn, serious, and impressive manner in the front room of the publick house, the said Jonathan alone being present besides the parties and the magistrate."[15]

The court record then stated that "immediately after the ceremony took place" Field returned to his home in Fayetteville and Mary Almira, with Mr. Bradley, drove "to the residence of her mother in Windsor" where "nothing was communicated to her mother or friends in relation to the marriage at Putney."[16]

However, sometime within the next two weeks, the family of Mary Almira learned of the ceremony at Putney. Jeremiah Clark, Mary's fiancé, was immediately summoned from Massachusetts, a family conference was held, and a letter drafted and forwarded to Roswell Field through the family lawyer. It read:

> To Mr. Roswell Field:
>   Sir: Moments of deep consideration and much reflection have at length caused me to see in its proper light the whole of my late visit to Brattleboro. That I have been led by you and others to a course of conduct which my own feelings, reason, and sense entirely disapprove, is now very clear to me. I therefore write this to inform you that I am not willing on any account to see you again. Neither will I by any course you can adopt be prevailed upon to view the matter in a different light from what I now do. I leave you the alternative of forever preventing the public avowal of a disgraceful transaction, of which you yourself said you were ashamed. Mary A.P.[17]

When the letter was handed to Roswell Field by the Torrey family attorney, Field instantly called it an "impudent forgery" and wrote a return reply urging that the Putney marriage be made public and an end put to the engagement of Jeremiah and Mary Almira. Before receiving a reply, he left immediately for Windsor, where his reception at the Torrey residence was anything but cordial.[18]

On entering the parlor where the family had gathered, he extended his hand to Mary Almira and "asked her how she did." But she looked at her mother and rejected his hand. Mrs. Torrey rebuffed a similar gesture. When he asked for a few private moments with his wife, the family retreated to the hallway outside the room, but kept the door open so that the conversation could be heard.[19]

14. Ibid.
15. Ibid.
16. *Clark v. Field,* in 6 *Vermont Reports,* 467, VSC.
17. Ibid., 470.
18. Field pleading, *Clark v. Field.*
19. Ibid.

In answer to Roswell Field's questions about the letter he had received, Mary Almira replied that upon coming home and thinking it over she found that she *did* love Jeremiah Clark, that Clark had been very kind to her, and that she ought to marry him.

Roswell asked how she could do that since she was already married.

"Why," said Mary Almira, "you can give up the certificate; let it all go and nobody will know anything about it." Pleading further, she added, "Come, now, you've got the certificate in your pocket, and you can give it up just as well as not and let me marry Jeremiah."[20]

This Field refused to do, and the private interview was interrupted by the mother who in great agitation echoed Mary Almira's plea for Field to give up the marriage certificate "and let things be as if they had never been."[21]

As the family quickly returned to the room, Field restated his position that he would not give up the certificate and that if Mary Almira attempted marriage with another he would publish the Putney marriage in every parish church and newspaper in New England. He turned and left; after remaining in Windsor for three days and feeling that nothing was to be gained by exposing "himself to renewed insults," he returned home to Fayetteville. A week later Mary Almira and Jeremiah Clark were married and after a brief residence in Boston, sailed for Europe. Upon her return, Mary Almira was several months pregnant with Jeremiah Clark's child.[22]

From the detailed court account of Roswell Field's courtship of Mary Almira, there can be little doubt that he was very much in love with her and had suffered a deep hurt and humiliation in the rejection he received from the young lady and her family. A person less emotionally involved than Field might have been inclined to take Susanna Torrey's suggestion, tear up the wedding certificate, and, as Mrs. Torrey said, "let things be as if they had never been." Or perhaps, if the person were legally inclined, they might have had the Putney civil marriage formally annulled, considering it a turn of good fortune to have been given the opportunity of being freed from a marriage to a young lady who was quite clearly immature. Had Field done so, he would have spared himself a great deal of future anguish and avoided what his family and friends, when speaking of Roswell Field among themselves, would later refer to as that "unhappy incident."[23]

20. Ibid.
21. Ibid.
22. Slason Thompson, *Study in Heredity,* 29; The quote is from Field pleading, *Clark v. Field.*
23. In his pleading, Roswell Field quotes Mary Almira's brother, Colonel Francis E. Phelps, as describing Mary Almira as an "unprincipled girl" who after her father's death when she was young "had grown up without government or discipline, that she always had her own way." *Clark v. Field*; Judge Frank L. Fish, when speaking of the Phelps-Field cases in his address to those attending the dedication of Field's portrait in the Windham County Courthouse in 1923, described it as the "unhappy incident." Fish, "Roswell Field," 236; Melvin L. Gray, executor of

While the humiliation of the rejection was certainly much on Field's mind at the time, more salient and weighty in influencing the course of action he was about to undertake was his firm belief in the legality of his civil marriage.[24] To Field, the marriage certificate represented a legal and binding contract between himself and Mary Almira and this took precedence over any other consideration. It appeared not to matter to him that even though his marriage might be legal, it had never been consummated. Nor did it seem to matter that his resolute belief in the validity of the Putney marriage made Mary Almira's subsequent marriage to Jeremiah Clark illegal and made her a bigamist before the law. Further it made her children from this marriage, to use the common New England term, bastards. The only thing that seemed to matter to Field was the law; in Field's judgment the law was on his side and his marriage was not only valid but binding. For his remaining years in Vermont, Field always called Mary Almira "his wife" and referred to her as "Mrs. Roswell M. Field."[25]

Therefore, from Field's point of view his wedding certificate was a legally binding civil contract, and this was all that really mattered. And just as he would some twenty years later tenaciously hold to the sanctity of Missouri's laws on slave freedom on behalf of his client Dred Scott, here in Vermont in 1832 he held to the sanctity of his civil marriage contract; to uphold its legal validity he would take his cause, if necessary, all the way to the Vermont Supreme Court. Those, like Susanna Torrey, who disavowed the sanctity of such a legal contract, would suffer the consequences for their debasement of the law. In Roswell's eyes Susanna Torrey was asking him to commit a crime and to "acquiesce and consent to the prostitution and adultery" of his wife.[26]

While anger, humiliation, and perhaps jealousy most assuredly drove Field, his subsequent actions were deliberate and calculating. The course he was about to embark upon, and to which he would devote a good part of the next nine years, was assiduously designed to achieve two objectives: first, "to bring the facts before the publick," and, second, "to test the validity of . . . [his] marriage at Putney in law."[27] What is less clear, however, is whether Field comprehended the likely

Field's estate and one of Field's closest Missouri friends, does not mention the Vermont Supreme Court cases in his biographical sketch of Field written in 1898 for A. J. D. Stewart's *History of the Bench and Bar of Missouri.* W. V. N. Bay, however, in his *Reminiscences,* published in 1878, does mention the cases.

24. Just why Roswell Field was considered an undesirable husband for Mary Almira Phelps by her family is somewhat surprising, but most likely Clark's wealth and social standing exceeded Field's. Field in his pleading in *Clark v. Field* quotes Dr. Edward E. Phelps as saying that Mary Almira "loves the whole of the other sex indiscriminately and would be just as happy with one man as another." To this Field asked why the family was in such anxiety as to her choice of husband. The doctor then replied, "Why damn it, sir, we have our preferences."

25. For example, in the legal action brought by Roswell M. Field and Mary A. Field, his wife, against Susanna Torrey.

26. Field pleading, *Clark v. Field.*

27. Ibid.

consequences of his actions, just as it would be unclear twenty years later, when he employed much the same strategy, whether he comprehended the consequences of taking a Missouri slave's case for freedom to the United States Supreme Court.

Within the first year following his marriage at Putney, he undertook a number of actions, both in the courts and in the newspapers, to achieve his two objectives. One of his first actions was his appearance before the Grand Jury of Windsor County, where he presented "a statement of the facts and circumstances connected with the abduction and prostitution of Mary Almira." The jury, having heard the facts, presented a bill of indictment against Mary Almira's two brothers, Mrs. Torrey, and Jeremiah Clark for a "conspiracy to carry the said Mary Almira without the State of Vermont, and to cause her to commit whoredom and adultery with said Jeremiah."[28]

Field then followed Mary Almira and Jeremiah Clark to Boston where he "presented to the Grand Jury of the City of Boston a written statement of facts in relation to the cohabitation of said Mary Almira with said Jeremiah in adultery." However, before any action could be taken, the couple "withdrew from the vicinity of Boston, left New England, and in a short time there after took passage, at the City of New York, in an outward-bound vessel."[29]

On his return to Vermont, Field took his next legal step and secured an indictment of Mary Almira's brother, Edward E. Phelps, in the United States District Court for having opened a letter Field sent to Mary Almira at Windsor. The newspaper at Fayetteville, edited by Field's good friend Zebina Eastman, noted that the case, even though centered in Windsor County thirty miles distant, was of "considerable interest" locally because "of the known connection of the circumstances, out of which it has grown, with the abduction and second marriage of the lady," Mrs. Roswell Field. The newspaper reported that Mary Almira's brother was found innocent of these mail fraud charges after the jury deliberated for thirteen hours, but added, perhaps as an editorial comment on the jury's verdict, that "on the same day" a thirteen-year-old black boy, who had tampered with the mails, "was sentenced to two years imprisonment at hard labor in the State Prison."[30]

Field's friend Eastman reported on still another court case that Field instigated in Windsor County, described in the newspaper as "R. M. Field and his wife against Green and Hatch," but made no mention of what the case involved, other than that it was related to "the validity of the marriage between the plaintiffs had before Asa Keyes, Esq., at Putney, on the 15th of Oct. 1832." The newspaper went on to relate that "it is well known that the lady, shortly after the marriage, was carried into a foreign jurisdiction by two female relatives and consigned in keeping to a young man of Boston" with the intent "to ruin and debauch the young lady."[31]

28. Ibid.
29. Ibid.
30. Ibid.; *Vermont Free Press,* June 7, 1834.
31. *Vermont Free Press,* June 7, 1834.

According to the newspaper account Field was "disappointed" that the courts did not rule on the legality of the Putney marriage, but the newspaper added that "it is understood that, in consequence of the very many misrepresentations circulating in the community on the subject of this marriage, Mr. Field will institute farther proceedings in law, calculated to bring the facts before the public. It is said also that in connection with the main action in this singular case, several interesting episodes are in a course of development."[32]

One of these predicted "interesting" episodes was the case of *Roswell M. Field, and Mary A. Field, his wife, v. Susannah Torrey,* which was filed in Windham County and which would reach the Vermont Supreme Court in 1835. But before the case was heard in the Chancery Court in Windham County, Field had the charges against Susanna Torrey published on May 17 and 24, 1834, in the pages of the *Vermont Intelligencer* of Bellows Falls, a town not far from Windsor, where Field was probably confident the charges would be seen and read not only by Susanna Torrey herself, her relatives, and friends, but by every literate adult in the county.[33]

Samuel H. Taylor, editor of the *Vermont Intelligencer,* later said he "had some surprise over the phraseology" of what Field was asking him to publish, but he was assured by Field that the chancellor of the court had read the "court notice" and had ordered its publication in his newspaper. The chancellor later testified that he had signed the order to make a public notice of the charges without reading them and that when he later saw the material in the newspaper, "I found to my astonishment that it contained very objectionable matter." As events later unfolded, the circumstances surrounding the publication of Field's charges against Susanna Torrey in the Bellows Falls newspaper would be important, for in a subsequent suit—this one also destined to reach the Vermont Supreme Court—Susanna Torrey charged Field with libel.[34]

The basis of Field's suit against Susanna Torrey was that Torrey, as administrator or bailiff of her daughter's inheritance from her father, had failed to provide an accounting of these inherited assets, either to Mary Almira or to Roswell Field as her husband, and that Susanna Torrey had continued to reap the benefits of Mary

32. Ibid.

33. *Roswell M. Field, and Mary A. Field, his wife, v. Susannah Torrey,* in 4 *Vermont Reports,* 371, VSC; Copies of the *Bellows Falls Intelligencer* for this period are not extant, nor is the published material contained in the reports of the Vermont Supreme Court. A printed copy of the published material, however, is contained in a booklet entitled *Trial For Libel,* an undated copy of which is located in the Field Collection at the Jones Library. This undated booklet was printed by E. C. Church, and covers, according to the printer, "A scandal case in which a very large number of very good people were mixed up, and created much excitement in its day." M. D. Gilman, ed., *The Biography of Vermont Or A List Of Books And Pamphlets Relating In Any Way To The State.*

34. *Susanna Torrey v. R. M. Field,* in *Trial For Libel,* Field Collection, JL; *Susanna Torrey v. Roswell M. Field,* in 5 *Vermont Reports,* 352, VSC.

Almira's inheritance even after her daughter came of age.[35] While the matter of Susanna Torrey's performance as administrator of her husband's estate was the stated legal issue involved in the suit, Roswell Field quite obviously had another objective in mind, and this was the opportunity the suit afforded to expose Susanna Torrey's life to public view. In this endeavor, Field showed how ruthless he could be.

Susanna Torrey, Field asserted in his legal action, had been employed by Mary Almira's father, Dr. Elisha Phelps, after the doctor's wife, Molly, had become afflicted with a "virulent and inveterate disease by which her eye-sight was greatly impaired." Torrey was at that time, Field stated, a "spinster, then commonly called Suky Eastman, a milliner or tailoress of Hanover." She was hired by Dr. Phelps to replace a previous servant, Hopy Talbot of Pocatapaug Flats with whom the doctor had had intimate relations, and "to take up her residence at the mansion house of said Elisha, to minister unto his wants and necessities as a house-keeper and hand-maiden" providing the same services as had Hopy Talbot. Elisha Phelps died when Mary Almira was five years old, and at that point, according to Field, Susanna "contriving, by sheer craft to cut off a large part" of Mary Almira's inheritance, "began to give out in speeches that she had been lawfully married to" Dr. Phelps and "to claim that, as his widow, she was entitled to dower in his estate." Furthermore, Field said, "Susannah Eastman, spinster, now Mistress Susannah Torrey of Windsor County, by divers artful, cunning and fraudulent pretenses" acquired valuable tracts of land from the estate of Dr. Phelps.[36]

Field raised questions as to whether Dr. Phelps had ever been legally divorced from his first wife, and also whether he had ever legally married Susanna. Field wrote that Elisha was "moved and seduced by the wanton and lascivious blandishments of said Susannah, who was then by her craft, contriving to make breaches between Elisha and his wife Molly." Susanna threatened Elisha's wife, Molly, with depositions she had taken "proving the act of adultery of said Elisha with said Susannah and other women" in order to convince Molly to seek a divorce from her husband. And, Field charged, Elisha "unmoved by the tears and supplications of said Molly, and led by evil passions artfully excited by said Susannah, also threatened to sell all of his property and effects, and escape with his harlot beyond the seas, leaving said Molly without home or shelter, and doomed to wander a blind beggar on the earth." Field stated further that "Elisha and Susannah never did intermarry after the date of such pretended divorce, and that their cohabitation was, in its inception and continuance, altogether meretricious and unlawful."[37]

It does not take much imagination to envision the reaction in Windsor County when these charges appeared in print on the pages of the *Vermont Intelligencer*. In addition, there were the mischievous questions raised in the minds of readers by

35. *Field v. Torrey.*
36. Ibid.
37. Ibid.

the names listed as instigators of the suit, "Roswell M. Field, and Mary A. Field, his wife."

After the chancery court heard the charges in the case, the court artfully dodged the sensitive issues involved, ruling simply that it was the court's opinion that the case properly belonged in the probate court, not the chancery court. However, on appeal to the Vermont Supreme Court, that court ruled that the "probate court is not clothed with all the power" and reversed the lower court's ruling and sent the case back to the chancery court.[38]

But Susanna Torrey probably had no intention of making a public accounting of her handling of Elisha Phelp's estate—certainly not to Roswell M. Field—and, in a counter move, immediately filed a libel suit against Field for ten thousand dollars, which, among other things, charged that Field "falsely, wickedly and maliciously did compose and publish and cause . . . to be published false, scandalous, malicious and defamatory libel" concerning her relationship with Elisha Phelps. To help win her case, Susanna Torrey hired, according to Field's defense attorney, the "most distinguished" array of legal talent the state of Vermont afforded.[39]

The case came to trial on November 28, 1835, at Woodstock in Windsor County and continued for several weeks with numerous witnesses offering depositions and testimony on both sides. Field based his defense on not only what he claimed was the "truth of the facts" of the charges made against Susanna Torrey but also the fact that publication of the charges in the Bellows Falls newspaper was made "under order in chancery."[40]

Strangely, nowhere in the trial was Field's marriage to Mary Almira a subject of contention, even though Field's attorney "read a record of marriage between the defendant and Mary Almira Phelps at Putney on the 15th of October, 1832." One of Susanna Torrey's attorneys, however, did touch on the marriage in his closing statement to the jury:

> The defendant said that he married the daughter of the plaintiff. For this very reason, he deserves a double punishment for his wanton and brutal outrage on filial reverence and piety. He charges in the pleas that the plaintiff had endeavored to make an adulteress of her daughter. What an atrocious charge! The whole conduct of the defendant is marked with unexampled malignity towards this virtuous and respectable matron, a demon thirsting for the plaintiff's destruction. Oh gentlemen, if you could but know the savage and ruthless warfare he has waged against this venerable, unoffending, widowed lady, how he has endeavored to bow her grey head with sorrow to the grave, you would consider any amount of pecuniary damages a poor equivalent for her manifold and aggravated sufferings.[41]

38. Ibid.

39. *Torrey v. Field*; *Trial For Libel*, 26; Field's attorney for both the state supreme court trials and the trials in Windsor County was Charles Coolidge, who at one time served as state's attorney for Windsor County, *Vermont Free Press*, October 25, 1834.

40. *Trial For Libel*, 25.

41. Ibid., 28.

Apparently, Susanna Torrey's array of legal talent failed to convince the Windham County jury, for they found for Roswell Field. The case was immediately appealed to the Vermont Supreme Court, where it was heard in February 1838, and where, after a lengthy weighing by the court of the privileges and immunities of published court orders by newspapers, the decision of the lower court was upheld.[42]

The proceedings of the Vermont Supreme Court in this case cover more than sixty printed pages in book five of the *Vermont Reports,* and these proceedings are in turn dominated by the ten special pleadings in bar made by Roswell Field.[43] These pleas relate in detail Field's description of the actions of Susanna Torrey, and while they are written in the vernacular of a lawyer they reflect not only Field's skill as an attorney but also the creativity of someone obviously well versed in English literature and exceptionally fluent in the English language. Paragraph by paragraph, the pleadings reveal the marked brilliance of Roswell Field's mind as he tells—in almost Dickensian fashion—his version of the pathetic seduction of Elisha Phelps by his servant Susanna. Writes Attorney Roswell Field:

> And the defendant further says, that said Susanna, being a woman of talents, and of great show of piety, virtue, and respectability, did, to wit, at Hanover aforesaid, in the tailor's-shop of one George Walton there situate, and in a certain bed-room adjacent thereto, to wit, on the 9th day of September, 1797, in the night time, and at divers other times and places, by many wanton and lascivious blandishments, and by divers artful and wicked practices, tempt, stir up, incite, seduce, instigate, provoke, and persuade said Elisha, unlawfully and wickedly to get and procure a false, fraudulent, covinous and collusive bill of divorce, wrongfully and unjustly dissolving the marriage between said Elisha and said Molly, to the end that said Susanna and said Elisha might have their intercourse, connection, and copulation together, under the false and feigned color, guise, and pretence of lawful, holy, and sacred matrimony.[44]

Within a few years after the Vermont Supreme Court ruled on *Susanna Torrey v. Roswell M. Field,* the *Vermont Reports* covering the proceedings of the case came to the attention of Justice Joseph Story of the United States Supreme Court. Story did not comment on the case itself nor on the decision of Vermont's highest court, but he was greatly impressed by the pleadings of Roswell Field. He pronounced them "masterpieces of special pleadings."[45]

More than five years had now elapsed since Mary Almira and Roswell had stood before Justice of the Peace Asa Keyes at Putney to exchange marriage vows, and the legality of the marriage—even with all of the court litigation—had not been

42. *Torrey v. Field,* in 5 *Vermont Reports,* 352–417, VSC.

43. Ibid.

44. Ibid., 372.

45. Fish, "Roswell Field," 232; Justice Story made a study of special pleading and developed such an interest in that branch of law that for many years it was his favorite subject, and he wrote several published works still used by students of the law. Story, ed., *Miscellaneous Writings,* 82.

tested. Field had still not achieved the goal he had set for himself back in 1833 to "test" in law the validity of his marriage, although he was soon to achieve that objective.

In 1835, a suit that had earlier roots in Massachusetts was filed at Windsor by Jeremiah Clark and Mary Almira seeking an injunction to restrain Field from obtaining any of Mary Almira's property. To seek an injunction would require a legal test of the validity of the Putney marriage, for by Vermont law husbands had claims to the assets of their spouses. As this suit moved forward in litigation, there seemed to be little room left for a court of law to avoid ruling on the issue.

The case came to trial at Woodstock in Windsor County in June 1839 with Mary Almira testifying that her marriage at Putney was a "nullity." She informed the court that during her visit to the Field house in 1832, Roswell Field had sought by "various artifices and persuasions at various times and in various ways, to induce the said Mary to violate & depart from her said engagement with said Clark and accept him, the said Field, as her suitor and lover instead."[46]

Mary Almira said she "complained" to Roswell's sister about Roswell's attentions, which she claimed were "painful to her feelings & took advantage of her youth and inexperience." She explained her belief that Roswell's sister and Jonathan Bradley and his wife had conspired to prolong her planned visit at the Field house, leaving her frequently alone and "exposed to the designs and practices of the said Field." She said that after she returned to Brattleboro "she was pursued by said Field" and that the Bradleys received Field into their home even though they knew she was under "solemn contract to another man." She said that when she was about to retire from the parlor and escape from Field's "painful importunities" the "said Field with force and violence restrained her & demanded a promise of marriage with him & said she need not ask for aid as no one in that house would hear her & he threatened the most brutal course unless such promise were instantly made."[47]

She claimed that on the next day, as Jonathan Bradley was driving her home to Windsor, he "by artful & cunning devises, arguments, solicitations and threats & by exciting her fears, set about inducing & in fact actually did induce said Mary to consent that a marriage ceremony should take place between her and said Field at a certain tavern at Putney which marriage was to be subject to her future consent. And this said Bradley induced her to believe & she did believe, that the same would be a perfect nullity" and the "marriage would not be binding unless she gave her future consent . . . in which case another & legal marriage was to take place after publishing of bans & in presence of her friends."[48]

In short, Mary Almira told the court that the "marriage ceremony between the said Field and the said Mary was obtained by the force, violence, fraud and

46. Clark pleading, *Clark v. Field*.
47. Ibid.
48. Ibid.

circumvention of the said Field, his confederates and associates." Furthermore, she claimed that it was agreed that the legality of the marriage "was at the option of said Mary" and that she later wrote Field that "it was her wish the ceremony was to be considered a nullity."[49]

In reply, Roswell Field through his attorney argued that "there can be no condition whatever annexed to a ceremony of marriage. It is a union of parties or it is nothing." He argued further that such a contract cannot be based on the belief of one of the parties as to its legality. "Both are bound, or neither," he said.[50]

The chancery court reached its decision on July 2, 1839. The finding was for Mary Almira, the court ruling that the marriage "between Roswell M. Field and the said Mary Almira, the same was and is null and void and of no effect or binding force whatever, either in law or equity." The case was then appealed to the Vermont Supreme Court, where Chief Justice Charles K. Williams, recognizing the "deep sense of injury . . . evidently felt and expressed by the parties in this controversy," announced the court's decision.[51]

The justice noted that since the suit was first instituted, Jeremiah Clark had died and that Mary Almira therefore could not be said to be "living in adultery with him." The justice added, "If the marriage at Putney is legal, she was an adulteress, and the defendant, possessing those honorable feelings which are attributed to him, could not live with her or receive her as his wife." But he added, "These consequences, however, cannot alter the facts, and upon them we must found our decision, leaving the parties to the consequences of their own actions, whether for good or evil."[52]

Said Justice Williams, "The evidence is satisfactory to us, that the parties did not, by the ceremony at Putney, intend a marriage, as far as we can learn their intentions," although the justice noted that Mary Almira "was pleased with the society of Mr. Field and not reluctant to receive his attentions. How far it was consistent with the rules of propriety and morality, for the defendant, knowing of her engagement to address her, or for her to receive his addresses, does not belong to this court to decide." The justice further stated:

> We are not disposed to animadvert of the conduct of the parties, or of their respective friends and connections, nor to pronounce any opinion further than is required to show the grounds of our determination. The immediate parties may find some excuse or palliation in the thoughtlessness of youth, the strength of affection, the pangs of disappointment and blighted hopes, in versatility of feelings to which all are subject . . . The conduct of the friends of either is not to be judged of, nor censured, in consequence of the unfortunate results which have attended this truly unfortunate

49. Ibid.
50. Statement of Field's attorney, *Clark v. Field,* in 6 *Vermont Reports,* 461, VSC.
51. Ibid.
52. Ibid.

case. . . . We inquire not as to the conduct of others, we censure them not, nor do we say anything as to the parties before us, except what has been thought necessary in deciding the case."[53]

The justice concluded that "the consent in this state must be declared before one authorized to solemnize a marriage, with a present intention to be husband and wife by the solemnization, and usually, with the intention of cohabiting together thereafter as husband and wife, in pursuance of the vows pledged at the time. This we do not consider was the case with these parties, and that it was viewed in no other light than in the nature of a promise or engagement." The decree of the chancellor in favor of Mary Almira, he said, is affirmed.[54]

It took Roswell Field almost nine years to test in law the legality of his Putney marriage to Mary Almira Phelps, and while he most assuredly was not pleased with the decision, he was probably not surprised when he later learned of it. For by July 1841, when Chief Justice Williams read the decision in the court at Montpelier, Roswell Field had long since departed Vermont and was probably at work in his Chestnut Street law office in St. Louis, some one thousand miles distant. He had left his native state for the West in the summer of 1839, immediately after the chancery court ruled his marriage to Mary Almira a nullity.[55]

Eighty-four years later, in 1923, an oil portrait of Roswell Field was hung above the judge's bench in the Windham County Court House at Newfane. In ceremonies marking that event, the Honorable Judge Frank L. Fish said that had Roswell Field remained in Vermont he would have "gone down in our legal history as one of our greatest lights in the law."[56]

53. Ibid., 476.
54. Ibid., 473.
55. Slason Thompson, *Study in Heredity,* 35.
56. Fish, "Roswell Field," 236; In the surviving Field family correspondence, there is nothing that reveals why Roswell Field in leaving Vermont selected St. Louis to live and practice law.

Roswell Martin Field was born in Newfane, Vermont, in 1807, and moved to St. Louis in 1839. This photograph was taken about 1850 by a St. Louis photographer, probably shortly before Field became the attorney for Dred Scott. Courtesy Eugene Field House and Toy Museum.

Frances Maria Field, wife of Roswell M. Field, about 1851, three years after their marriage, shown here with her son Eugene. She was born in Newfane, Vermont, in 1826. Courtesy Eugene Field House and Toy Museum.

The Field family homestead in Newfane, Vermont, where Roswell Field lived as a young man. The house was built in about 1825 and was destroyed in a fire early in the twentieth century. The law office of Roswell Field's father, Martin Field, can be seen in the far right. Courtesy Historical Society of Windham County.

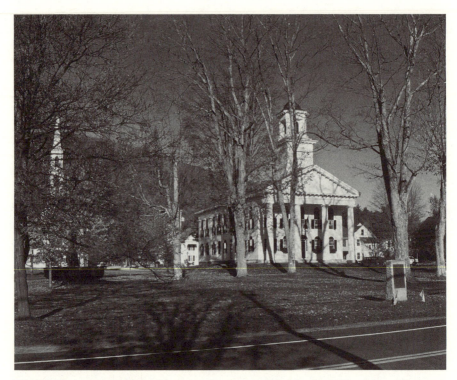

The Windham County Courthouse on the commons at Newfane, Vermont, as it appears today. Roswell Field's portrait hangs on the wall above the judge's bench in the courtroom on the second floor. In this courthouse Field practiced law during the 1830s before moving to St. Louis.

MARTIN FIELD.

Martin Field, Roswell Field's father, came to Newfane, Vermont, as a young attorney in 1800. He was also a naturalist whose collection of local minerals and fauna was at that time one of the largest in the state. He died in 1833. Courtesy of Eugene Field House and Toy Museum.

EUGENE FIELD'S GRANDMOTHER.

Esther Kellogg Field, Roswell Field's mother, was born in Massachusetts in 1780 and was thoroughly trained in the discipline and religious faith of her Puritan ancestors. Thrifty and industrious, she was the respected matron of the Field family for thirty-four years after the death of her husband. Courtesy of Eugene Field House and Toy Museum.

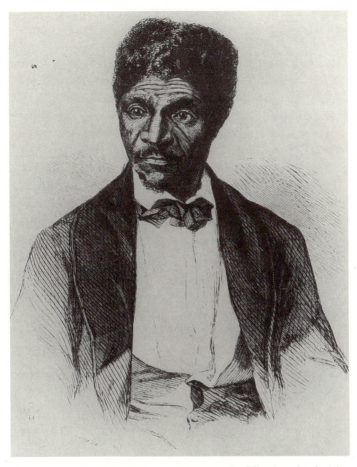

Dred Scott as he appeared in 1857 immediately following the decision
of the United States Supreme Court that denied Scott his freedom.
This sketch was published in a New York newspaper. Courtesy of
Jefferson National Expansion Memorial—National Park Service.

Harriet Scott, wife of Dred Scott, in 1857. Her suit for freedom moved through the courts in tandem with that of her husband. She was also denied freedom by the Supreme Court. Courtesy of Jefferson National Expansion Memorial—National Park Service.

Eliza and Lizzie Scott, daughters of Dred and Harriet Scott, were kept in hiding by their parents during the many years the Dred Scott case was in litigation. They were given freedom in 1857 by Taylor Blow. Courtesy of Jefferson National Expansion Memorial—National Park Service.

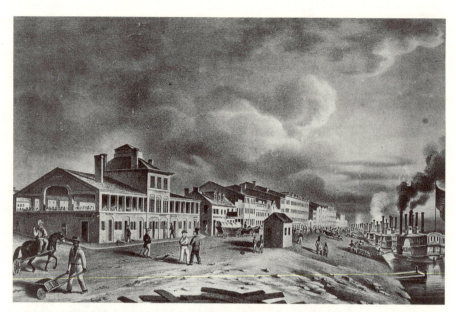

A lithograph by J. C. Wild shows the levee in St. Louis in 1840, a year after Roswell Field arrived in the city from Vermont. The buildings on the left were located on what was then called Front Street. Courtesy Missouri Historical Society.

Ruins of downtown St. Louis after the Great Fire of 1849. Roswell Field's law office on Chestnut Street was destroyed in the fire, which came within a block of destroying the Field house on Collins Street as well. Courtesy Missouri Historical Society.

The courthouse in St. Louis in 1851 at the time of the first state trial in Dred Scott's suit for freedom. Work began on the courthouse in 1839, the year of Roswell Field's arrival in St. Louis. The old courthouse still sits beside the uncompleted new structure. Courtesy Missouri Historical Society.

Lynch's Slave Pen in 1855 when Roswell Field was attorney for the Scott family. Located at Fifth and Myrtle Streets, the building was used during the Civil War as a prison for numerous prominent St. Louis citizens who were sympathetic to the Southern cause. Courtesy Missouri Historical Society.

634 South Fifth St. St Louis
Birthplace of Eugene Field

The Fields' home at 634 South Fifth Street, shown as it looked in about 1890 before restoration, and some thirty years after the Fields moved out. Now a museum, it is the oldest surviving residential building in downtown St. Louis. Courtesy Eugene Field House and Toy Museum.

Justice Hamilton R. Gamble dissented from the opinions of the other two justices when Dred Scott was denied freedom by the Missouri Supreme Court in 1852. Gamble, a friend of Roswell Field's, was later named provisional governor of Missouri during the Civil War. Courtesy Missouri Historical Society.

Dred Scott's trial in the federal court in 1854, with Roswell Field as attorney, was held on the second floor of this commercial building on South Main Street, depicted here in an ad from a city directory. Courtesy Jefferson National Expansion Memorial—National Park Service.

On May 15, 1854, after the Federal Court in St. Louis denied Dred Scott his freedom, Roswell Field, failing to obtain a new trial, wrote and filed this bill of exceptions with Judge Robert Wells. With this action, Field moved Scott's case to the United States Supreme Court. United States District Court, Eastern Missouri Division.

Dred Scott's case for freedom was argued before the United States Supreme Court in these chambers located on the lower floor of the Capitol in Washington, D.C. Now restored to the 1857 period, the center chair behind the bench was the one used by Chief Justice Roger Taney when he read his decision before a crowded courtroom on Friday, March 6, 1857. Courtesy Architect of the Capitol.

Know all Men by these Presents, *That We,*

_____ *as principal, and*

_____ *as securities,*

are held and firmly bound unto the State of Missouri, in the just and full sum of _____ *hundred Dollars, lawful money of the United States, for the payment of which we bind ourselves, our heirs, executors and administrators, firmly by these presents, sealed with our seals, and dated this* ___ *day of* _____ *A.D. 18__*

The condition of the above Obligation is such, that whereas the said _____ *has applied to the County Court of St. Louis County for, and obtained a license to reside in the State of Missouri, during good behavior: Now, if the said applicant shall be of good character and behavior during* ___ *residence in the State of Missouri, then this obligation to be void, else of full force and virtue.*

After the Supreme Court decision, Dred Scott's owners, Dr. and Mrs. Calvin Chaffee of Massachusetts, signed over the Scott family to Taylor Blow. As required by law, Blow had to sign this freedom bond for one thousand dollars to permit Dred Scott to live as a free black in Missouri. Courtesy Missouri Historical Society.

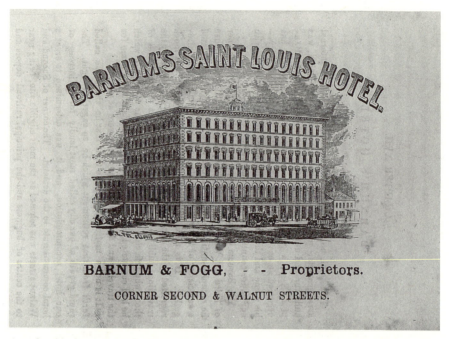

As a free black person, Dred Scott during the last year of his life worked as a porter at Barnum's Hotel on Walnut Street. Here, according to tradition, Scott became a celebrity, sought out by guests wanting to meet the famous slave. Courtesy Missouri Historical Society.

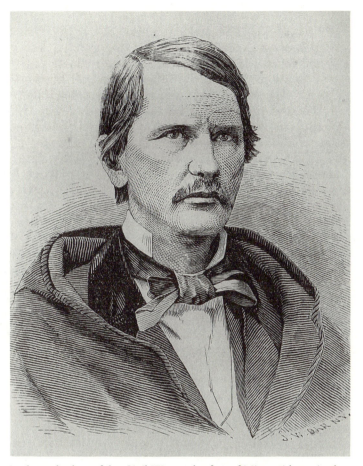

In the early days of the Civil War, as the fate of Missouri hung in the balance, Roswell Field worked closely with Francis P. (Frank) Blair to keep Missouri in the Union. Blair was president of the "Committee of Safety" and helped raise federal troops for President Abraham Lincoln. Courtesy Missouri Historical Society.

After capturing Camp Jackson in May 1861, Federal volunteers returning to the city are mobbed and fired upon by Secessionist supporters at Fifth and Walnut Streets. Throughout the Civil War, St. Louis remained under martial law. Courtesy Missouri Historical Society.

A painting by Thomas Satterwhite Nobel entitled "Last Sale of the Slaves, 1860" depicts the public auctioning of slaves on the steps of the St. Louis Courthouse. Courtesy Missouri Historical Society.

Slave Law

Roswell Field was—as his fellow New Englanders might have said—a finished scholar. By the time he left Vermont for St. Louis in 1839 he could read Greek, Latin, French, German, and Spanish, two of which—German and French—he spoke with "great facility." He was thoroughly familiar with English literature and had also acquired, to the extent it existed in that day, a broad knowledge of science. Jurisprudence, however, was his vocation, and he was said to be not only an eloquent advocate but also a learned lawyer who displayed a mastery of legal principles. No man in Vermont, it was observed, had ever before brought to the bar of that state a "greater amount of exact legal learning, or clothed it with a more impressive and attractive logic."[1]

Yet as impressive as Roswell Field's judicial credentials were in his native state of Vermont, when he arrived in St. Louis in the fall of 1839, these legal attainments would have been deemed deficient by Missouri judicial standards in at least one minor, but important, aspect—Field probably knew very little about slave law.

This deficiency was certainly not Field's fault. Born and educated in Vermont and trained in his uncle's law office in the small town of Rockingham where there was no slavery, Field could not have been expected to have been well versed in slave law.[2] Vermont, which came into the Union in 1791 as the fourteenth state,

1. *Centennial Proceedings,* 47; Hyde and Conard, *Encyclopedia of the History of St. Louis,* vol. 2, 741.
2. Slave law or the law of slavery are terms often used to cover the vast body of laws in the pre–Civil War Southern states that related to black slavery. Paul Finkelman, *Slavery in the Courtroom, An Annotated Bibliography of American Cases,* 5.

had adopted a state constitution prohibiting slavery, reaffirmed in a later statute that declared "the Idea of Slavery is expressly and totally exploded from our free Government." No one, Vermonters believed, "ought to be beholden by law to serve any person as a servant, slave, or apprentice after he arrives at the age of twenty-one."[3] Missouri, by contrast, had entered the Union in 1821 on a fiat from Congress that expressly permitted slavery.

The consequence "was the gradual development of a law of slavery in the South and a law of freedom in the North."[4] While the laws of both Northern and Southern states were similar in most respects, "the legal systems of the slave and free states diverged quite sharply on questions involving the status of Negroes." In Northern states like Vermont it was presumed by law that all people were free. In Southern states like Missouri it was presumed that all people who were black were slaves.[5]

Just how well Roswell Field understood this conflict in law between that of Vermont and that of Missouri is unknown, but the contrast in social conditions that gave rise to Southern law would have been graphically illustrated for him on that fall day in 1839 when he first stepped from the boat onto the St. Louis levee. As far as his eye could see in either direction, the stone levee, some 150 feet wide, served as a wharf onto which, it seemed, mountains of crates, barrels, bales, and boxes of every description were being disgorged from dozens of steamboats moored at the river's edge, their tall stacks belching clouds of black smoke and soot that often obscured the nearby warehouses and commercial buildings. For Field, the scene was not too unlike one he had observed earlier in his life on the wharves of New York and Boston, except that here in St. Louis the laborers who brought life to this panorama were not white men but black men, and Field would have known without asking that they were slaves.[6] Men in bondage, their arms and backs glistening with sweat, were carrying the cargoes from boats to the levee and

---

3. Ludlum, *Social Ferment*, 135; *Vermont Reformer*, July 31, 1903; Edgar J. McManus, *Black Bondage in the North*, 160.

4. Paul Finkelman, *An Imperfect Union, Slavery, Federalism and Comity*, 2; Thomas R. R. Cobb wrote the only treatise on slave law. A reporter for the Georgia Supreme Court, Cobb also drafted the Confederate Constitution. Mixing racist theories with legal arguments, an article in his treatise reads, "As all the negroes introduced into America were brought as slaves, the black color of the race raises the presumption of slavery, contrary to the principles of common law, which would presume freedom until the contrary is shown." Kermit L. Hall, William M. Wiecek, and Paul Finkelman, *American Legal History*, 191.

5. "At the founding of this country, conflict of laws was one of the most undeveloped fields in Anglo-American jurisprudence. Indeed, not until the publication of Joseph Story's *Commentaries on the Conflict of Laws* in 1834 was there a generally accepted treatise on the subject in the United States." Ibid., 13.

6. A visitor to St. Louis in 1832 noted, "The greater part of the workmen in the port . . . are negroes . . . [and] are all slaves." Maximilian, Prince of Wied, *Travels in the Interior of North America, 1832–1834,* in Reuben Gold Thwaites, ed., *Early Western Travels 1748–1846,* vol. 22, 216.

to the many waiting dray wagons. Whether this first view of the St. Louis levee was what Field had envisioned a month earlier back in Vermont as he packed his trunks and bade his farewells can only be surmised.

Most likely Field was not greatly impressed by his first view of the city that he had chosen as his new home. Not many people were. From the river St. Louis was not striking, with few church steeples or other tall structures and no hills to offset the rather squat assemblage of clustered buildings that extended more than seventy city blocks along the western bank of the river.[7] But while the city was sometimes viewed as lacking in appearance, it was more often seen as a city of great commercial vitality and one with a promising future.

In 1839 St. Louis had about twenty-two thousand inhabitants, having grown by 250 percent during the preceding decade. It was expected to double in size to fifty thousand over the next decade, giving St. Louis, it was hoped, "first rank among the first cities of the Union" and turning it into the "commercial emporium of the valley of the Mississippi." One writer boasted that not until "our mighty rivers . . . should cease to flow . . . will St. Louis be arrested in her upward march to greatness."[8]

The city's early French heritage was quickly being diluted by the influx of Americans from the East and by large numbers of immigrants from Germany and Ireland. Charles Dickens, the English novelist, who visited the city in 1838, observed:

> In the old French portion of the town, the thoroughfares are narrow and crooked, and some of the houses are very quaint and picturesque: being built of wood, with tumble-down galleries before the windows, approachable by stairs or rather ladders from the street. There are queer little barbers' shops and drinking houses too, in this quarter; and abundance of crazy old tenements with blinking casements, such as may be seen in Flanders. Some of these ancient habitations, with high garret gable-windows perking into the roofs, have a kind of French shrug about them; and being lop-sided with age, appear to hold their heads askew, besides, as if they were grimacing in astonishment at the American Improvements.[9]

St. Louis in the 1830s also retained much of the flavor of the frontier; Indians were common on the streets, many newly arrived from as far west as the Rocky Mountains. Since the city was the western office for Indian affairs, Indians often arrived in thirty- to fifty-member delegations from various western tribes and congregated on the street corners, wearing their traditional clothing and armed with tomahawks and lances. A visitor observed:

7. A St. Louis directory shows the city extending for some seventy blocks along the bank of the river and inland for about eighteen blocks at its widest point. *St. Louis Directory for the Years 1838–39.*

8. *St. Louis Directory for the Years 1840–41,* introduction; *Directory 1838–39,* x.

9. Charles Dickens, *American Notes and Pictures From Italy,* 151.

It was highly interesting to . . . observe so many of these Indians together. They
were by no means grave and still; on the contrary, they were very cheerful, and often
laughed heartily. If one went up to them familiarly, and spoke to them, many of
them had a very agreeable, friendly expression; others were cold, and appeared to
us, hostile.[10]

But St. Louisans were little interested in the past. Their focus was on the city's
ongoing commercial and industrial development.

St. Louis has two Iron Foundries . . . there are, besides, two White Lead Mills, a Type
Foundry, a Sugar Refinery, Two Planing Machines, nine Saw Mills . . . and two steam
and one water Flouring Mills . . . and a Bagging and Bale Rope Factory.[11]

According to the city directories of the day, St. Louis was also proud of its thirteen
churches, two of them described as African; that was as close as the directories
ventured in calling attention to one of the city's more obvious characteristics:
slavery. Among the hundreds of proprietors of businesses and the even larger
number of craftsmen listed in the 1839 directory, two names were notably absent:
Bernard M. Lynch, proprietor of Lynch's Slave Pen on Locust Street between
Fourth and Fifth, and Corbin Thompson, who ran the city's other slave market at
3 South Sixth.[12]

Slaves were to be seen everywhere in St. Louis. Prince Maximilian, a German
naturalist who visited the city in 1832 on his way up the Missouri River with artist
Carl Bodmer to study the western Indian tribes, wrote in his journal about St.
Louis's black population:

Everywhere they are a demoralized race, little to be depended upon; and the manner
in which they are treated is generally not as good as has been represented. We were
witnesses of deplorable punishments of these people. One of our neighbors at St.
Louis, for instance, flogged one of his slaves in the public streets, with untiring arm.
Sometimes he stopped a moment to rest, and then began anew.[13]

On the east steps of the city's courthouse, where Field would try his cases and
where the city's law library was located, slave auctions were a frequent occurrence.
Here black slaves were sold to the highest bidders.

Before the sale slaves were told what ages to give. On the block the slave was expected
to be happy, lively, and ready to boast about his accomplishments; if he refused he
was lashed. At the courthouse auctions, prospective buyers often examined the slaves

10. Maximilian, *Travels,* 226.
11. *Directory 1840–41,* introduction.
12. Trexler, *Slavery in Missouri,* 48.
13. Maximilian, *Travels,* 216.

just as they would horses—checking their teeth, feeling their muscles, and looking at their backs for lash marks which might indicate an unruly slave.[14]

The number of slaves sold at the courthouse and other auction sites in the city was probably quite large, often attracting large crowds and lasting several hours. Typical of such an auction, was an order of the probate court in 1844 requiring the sale of nine slaves to settle an estate.

> At auction on the fifth-teenth day of April eighteen hundred and forty-four between the hours of ten o'clock in the forenoon and five o'clock in the afternoon of that day, at the eastern door of the Court House in the City of St. Louis, to the highest bidders for cash, the following named slaves belonging to the estate of Antoine DuBreuil, deceased, viz., Philip, Joe, Celeste and her infant, Marie Louise and her infant, Ignace, Julie and Frank . . . [15]

The Rev. William Greenleaf Eliot, a Unitarian minister, noted that it was not uncommon in St. Louis to see gangs of black slaves chained together and being led to the levee, where they would be put aboard steamboats destined for the cotton and rice plantations of the lower Mississippi. The sight of these gangs became so repugnant to some citizens that the transfers from the slave pens to the levee were done early on Sunday mornings, when no one was on the streets.[16]

It was perhaps after witnessing scenes like these on the streets of St. Louis during his early days in the city that Field sought refuge among a local cadre of New Englanders, who like himself were newly arrived migrants to the city. During those years St. Louis had many boardinghouses, in part because of the large number of new arrivals to the city, but also because of the poor condition of the city's hotels, whose squalor was equaled only by their high room rates. Proprietors of these boardinghouses often attracted newcomers who shared common interests and customs with them, and who in many instances had migrated from the same states and countries. This amenity made the boarders feel welcome and eased their adjustment to life in a strange city. Newly arrived Germans sought out boardinghouses run by Germans in which the German language was understood and back-home food served. The many Irish immigrants did likewise. Very likely it was such a boardinghouse catering to native Virginians that the Peter Blow family sought to establish when they arrived in St. Louis in 1830 with their slave Dred Scott and rented the large house from Peter Lindell, which they named after that famous Virginian, Thomas Jefferson. Immediately after his arrival Roswell Field boarded first with a German family and a short time later took room and board in the home of "a Yankee woman" whose "bill of fare," he said, was so ample that he

14. Van Ravenswaay, *Informal History*, 402.

15. Order of the Probate Court of St. Louis County, March 20, 1844, Slaves and Slavery Collection, MHS.

16. Van Ravenswaay, *Informal History*, 401.

remained as a boarder in her house for eight years, and according to the Yankee woman, became like another brother in the family.[17]

It was probably a similar wish to be among those who shared his New England heritage that prompted Field, upon his arrival in St. Louis, to enter into a law partnership with Myron Leslie, who, like Field, was a young attorney from Vermont. Leslie had left Vermont in 1834 and, after several sojourns along the way west, had arrived in St. Louis a year before Field. Leslie had been practicing with an attorney named F. W. Risque, but apparently the partnership was not mutually satisfactory. Roswell Field replaced Risque, and the new law firm of Leslie and Field came into being with offices located at 39 Chestnut Street.[18]

One historian reports that the new firm "was regarded as one of the strongest at the St. Louis bar," and perhaps it was, although given the contrasting personalities of the two partners and the fact that the partnership lasted only a few years and then evaporated, this probably reflects a little hyperbole. What is better documented is that Roswell Field, after this brief partnership with Myron Leslie, never again entered into a partnership with any attorney, preferring to practice his vocation in his name only for the remainder of his life.[19]

The three years spent in partnership with Leslie were difficult and perhaps even painful ones for Field. How much can be attributed to the partnership and how much can be attributed to Field himself is open to conjecture. Most likely both contributed to the unhappy—and possibly depressive—state Roswell Field found himself in during his early years in St. Louis.

The sources of this melancholia can perhaps be traced back to Vermont, and more specifically to Field's reasons for leaving Vermont and moving west. His Vermont friend Zebina Eastman had noted back in Vermont that Field had a "western passion." But was this passion strong enough to attract Field away from a way of life he obviously cherished to an uncertain life in an unfamiliar frontier city? Financial considerations could also have prompted Field's migration, for when Field first arrived in St. Louis he had very little money. Had poor economic conditions in Windham County, or the Panic of 1837, made his Vermont law practice unprofitable? Or, lastly, could the move west have been spurred by the disappointing outcome of his eight-year legal struggle with Mary Almira Phelps over their Putney marriage? Certainly, Field's move west in the fall of 1839 followed almost immediately upon the ruling in July 1839 by the circuit court that Field's marriage was null and void.

17. Bay, *Reminiscences*, 237; Charles K. Field to his wife, May 19, 1848, Field Collection, JL; Listings in the city directories and newspaper advertisements reflect the large number of boardinghouses.

18. Bay, *Reminiscences*, 349.

19. Ibid.; Field had other attorneys working in his office from time to time, and may also have had law students on occasion, but neither the city directories nor the court records indicate he ever formed a partnership with these attorneys.

The last-named may be the most likely explanation, and this is the one given by a family biographer who wrote, "Having exhausted the processes of the law and failed, Roswell Field had no more use for the state whose courts could not preserve inviolate the divine ordinance of marriage and he determined to emigrate." This conclusion takes on added credibility when viewed against Field's depressed mental state after his arrival in St. Louis. A St. Louis attorney who knew Field personally noted that the adverse court verdict "had a marked effect upon his character and almost made him a cynic. For years he withdrew from society, and scarcely ever mingled with people." To make matters worse—and no doubt adding to Field's emotional trauma—Mary Almira Clark, now that her husband was dead, made a visit to St. Louis in the hopes of "renewing her earlier pledge." Field refused to see her.[20]

Field withdrew not only from society during his early years in St. Louis, but also, it appears, from active participation in court. In setting up the partnership with Myron Leslie, Field's role in the partnership seems to have been in some fashion subservient to Leslie's. The very name selected for the partnership—Leslie and Field—would seem to make that explicit. Furthermore, among the cases before the courts during the period of their partnership, Myron Leslie's name is frequently listed in various court actions, while that of R. M. Field appears only rarely. Perhaps the partners had an agreement whereby Leslie would handle the cases in the courtrooms, and Field would handle the more detailed preparatory or book work in the office.

Such a division of legal talents would not have been inappropriate, for Leslie, unlike Field, had received "a very moderate education." Also, unlike Field, he had "little or no knowledge of the classics and was far from being even a good English scholar." A biographer noted that Leslie boasted of having once run a sawmill in Vermont, of having rafted on the Susquehanna River, and of having studied law "but with whom we are not advised."[21]

But in the courtroom Myron Leslie excelled. "His style of speaking," it was said, "abounded in wit, sarcasm and irony . . . [and] once thoroughly aroused, his mind flashed with dazzling brightness and he carried everything before him."[22]

There were few lawyers who surpassed Leslie in the cross-examination of a witness. Leslie, it was noted, "assumed an air of indifference, and without giving the witness any reason to suppose that he entertained any doubt respecting the

20. Slason Thompson, *Study in Heredity,* 12; Bay, *Reminiscences,* 239, 240; Another source says Mary Almira later married a merchant from Windsor County, Vermont, and moved shortly thereafter to St. Louis. "There she lived for several years, moving in the finest social circles (though never meeting Mr. Field) and where she died suddenly of heart disease beloved by all who knew her." Charles Kellogg Field III, *Field Family,* 61.

21. Bay, *Reminiscences,* 349.

22. Ibid.

truth of his statement, he was in-geniously weaving a net-work in which to entangle him."[23]

But Leslie had a major weakness and it was one that Field would have quickly detected: Leslie was a drunkard, a weakness whose "iron grasp" would bring Leslie "to his grave" within a few years. These "intemperate habits," as they were then politely described, occurred not only in taverns and on the streets but in the courtrooms as well, making Leslie "unpopular" with both court judges and the firm's clients. Such actions probably had a significant adverse impact on the fortunes of the law firm, for a fellow St. Louis attorney recalled having heard Field "state on several occasions that during his first six years of his residence here his practice did not yield enough to pay his room and board bill, and he was forced to rely on remittances" from his family.[24]

Perhaps the firm's shaky financial condition explains why, in the fall of 1840, a year after Field's arrival, the Leslie and Field law firm appeared before the St. Louis Circuit Court to defend a local slave-owner, Murry McConnell, accused of taking Josiah Cephas, a "colored boy aged two years," and his mother, Diana, from the free state of Illinois and holding them against their will in slavery in Missouri.[25]

For Roswell Field this was his first slave case; that he should have represented a slave-owner rather than a slave may seem somewhat strange, especially considering his later fame as the attorney for history's most famous slave, Dred Scott. Unfortunately, the answers to most of the questions raised cannot be answered. For example, exactly who was the primary attorney in the case? And who in the law firm—Roswell Field or Myron Leslie—made the decision to represent Murry McConnell? Or perhaps Murry McConnell had been a long-standing client of the firm and the partners felt an obligation to represent him in any type of court action.[26] Or—and this is not totally unlikely—the law firm was so badly starved for money that any case was welcome.

Nowhere in the case papers does Roswell Field's name appear alone on documents, while that of Myron Leslie appears twice by itself. On April 9, 1841, the clerk of the court noted, "Now on this day comes Myron Leslie, attorney, and

23. Ibid.

24. Ibid., 250; Bay quotes Field as saying he obtained money from his father back in Vermont, but Martin Field was dead at this time and if Field got money from back home it was probably from someone else in the family. Ibid., 237.

25. Leslie and Field were attorneys for Murry McConnell in two suits during the fall court term of 1840: *Josiah Cephas by his next friend, Diana Cephas, v. James Scott and Murry McConnell,* docket no. 145, and *Diana, a woman of color v. James Scott* (and later Murry McConnell), docket no. 146, SLCC.

26. Just who Murry McConnell and James Scott were is uncertain. When the sheriff attempted to serve a summons, Scott was found not to be in the county. Murray McConnell, whose first name is often spelled Murry, was described as a lawyer, but no attorney by that name is listed in city directories, only an "M. McConnell" whose occupation was that of exchange broker.

voluntarily enters the appearance of Murry McConnell to this action." Linking Leslie even more closely to the case is his signature "Myron Leslie, attorney for defendant" on the bottom of a notice concerning depositions. His signature matches perfectly the handwriting on other documents bearing the firm's name.[27]

While this implies that Myron Leslie, and not Roswell Field, probably served as the primary attorney for the defense of Murry McConnell, it would be wrong to assume that Field did not in some fashion participate in the case, or that he was not involved. For all that is known, Field may very well have considered the law to be on the side of Murry McConnell. Field was certainly familiar with the case, and probably would have shared in any financial remuneration the firm earned in handling the case.

For Field, at least, the defense of Murry McConnell would have brought him to the very heart of Missouri slave law. And just as the roots of Vermont's laws extended back to the early days of colonial settlement and English common law, so also did the roots of Missouri's slave law go back to these same early colonial days. In large part, Missouri slave law was closely patterned after that of Kentucky, which in turn was closely patterned after that of Virginia.[28] And the Virginia law on slavery had its origins during those dim years of the early 1600s, when Africans first arrived on the shores of North America.

Laws grow out of the customs and practices of a people and develop into law when these customs and practices become binding and enforceable by authority. Just when and where the custom evolved whereby whites and blacks held in bondage on the Virginia plantations of the early 1600s were first viewed as distinct from one another is uncertain. It is generally agreed that at least initially both white and black servants were treated alike, working out their years of bondage and then being freed. However, the first indication of "outright enslavement" appears in 1640 when three Virginia servants were captured after fleeing to Maryland. In pronouncing sentences, the General Court of Virginia ordered the two white servants to serve their masters for an additional year as a penalty, but "the third being a negro" was sentenced to serve his master "for the time of his natural life."[29] From such obscure beginnings slave law grew, and like a microscopic cancer cell that through metastasis spreads throughout the body, slave law slowly expanded, eventually infecting almost the whole judicial fabric of the American South.

The legal issues involved in Diana Cephas's suit for freedom in the Missouri courts clearly fell within this Southern judicial fabric, for her case involved an issue at the very heart of slave law—freedom. As slavery gained statutory recognition, other issues such as miscegenation and manumission arose. Later questions included

27. Record book 12, 151, SLCC; Notice on taking of depositions, acknowledgment signed by Myron Leslie, undated, *Josiah Cephas, by his next friend, Diana Cephas, v. James Scott and Murry McConnell*, docket no. 361, November term 1840, SLCC.

28. Finkelman, *Imperfect Union*, 217; Trexler, *Slavery in Missouri*, 265.

29. Winthrop D. Jordan, *White over Black*, 44, 75.

whether slaves were real or personal property, and what rights, if any, they had. If slaves were simply property, could they be held accountable for crimes and judged by the same laws as their masters? Could slaves own property or enter into contracts such as marriage? Could they testify in court against a white person? Could a slave sell his labor or did his or her labor belong to the master? And, of course, there were a multitude of questions centering on the slave's very humanity and moral condition, such as the one Oscar Shafter sought to answer in the pages of the *Vermont Free Press*—"Is the African Negro A Man?"

According to Missouri slave law, the first step Diana Cephas had to take to obtain freedom for herself and her child was to appear before the court and file a petition. For Diana, this in itself would have been no simple task, requiring not only a strong element of courage but also a lawyer—and a white lawyer at that—for there were no black lawyers in Missouri. Furthermore, Diana could neither read nor write and she probably had little idea of the legal processes involved. She also had no money.

Fortunately for Diana, there were in St. Louis lawyers willing to assist slaves in obtaining their freedom. One of these was Francis B. Murdoch, the city attorney who had sought in the court at Alton the conviction of those responsible for the murder of Elijah P. Lovejoy and who afterward had moved to St. Louis to practice law.[30] Just how and by what means Diana Cephas made contact with Francis Murdoch and told him her wishes is unknown, just as it was no doubt unknown to her owners in 1840. As a slave, Diana was involved in a very risky undertaking, and her actions would have required secrecy. Had her owners become suspicious, she could have been severely punished, chained up, or moved away from St. Louis. As property, Diana Cephas and her son Josiah were worth about eleven hundred dollars, an investment McConnell would not have wanted to forfeit.[31]

Accordingly, on October 22, 1840, two petitions written by Francis Murdoch and signed with an "X" by Diana Cephas were presented to Luke Lawless, judge of the St. Louis County Circuit Court.[32] One was on behalf of Diana Cephas and the other was for her two-year-old son, Josiah. The petitions asked the court to grant them leave to sue as poor persons in order to establish their rights to freedom.

In this petition, the mother told the court that she and her son had been born slaves in the state of Maryland and brought to Illinois in the spring of 1839 by their master Mark Delahay and his wife. There they settled at the town of Naples on the

30. *History of Madison County,* 188; "Not only did immigration to Alton cease as a sequence of the riot, but many men who had settled there who held anti-slavery views . . . sought new homes." E. T. Norton, ed., *Centennial History of Madison County, Illinois and Its People 1812–1912,* 60.

31. Deposition of Mark Delahay who brought the slaves from Maryland and sold them in St. Louis for eleven hundred dollars. *Josiah Cephas v. Murry McConnell,* SLCC.

32. *Diana, a woman of color v. James Scott,* and *Josiah by his next friend, Diana Cephas, v. James Scott and Murry McConnell.* Fall term, 1840, SLCC.

Illinois River in July 1839. Her master, she said, made Naples his "place of abode" and hired out Diana "to labor and received the rewards of her labor." A month after their arrival Delahay's wife died, and six months later Delahay went south, leaving Diana and her son behind. In February 1840, Murry McConnell, "pretending to be the owner" of Diana and her son, came to Naples and took mother and child by steamboat to St. Louis, where they were both held in slavery.[33]

Considering the ideological credentials of the judiciary in St. Louis in 1840, it would have been difficult for Diana Cephas to have found a judge with a stronger proslavery reputation than Judge Luke E. Lawless. Yet Diana was fortunate that her suit for freedom was filed within the jurisdiction of Missouri, where the conflict between the laws of free and slave states regarding slave freedom had been largely resolved in earlier court decisions, a precedent that was difficult for even a proslavery judge like Luke Lawless to disregard. Furthermore, Diana also had the benefit of trial by jury and was therefore not solely dependent upon the individual caprice of a judge. And while jury membership was limited to white males only, jurors were often seen as fairer than many Southern magistrates and judges.[34]

Four years earlier, in 1836, Judge Luke Lawless had been the target of many of Elijah P. Lovejoy's antislavery newspaper articles. Lovejoy's editorial attacks against Lawless focused on the judge's strong proslavery statements and his judicial leniency toward violent proslavery groups, such as the mob that had broken into the St. Louis jail, taken hold of a free black prisoner named Francis McIntosh, and burned him alive on a vacant lot on Chestnut Street. In turn, Lawless retaliated against Lovejoy by encouraging St. Louis proslavery mobs to make repeated attacks on Lovejoy's printing shop, driving the editor out of St. Louis and across the river to Alton, where Lovejoy was later killed.[35]

But Judge Lawless's proslavery sympathies can nowhere be detected in the court records involving Diana Cephas's suit for freedom. On receiving the petitions for freedom from the two slaves, Judge Lawless, following Missouri legal precedents, took prompt action holding that in his opinion the petitions contained "sufficient matter to authorize the commencement" of suits. Judge Lawless also allowed Diana "to sue as a poor person to establish her right to freedom" and assigned to Diana

---

33. *Josiah Cephas v. Scott and McConnell,* SLCC.

34. Eugene D. Genovese, *Slavery in the Legal History of the South and Nation,* in Paul Finkelman, ed., *Law, the Constitution and Slavery,* vol. 2, 143.

35. Van Ravenswaay, *Informal History,* 285; Biographical sketches of early St. Louis lawyers are often quite colorful. For example, of Judge Lawless: "In going home from court he would frequently walk several squares beyond his house, and not discover his mistake until he met some acquaintance who would inquire where he was going. In shopping with Madam Lawless, if his attention was drawn to anything of interest passing on the street, he would sometimes walk off and forget where he left her. Not infrequently he would leave home without a hat and not be sensible of it until some one reminded him of it. When invited out to dinner, he seldom could recollect the hour appointed and appeared either too early or too late." Bay, *Reminiscences,* 443.

and her son as counsel the law firm of Risque, Murdoch, and A. King. Murdoch and his firm would serve as counsel to the slaves without compensation.[36]

As in similar Missouri slave suits for freedom, Judge Lawless further ordered that "Josiah and the said Diana have reasonable liberty to attend the said counsel and the court as occasion may require, that [they] not be removed out of the jurisdiction of this court and that [they] not be subject to any severity on account of [their] application for freedom."[37] This action was taken to protect the slaves from any retaliation by their owners and to assure that the owners would allow the slaves time to visit their attorney and to appear in court.

According to Missouri law, slave suits for freedom took the standard form of a suit for damages, with the slave charging trespass for false imprisonment. To win his freedom, the slave had to prove that before and during his imprisonment, or bondage, he had been a free person, and that as a free person, he was still being held in slavery when he filed the suit.[38] Therefore, as required by statute, Francis Murdoch filed two similar individual declarations initiating actions of trespass. Josiah's declaration charged that Murry McConnell:

> With force and arms assaulted the said plaintiff and him then and there took and imprisoned, and restrained him of his liberty and held him in servitude . . . against the law of the land and against the will of said plaintiff [who] . . . was, and still is, a free person, and that the said defendant, held and still holds him in slavery—Wherefore, the said plaintiff saith he is wronged and hath damages to the amount of ten dollars and wherefore he brings suit.[39]

Following this declaration, Diana's next legal step was to prove to the court, in a trial before a jury, that she and her son were indeed free persons. In a Northern court this would not have presented a legal question, since all people were presumed free before the law. However, in Southern courts, where it was presumed that all blacks and mulattoes were slaves, Diana and Josiah had to prove, despite the color of their skin, that they were free.

Fortunately, Missouri law had from almost the creation of the state in 1821 clearly established the criteria by which a black person residing in the state might be considered free. One way was by manumission, whereby the owner of a slave, with the permission of the courts, could free his slave. This, however, was a privilege and not a right, since free blacks were considered dangerous to society. Furthermore, to assure that slaves being freed did not become a burden on society, the person

36. Ferdinand W. Risque, like Murdoch, had the reputation of being a slave lawyer. Before joining the Murdoch partnership he had been a partner with Myron Leslie. Bay, *Reminiscences*, 349.

37. *Josiah Cephas v. Scott and McConnell*, SLCC.

38. Fehrenbacher, *Dred Scott*, 251.

39. *Josiah Cephas v. Scott and McConnell*, SLCC.

who manumitted them had to furnish bond to the court, and the slave had to be "sound in mind and body" and not too young or too old.[40]

Another way a slave might obtain freedom was to sue for it in the courts and convince a jury why he or she was entitled to freedom. Missouri law was quite helpful in assisting a slave in such an undertaking. Legal counsel, if needed, was provided by the courts, and if a master subjected a slave to severe punishment for bringing suit, the slave could be taken by *habeas corpus* and placed under the protection of the courts. Furthermore, jurors were instructed that the "weight of evidence lies with the petitioner [slave]" and appeals could be made to a higher court.[41]

At the heart of most suits for freedom was the conflict in law as it related to the dissimilar status of blacks in free and slave states. There was no conflict in law as long as black persons stayed where they belonged: that is, in the slave state in which they were born. Problems arose when black people moved—or were taken—across state lines between free and slave territory. In such instances disputes developed, requiring the courts to step in and resolve the issues. The judicial roots of this conflict extended all the way back to the very founding of the country, with the enactment of the Fugitive Slave Law. That law required the Northern free states to respect Southern slave property and return slaves who escaped into the North. Had Diana Cephas and her child, for instance, not been taken out of Maryland and into a free state such as Illinois, there would have been no grounds for a suit for freedom. At the heart of the comity question was the very foundation of the Union itself, which required the free movement of people and property across state lines as set forth in Article IV of the Constitution. Without the mutual respect for the laws of other states, the Union itself would founder.[42]

Missouri was forced to face these issues of comity from its very inception. Created as a slave state, it was bordered by free territory on two sides and crossed by large rivers that provided easy transit for blacks, both slave and free. The issues were first raised in territorial days and quickly came to the forefront shortly after Missouri became a state. In 1824 a case, *Winny v. Whitesides,* reached the Missouri Supreme Court that would set the pattern for all future suits for

40. Trexler, *Slavery in Missouri,* 209.

41. Ibid., 211; A statute "to enable persons held in slavery to sue for their freedom" was passed in the Missouri General Assembly on December 30, 1824. Gerald T. Dunne, *The Missouri Supreme Court,* 27.

42. The Fugitive Slave Law was enacted by Congress in 1793. When a fugitive from justice fled into another state it was the duty of the governor in that state to honor a request for the fugitive's return, as an appeal for interstate comity. The law also permitted a slave-owner to cross a state line to claim his runaway slave, and upon showing proof of ownership to a local magistrate, return the slave back home; Slave-owners, in arguing for comity between the states, frequently argued that a man and his slave traveling through or visiting in a free state were entitled to the same comity as a man traveling through a free state with his horse or cow.

slave freedom in Missouri.[43] Winny, a black slave, had in 1799 been taken by her master from the Carolinas to Illinois, and later from there into Missouri. In 1822, Winny petitioned for freedom in the Missouri courts, claiming her stay in Illinois territory entitled her to freedom. When the case came before the St. Louis County Circuit Court, the jury was instructed by the judge to find for Winny if they believed her master had "resided in Illinois with an intention" to make that place his home. Following this instruction, the jury granted Winny her freedom and the case was appealed to the Missouri high court. In appealing, Winny's masters argued, among other things, that Winny had forfeited her freedom by not suing for it when she resided in Illinois, and that in coming to Missouri she forfeited her rights to whatever freedom she might have had in Illinois.[44]

However, the Missouri Supreme Court, taking note of the interstate comity issues involved, ruled that Winny's return to Missouri did not re-create her slave status and that "personal rights or disabilities, obtained or communicated by the laws of any particular place, are of a nature which accompany the person wherever he goes." The court then concluded that when a person takes a slave into a free jurisdiction "and by length of residence there indicates an intention of making that place his residence and that of his slave . . . [he] does, by such residence, declare his slave to have become a freed man."[45]

In subsequent years additional slave freedom cases came before the Missouri Supreme Court and, while some reinterpretations were made, Missouri law basically held that a slave's claim to freedom was, with some minor exceptions, dependent upon the intent and duration of residence in a free jurisdiction. This was the heart of the issue in the case of Diana and Josiah Cephas before the St. Louis court in 1840.

Since no transcripts were made of court trials, it is impossible to determine from surviving court records exactly what arguments were presented to the jury by Francis Murdoch and Leslie and Field on behalf of their clients. However, the old court files contain copies of depositions taken from witnesses, and these offer some idea as to the likely positions taken by the opposing counsels.

For example, from a deposition taken of one Ross Hughes, a resident of Naples, Illinois, it is evident that Francis Murdoch intended to show that Diana and Josiah were not simply passing through Illinois on their way to Missouri, but resided there. In his deposition, Hughes related that Mark Delahay and his wife, while in Illinois, hired out Diana to Hughes. On one occasion Diana worked for Hughes for four weeks and on another occasion for three months. Sometime later, Murry

43. *Winny v. Whitesides,* 1 *Missouri Reports,* 472, Missouri Supreme Court (MSC).
44. Ibid.
45. Ibid.

McConnell arrived with a constable, and claiming Diana and her son to be his slaves, took them by boat to St. Louis.[46]

Leslie and Field, on the other hand, in defense of their client, took two depositions. One was that of Mark Delahay, who had brought Diana and her son from Maryland to Missouri, and the other was of the justice of the peace at Naples.

In his deposition, Delahay related that he had brought Diana and her son from Maryland to St. Louis where, on July 4, 1839, he sold them. Later, he said, he and his wife moved to Naples, and Diana, who had served as a nurse for Delahay's dying wife, accompanied them "of her own free will." In the second deposition, Royal Movens, a justice of the peace at Naples, related that McConnell had come to him in 1840 and under oath claimed that Diana and her son were "fugitive slaves in Illinois owing service" to him, had run off, and that they should be "dealt with as the law requires." To prove ownership, Movens said, McConnell showed him a bill of ownership. Acting immediately on the charge that the slaves were fugitive runaways, Movens convened a magistrate's court at Naples on the same day and "a trial was had upon said complaint" and "witnesses examined." The court then ordered the constable to seize Diana and her son Josiah and turn them over to the "personal custody" of McConnell. McConnell was ordered to remove the slaves "to the state of Missouri or to any other place or country where by law the owner may have power to take, possess and own slaves."[47]

From these two depositions it would appear that in defending their client against charges of trespass, Leslie and Field argued that the slaves, Diana and Josiah, were not taken to Illinois but rather fled there as runaway slaves, and that under the Federal Fugitive Slave Law they were required to be returned as slaves to their rightful owner. The question before the court was whether Diana and her son had fled to Illinois as fugitives or whether they were taken there and hired out for wages.

However, on July 19, 1842, a year before the case came to trial, Josiah Cephas died. A month later the court abated Josiah's suit.[48] With the death of Josiah, the case finally came to trial before the circuit court on September 18, 1843, and only Diana Cephas's plea for freedom was argued. Here, after deliberation, a jury of "twelve good and lawful men" granted Diana Cephas her freedom, and found Murry McConnell "guilty of the trespass and false imprisonment as claimed." The judge then ordered that Diana Cephas "be liberated and entirely set free."[49]

46. Deposition of Ross B. Hughes dated July 13, 1841, *Josiah Cephas v. Scott and McConnell,* SLCC.
47. Deposition of Mark Delahay dated April 18, 1841, *Josiah Cephas v. Scott and McConnell,* SLCC; Fugitive slave trial, February 22, 1840, Magistrate Court, Scott County, Illinois.
48. Record book 13, 224 and 328, SLCC.
49. Record book 14, 179, SLCC.

In obtaining her freedom, Diana Cephas joined the ranks of some sixty-five other former slaves who had successfully obtained their freedom through petitions to the circuit court of St. Louis in the wake of the legal precedent established in *Winny v. Whitesides* two decades earlier. However, during that period, another sixty-two slaves had tried for freedom in the courts and failed.[50]

While this verdict was a victory for Diana Cephas, it was a defeat for the law firm of Leslie and Field and for their client, Murry McConnell. In less than a year, however, Roswell Field would find himself once again involved in Southern slave law and back in court, this time as counsel—not for a slave master—but for a slave mother and her nine-year-old son.

In the fall of 1844, shortly after Field went into law practice for himself, he became the attorney for a slave named Martha Ann, who along with her son, James, sought freedom in the Missouri courts.[51] In many respects the suit was not unlike that of Diana Cephas, and like Diana, in filing her petition, Martha Ann told Judge John M. Krum that she was a poor person, unable to pay counsel fees. Judge Krum, in accordance with Missouri law, assigned Roswell Field as her counsel. While it is possible that Judge Krum made the assignment without personally knowing Field, perhaps randomly selecting Field's name from a list of attorneys, it is far more likely that Krum knew Field and had some inkling that Field's opinions about slavery would not make him adverse to serving as a counsel for a slave seeking freedom.

Certainly, Field knew the judge, for Krum, like Francis Murdoch, had participated in the trials held at Alton following the murder of Elijah Lovejoy. Murdoch had been the city attorney and Krum had been mayor. And like Murdoch, Krum had left Alton afterward and in 1843 was named judge of the St. Louis County Circuit Court.

In her suit for freedom, Martha Ann filed the customary plea of trespass in which she claimed that her master, Hiram Cordell, "with force and arms" made an "assault upon her, imprisoning her and depriving her of her liberty." The plea, typical for a slave freedom suit, was written and signed by Roswell Field as "her Attorney, assigned by the court."[52]

Martha Ann's claim to freedom was based, as was that of Diana Cephas, on residency in a free state, and in her petition she stated that she had been the slave

50. Robert Moore Jr., manuscript, unpublished research by a historian with the National Park Service in St. Louis, comprised of compilations of freedom suits, emancipations, and manumissions in the St. Louis Circuit Court prior to the Civil War. Some of Moore's research was reported in the quarterly publication of the Missouri Historical Society entitled "A Ray of Hope Extinguished, St. Louis Slave Suits for Freedom" by Robert Moore. Similar research has also been undertaken by Melvina Conley, supervisor of the accounting department and archives for the court.

51. *Martha Ann, a person of color v. Hiram Cordell,* April 18, 1844, record book 15, 4, SLCC; *James, a person of color v. Hiram Cordell,* April 18, 1844, record book 15, 5, SLCC.

52. Plea of trespass, *Martha Ann v. Cordell,* SLCC.

of a Dr. John Young and his wife, who took her to Galena, Illinois. Here, she said, she was "held as a servant to his family" and kept "continually employed as a slave there for a period of six months." Returned later to St. Louis, where Dr. Young and his wife died, she became the property of Hiram Cordell, administrator of the estate.[53]

Two individual suits for freedom were filed by Field: one for the mother, Martha Ann, and the second for her son, James. James based his claim on the contention that he had been born of a free mother. However, by a strange turn of events, and a mistake by Cordell's attorney, James received his freedom almost immediately. The attorney for Cordell, in answering the two summonses issued by the court, responded to only one, that of Martha Ann, and later told the court that he supposed "that there was but one suit"—that of the mother—and that "the defense in that case would be a defense to both." This mistake proved costly to Cordell, for the nine-year-old boy was freed by the court on a "final judgment of liberation upon default."[54]

But Martha Ann's suit for freedom continued in the court, and in preparing for her trial Field obtained several depositions attesting to Martha Ann's residence in Illinois. One was of a Dr. Albion Crow, who said he remembered that in the years 1827 and 1828 Dr. Young lived in Galena, where he practiced medicine and that "there lived in his family a negro girl by the name of Martha or Martha Ann."[55]

The case came to trial on January 21, 1846, before Judge Krum; as the court record reports, "after hearing the evidence and arguments of counsel" the jury was "unable to agree upon a verdict" and was "discharged and the case continued until the next term of court."[56]

Again, as in the suit of Diana Cephas, there were no transcripts made of the trial, and the respective arguments made during the litigation must be reconstructed from the few surviving court records. In this case, the only clues as to what might have transpired in the courtroom that day are derived from the wording of the opposing counsels in the charges they wrote for presentation to the jury.

Field's proposed charge to the jury on behalf of Martha Ann was that "if the jury find that Dr. Young while the owner of the plaintiff as a slave took her to Galena in the State of Illinois to work and held her there in service, the plaintiff thereby

53. Petition, *Martha Ann v. Cordell*, SLCC.

54. Petition, *James v. Hiram Cordell*, SLCC; Missouri law held that the maternal line of descent determined the slave status of a black person, applying the principle of *partus sequitur ventrem* (literally, what the child that follows the pregnancy). Slave marriages had no legal basis in Missouri law, and it was easier to determine a black child's mother than the father. The Missouri Supreme Court, however, preferred to consider the law humane rather than practical in origin. Emil Oberholzer, "The Legal Aspects of Slavery in Missouri," 39; Judgment by default, *James v. Cordell*, in record book 15, 325, SLCC.

55. Deposition of Dr. Albion Crow dated April 13, 1845, *Martha Ann v. Cordell*, SLCC.

56. Record book 17, 47, SLCC.

became entitled to her freedom and the jury ought to find for the plaintiff."[57] The issue, as Field saw it, was clearly residency by a slave in a free state.

The charge to the jury by opposing counsel, on the other hand, stated, "Before the jury can find for the plaintiff in this case, they must be satisfied from competent testimony that the slave plaintiff in this case is *the identical one* [underlined in original] spoken of by the witnesses and in the depositions and that if there is no evidence of such identity, that they must therefore find for the defendant."[58]

From this charge to the jury, it is evident that Cordell's attorney was arguing that the black woman who resided in Illinois two decades earlier was not the same Martha Ann who was now a slave of Hiram Cordell in St. Louis. They were, Cordell's attorney probably argued, two different women. Had Martha Ann been allowed to take the witness stand, she perhaps could have convinced the jury that she was indeed the same Martha Ann who was taken as a slave into Illinois. That would have been illegal, however, for blacks, slave or free, were not allowed by Missouri law to testify in court against whites.[59]

On May 6, 1846, the trial was held before a jury, and the following day the jury again reported to the court that they were "unable to agree upon a verdict," following which the jurors were discharged and the case continued.[60]

A year elapsed before Martha Ann's case for freedom came up again in court, and during that interval a new judge was appointed to the bench. His name was Alexander Hamilton, and in the following decade, as judge of the St. Louis County Circuit Court, he would leave his mark on American history as the judge who presided over the state trials of a slave named Dred Scott and who twice granted freedom to Scott in his long legal struggle to escape bondage.[61] Of perhaps lesser historical significance, Judge Alexander Hamilton was also to become a close personal friend of Roswell Field.

Biographical sketches of Hamilton and Field make no note of this friendship, nor is it mentioned by historians writing about the Dred Scott case, but the nature of the friendship was obviously of sufficient intimacy to prompt Field, before he died, to name his friend Alexander Hamilton as guardian of his youngest son, Roswell. Mary French, Field's niece, wrote at that time, "I am rejoiced that Judge Hamilton has accepted the guardianship of Roswell. He was such a true friend of my uncle."[62]

57. *Martha Ann v. Cordell,* SLCC.
58. Ibid.
59. Trexler, *Slavery in Missouri,* 210.
60. Record book 17, 280, SLCC.
61. Hyde and Conard, *Encyclopedia of the History of St. Louis,* vol. 2, 976.
62. Expenditures "for use of my ward, Roswell Field" signed by A. Hamilton. Estate of Roswell M. Field, no. 8870, SLPC; Guardian Records for Roswell Field, no. 6718, SLPC; M. F. French to Melvin Gray, September 13, 1869, Roswell Field estate, SLPC.

Alexander Hamilton, a native of Philadelphia, was seven years younger than Field and came to St. Louis, like Field, as a young attorney.[63] Hamilton was said to have had a "classical and cultivated taste" and "his memory was stored with the treasures of literature"—interests that probably meshed amicably with those of Roswell Field. Whatever else it was, the friendship provides a hitherto unknown link—coincidental though it might be—between what historians call the two separate Dred Scott cases; between *Scott v. Emerson* in the state courts, and *Scott v. Sandford* in the federal courts.[64]

After three years of litigation, and two hung juries, Martha Ann's third trial for freedom came up before Judge Hamilton during the 1847 spring term, which, before it ended, would also include Dred Scott's first trial for freedom. When Martha Ann's trial took place on May 13, Dred Scott's attorney was busy on that day obtaining a deposition from a witness in preparation for Scott's case, which would be tried on June 30 before Judge Hamilton. Martha Ann's third trial on May 13 ended as did her previous two trials, with a hung jury. And again Judge Hamilton ordered the case continued.[65]

Some two-and-a-half years would elapse before Martha Ann's case was heard again, for the fourth time, by a jury in Judge Hamilton's court. The date was December 12, 1849. This time, Roswell Field employed a different strategy on behalf of his client. Dr. Albion Crow of Galena, who almost five years earlier had stated in his deposition that he remembered Martha Ann when she lived in Illinois, was brought to St. Louis. Provided lodgings at a hotel, Dr. Albion was brought before the jury to testify on behalf of Martha Ann. Probably he said very little, simply pointing out Martha Ann in the courtroom and telling the jury that Martha Ann was the same black woman who lived in Illinois twenty years earlier. Dr. Albion's testimony apparently convinced the jury that the two women were indeed one and the same, for James Caldwell, foreman, reported that the jury of twelve men found Hiram Cordell "guilty in manner and form" as claimed by Martha Ann, and Judge Hamilton immediately ordered her freedom. Martha Ann could now share in freedom with her son James, the two joining the ranks of the growing number of former slaves who had, since *Winny v. Whitesides* in 1824, obtained their freedom in the St. Louis courts. As of December 1849, the number of such slaves freed by the court totaled seventy-six.[66]

63. Hyde and Conard, *Encyclopedia of the History of St. Louis,* vol. 2, 976.

64. Based on their close friendship, Hamilton may well have acquainted Field with the Dred Scott case long before Field officially became Scott's attorney. It perhaps also explains why out of the many attorneys in St. Louis, Field was singled out to take over the case in 1853, and how and in what way the transfer to a federal action was first conceived, questions that have long puzzled historians.

65. Record book 17, 592, SLCC.

66. Record book 19, 65, SLCC; Sheriff's summons, *Martha Ann v. Hiram Cordell,* SLCC; Record book 19, 65, December 12, 1849, SLCC; Slave cases for freedom in the St. Louis County Circuit Court prior to the Civil War, based on research by Conley and Moore.

In acknowledgment of her achievement, Martha Ann would have been granted a certificate by the county court of St. Louis that stated her name, age, height, and the darkness of her complexion. According to law, she would have been required to carry the certificate with her at all times. The certificate would have further declared that Martha Ann "is of the class of free negroes and mulattoes who are authorized by law to be licensed by said Court, to reside within the State of Missouri; that she is of good character and behavior, and capable of supporting herself by lawful employment; and having also obtained from said Court an order for a license to reside within the State aforesaid . . . so long as she shall be of good behavior, and no longer."[67]

---

67. Free blacks were generally a despised group in Missouri and an 1825 law stated emphatically, "No free negro or mulatto shall, under any circumstances, emigrate to this state from any other State or Territory." For free blacks already in the state or those granted freedom by the courts, Missouri established a licensing system in 1835 that entitled a free black to live within the state. Oberholzer, "Legal Aspects," 49; License of Jane Brackenridge, a free black of dark complexion, dated March 4, 1844, and issued by the County Court of St. Louis, Slaves and Slavery Collection, MHS.

The Emersons

Dred Scott was not in St. Louis when Roswell Field arrived there in 1839, having departed six years earlier in 1833 with his new master, Dr. John Emerson, a surgeon in the U.S. Army. When Field stepped ashore onto the levee at St. Louis, Dred Scott was living some eight hundred miles upriver at Fort Snelling in what was then Wisconsin territory.

Dr. Emerson purchased Dred Scott from Peter Blow, and while no record of the sale has been found, Henry T. Blow, Peter Blow's son, later confirmed in court testimony that his father had sold Scott to Emerson. Irene Emerson would later claim that her husband had purchased the slave out of charity to save him from abuse because Dred Scott had been "so badly beaten by one of the Blows." However, the Blow family, in its version of the sale, claimed that Dred Scott had such "a great dislike" of Emerson that when the slave heard that the sale had been agreed upon, he ran away and hid for several days in the Lucas Swamps at Twelfth and Pine Streets, "beyond the city limits where slaves used to meet and play cards." Neither account is based on documentary fact, although the story that Scott ran away following his sale to Dr. Emerson gains credence from a court summons issued to Charlotte (Blow) Charless and Peter E. Blow to appear in the St. Louis County Court on August 10, 1833, on complaint of Dr. Emerson. The nature of the controversy is not mentioned in the summons, which leads some to speculate that it involved Scott's disappearance after the sale. Whatever the complaint, it was quickly dropped.[1]

---

1. *St. Louis Daily Evening News,* April 3, 1857; Deposition of Henry T. Blow, *Dred Scott v. Irene Emerson,* November term, 1846, SLCC. Copies of these papers are in the Dred Scott File in the

Dred Scott was purchased by Emerson to serve as the doctor's body servant or valet, one of the accoutrements permitted military officers in those days. Army regulations entitled any officer to be accompanied by servants, each servant's expenses subsidized by the government equal to the "pay, rations and clothing" of a private soldier.[2] The servants could be used by the officer or hired out at wages.

Dr. Emerson, a native of Pennsylvania and about the same age as Dred Scott, had actively been seeking a military appointment, and when it finally came on October 15, 1833, it included orders for Emerson to report for duty at Fort Armstrong, which was situated on an island in the Mississippi River some three hundred miles north of St. Louis in Illinois. Dr. Emerson and his slave Dred Scott arrived at the fort on December 1, 1833, and it was probably the first time Scott had ever lived in free territory.[3] Illinois, unlike Missouri, had been part of the old Northwest Territory, and its constitution of 1818 prohibited slavery within its boundaries.

That Dred Scott was black and a slave apparently drew little or no attention at Fort Armstrong, where black servants, both bonded and free, were not an uncommon sight. Miles H. Clark, an officer in the army at Fort Armstrong with Dr. Emerson who would later testify on Scott's behalf in his suit for freedom, said rather matter-of-factly, "I know the negro named Dred. He was held in service there by Dr. Emerson as a slave from the time I first knew him."[4]

Living conditions at Fort Armstrong were rather bleak, and there was not much for the troops to do since the Black Hawk War had ended. Dr. Emerson, who was six-feet four-inches tall but whose rather colicky physiology made him prone to a variety of ailments, developed a slight disease of the foot that prevented him from wearing a shoe. For this and other reasons he told his superiors in Washington that he would very much like to return to St. Louis. Instead, in 1836 he received a transfer to Fort Snelling on the west bank of the Mississippi some five hundred miles in the opposite direction. Here again, as in Illinois, Scott went largely unnoticed, even though Fort Snelling was located in the old Louisiana territory far north of Missouri—a territory that had been declared explicitly free of slavery by the Missouri Compromise of 1820.

At the time of Scott's arrival, the largest slave-owner in the vicinity of Fort Snelling was Lawrence Taliaferro, an Indian agent for the area. Among his slaves

archives of the United States District Court, eastern division, St. Louis (USDC); Letter of Mary Dalton to Frederick T. Hill dated February 22, 1907, Dred Scott Collection, MHS; *Springfield Daily Republican,* February 12, 1903; "Dred Scott, Life of the Famous Fugitive and Missouri Litigant," typed manuscript written about 1891, T. W. Chamberlain Collection, MHS; Estate papers of Peter Blow, SLPC.

2. *Historic Fort Snelling Chronicles,* no. 2, 1975, pamphlet published by the Minnesota Historical Society.

3. Ehrlich, *They Have No Rights,* 17.

4. John D. Lawson, ed., *American State Trials,* vol. 13, 228.

was a young black woman of about fifteen or sixteen named Harriet Robinson, and Dred Scott and Harriet soon formed an attachment for one another. Before the year was out Dred and Harriet were joined in marriage and, with the sale of Harriet by Taliaferro, the couple became the property of Dr. Emerson.[5]

After the marriage, Dr. Emerson hired Dred and Harriet out to the families of officers at Fort Snelling. Catherine A. Anderson, wife of an army lieutenant at the fort, would later testify at Scott's trial for freedom that "during the whole time I knew them at Fort Snelling they were held in slavery by Dr. Emerson or by persons to whom they were hired by him. They were universally known there to be Dr. Emerson's slaves."[6]

But Dr. Emerson still wanted to return to St. Louis. The northern climate, he claimed, had crippled him with rheumatism, and after repeated requests for transfer he was finally ordered to Jefferson Barracks south of St. Louis in October 1837. The river was so low that he was forced to make most of the upper journey by canoe, leaving his belongings—including Dred and Harriet—behind. But he had no sooner arrived at Jefferson Barracks than orders came for him to proceed to Fort Jessup in western Louisiana.

Here old ailments returned, including respiratory problems that made it difficult for him to breathe. Apparently he had sufficient breath, however, to propose marriage to an attractive young lady from St. Louis named Irene Sanford. On February 6, 1838, after a whirlwind courtship, Dr. Emerson and Miss Sanford were married. Shortly after the marriage Emerson sent for his slaves, and Dred and Harriet made the long trip by steamboat from Fort Snelling to Fort Jessup.

For Dred and Harriet it was a voluntary return from free territory, where they had lived for five years, to slave territory, and if the slaves realized the significance of that fact, it apparently prompted no action on their part. On much of the trip down the Mississippi there was free territory on both sides of the river into which the slaves could easily have fled if they had so wished, but they did not avail themselves of the opportunity.

The Scotts had barely arrived in Louisiana when Dr. Emerson received orders to return to Fort Snelling. He booked passage on a steamboat to St. Louis for the Emersons and their slaves, and then on another boat from St. Louis to Fort Snelling. On this second lap, aboard the steamboat *Gypsey,* Harriet gave birth to a girl whom Dred and Harriet named Eliza. The child was born on the river far

5. *Historic Fort Snelling Chronicles*; Historians do not agree whether Harriet was sold or given to Dr. Emerson. Considering Harriet's value as a slave, it seems unlikely that Taliaferro would have given her away. Ehrlich notes that the marriage of Dred and Harriet was unique in slave history for "it was a civil ceremony performed by a justice of the peace." Walter Ehrlich, "Dred Scott in History," 5.

6. Lawson, *State Trials,* 229.

above the northern boundary of Missouri and well into free territory, a point that Roswell Field would later cite in testimony presented before the federal courts.[7]

After another two years at Fort Snelling, Dr. Emerson received orders to go to Florida, where the war with the Seminole Indians was in progress, and in the spring of 1840 Mrs. Emerson, along with the slaves, returned to St. Louis while Dr. Emerson proceeded to Florida alone. For Dred Scott, the return to St. Louis and slave territory represented a termination of his seven-year sojourn in free territory. For the remainder of his life he would never again set foot on territory free from slavery.

It is unclear exactly what Dred and Harriet did for the next six years of residency as slaves in Missouri preceding their court action for freedom. Mrs. Emerson lived on the estate of her father, Alexander Sanford, near St. Louis, during her husband's tour of duty in Florida. The slaves may have worked on Sanford's estate, or perhaps more likely were hired out for wages in St. Louis. Sanford would probably have been reluctant to expose his other slaves to the tales Harriet and Dred might have told about their lives in free territory.

Dr. Emerson returned from Florida in 1842, this time suffering from remittent fever. After discharge from the army, he died of consumption on December 29, 1843, leaving behind his widow and the couple's young daughter, Henrietta. John Emerson's will made no mention of the slaves Dred and Harriet, and he left everything to his wife with "broad authority" to use his estate for her benefit and that of their daughter.[8] While Irene Emerson sold off some of the land that she inherited from her husband, she did not sell either Dred or Harriet but kept them as slaves, using them as workers on her father's farm or hiring them out for wages either to her brother-in-law Colonel Bainbridge, or to residents in St. Louis. At one time during these years, Dred Scott said he was taken to a Texas military post by Mrs. Emerson's brother-in-law.[9]

Dred also related that during this period he sought to buy his freedom from Mrs. Emerson but that she refused.[10] Just why she refused is a question that has puzzled historians down through the years. Whatever her reasons, she never revealed them, and when she died in 1903, the questions remained unanswered.

There are perhaps two reasons why Irene Emerson declined to allow Dred Scott to buy his freedom, the reasons also perhaps explaining why, in later years, she

7. Ehrlich, *They Have No Rights,* 24; Statement of facts by R. M. Field and H. A. Garland, filed May 4, 1854, Dred Scott Collection, MHS.

8. Some historians have claimed that Emerson's will placed his estate in trust, which prevented his wife from disposing of the slaves. Fehrenbacher relates that Emerson left his entire estate to his wife with authorization "to sell all or any part of his land and tenements and to use the proceeds for her own and Henrietta's maintenance." Fehrenbacher, *Dred Scott,* 248.

9. *St. Louis Daily Evening News,* April 3, 1857.

10. Ibid.

fought so aggressively through her attorneys to block Dred and Harriet Scott's efforts to obtain their freedom. In his study on Missouri slavery, Harrison Trexler says that slave-owners held on to their slaves because they thought their slave investment was profitable, and also because they wanted to preserve the family dignity.[11] Irene Emerson's actions could be explained for both reasons.

The Sanfords were natives of Virginia and strongly proslavery. On their estate in north St. Louis County they used slaves for farm and household work. Alexander Sanford, the father, was active in proslavery circles and worked actively for the "protection of slave property against the evil designs of abolitionists." Irene Emerson's older brother, John F. A. Sanford, who watched over his sister's property and who would later be named defendant in Dred Scott's suit in the federal courts, was also strongly proslavery and was married to Emilie Chouteau, daughter of Pierre Chouteau Jr. and a member of one of the largest slave-owning families in St. Louis. For slave-owners like the Sanfords and Chouteaus there was a certain stigma attached to selling one's slaves unless absolutely necessary to meet a family financial crisis or to punish a recalcitrant runaway. The dignity of the family required nothing less.[12]

However, for Irene Emerson there may well have been equally compelling financial reasons for keeping Dred and Harriet in bondage rather than selling them or allowing them to sue successfully for freedom. Dred Scott was originally purchased by Dr. Emerson in 1833 for about five hundred dollars. Now, ten years later, after a six-year sojourn in free territory, Dred Scott's dollar value was greatly diminished. The years Dred and Harriet spent in free territory, which qualified them for freedom in Missouri courts, would have made their sale on the slave market difficult if not almost impossible. Purchasers of slaves in Missouri frequently asked for titles assuring the buyer that the slave had no hidden physical defects, was not prone to run away, and had not spent time in free territory. Irene Emerson could not have given such a title for Dred and Harriet Scott, and most likely both she and her brother, John Sanford, knew that. In fact, John Sanford was probably aware of a similar situation when Gabriel S. Chouteau, a relative, had the sale of a slave woman and her children forfeited for the same reason. On May 3, 1843, the purchaser, K. MacKenzie, wrote to Gabriel Chouteau:

> Being informed that the negro woman and children bid off by me at the Court House on Monday last claim they are free and that a suit has been instituted for the purpose of obtaining their freedom. Under the circumstances I decline to pay for

11. Trexler, *Missouri Slavery,* 28.

12. Notes on Sanford family by Mary Louise Dalton, Dred Scott Collection, MHS; Scharf, *History of St. Louis City and County,* vol. 1, 185; *St. Louis Weekly Union,* November 13, 1846; Notes on Sanford family by Dalton, Dred Scott Collection, MHS; Members of the Chouteau family were named as defendants in several slave suits for freedom in the St. Louis courts; Trexler, *Missouri Slavery,* 46.

or receive them because at the time of sale I understood that there was no dispute regarding the title to them.[13]

Even slave traders gave warranties on the slaves they sold. Bernard M. Lynch, who operated Lynch's Slave Pen on Locust Street at Fifth, gave this receipt in 1853:

Received of Geo. W. Berkley seven hundred dollars in full pay for a Negro girl named Charlote of yellow complexion aged about seventeen years. The above described Negro girl I warrant sound in body and mind, a slave for life and free from all claims, or claims whatsoever."[14]

Therefore, unable to sell Dred and Harriet Scott on the St. Louis slave market at a good price, Irene Emerson probably found it more profitable to hire the slaves out for wages. The hiring out of slaves in those days was a very common practice in St. Louis and it involved no loss in dignity. Besides, the annual financial returns were often very good, averaging about 14 percent of a slave's value. For Dred Scott's labor, Irene Emerson would have collected probably five dollars a month, and for Harriet Scott, part of whose time was taken by her small child, about four dollars a month. These wages earned by Harriet and Dred represented a steady monthly income for Irene Emerson. Furthermore, Irene Emerson might have speculated that the slaves also represented an investment that was likely to increase in value as the years progressed. In a few years, Dred and Harriet's daughter Eliza would be old enough to be hired out, and with Harriet Scott still a young woman, more children might be forthcoming, further increasing the value of her slave investment.[15]

Hiring the slaves out for wages required very little of Irene Emerson's time. Hiring contracts were "customarily made for a term of one year," but sometimes for several years, and called for the hirer "to furnish the slave with food, good clothing suitable to the season, and medical care, including the services of a doctor, if needed, and to return the slave, if alive, at the expiration of the term."[16] For Irene Emerson the only effort involved was collecting the wages earned by the slaves, and this responsibility she seems to have delegated to her father, Alexander Sanford.

All of which—while speculation—might help to explain why Irene Emerson refused Dred Scott's request to buy his freedom and why, after Dred and Harriet filed for their freedom in the Missouri courts, she encouraged her attorneys to use every legal strategy to keep them in bondage. It would also explain why, upon

13. Letter of K. MacKenzie to Gabriel Chouteau, May 3, 1843, Slaves and Slavery Collection, MHS.
14. Receipt from B. M. Lynch to George W. Berkley, October 8, 1853, Slaves and Slavery Collection, MHS.
15. Oberholzer, "Legal Aspects," 14; "Masters wanted their slaves to have children so that they could reap the potential capital gains at a later date." Hurt, *Agriculture and Slavery,* 263.
16. David D. March, *The History of Missouri,* vol. 1, 816.

leaving St. Louis for Massachusetts, Irene Emerson feigned such loving concern for the Scott family she was leaving behind, telling Dred Scott "that he was practically free, and the only thing she asked of him was that he take care of his wife and family well."[17]

17. *Springfield Daily Republican,* February 12, 1903; What Mrs. Emerson meant when she stated the Scotts were "practically free" is unclear. Perhaps she permitted the Scotts to find their own lodgings rather than live on the premises of those for whom they worked. She may also have meant that she permitted the Scotts to hire themselves out, or as the slaves described it, "hire their own time." Such practices, while illegal, were often more profitable than leasing out slaves on an annual basis. For the slaves themselves, such practices "created a new dimension of independence." Wade, *Slavery,* 48, 53; Lawrence O. Christensen, "Black St. Louis: A Study in Race Relations, 1865–1916," 9.

Real Estate Law

Sometime in 1842 or 1843, Myron Leslie and Roswell Field dissolved their law partnership and Field established his own law firm under the name R. M. Field. He moved into a separate office at 44 Chestnut Street, one door west from the former office of Leslie and Field.[1]

More significant, however, than the dissolution of a partnership and the move to a new office address, was the decision Field made during these years to focus his law practice on legal matters involving real estate. He would never find reason to change that focus; for the remainder of his twenty-five years as a practicing attorney in St. Louis, real estate law would be his specialty and the foundation upon which, in later years, his reputation as a lawyer would be based. History remembers Field as the attorney for the slave Dred Scott, but among the St. Louis attorneys with whom he practiced in the mid-1800s, he was, first and foremost, a real estate lawyer. Among that class, they said, Field "was justly considered as standing in the front rank of the bar of the city and State."[2]

Real estate law might seem a rather prosaic and lackluster field of jurisprudence, but in the 1840s in Missouri, real estate law was anything but dull, and if it has since become otherwise, that is because most of the land conflicts of that day have long since been put to rest. It was a field of law probably little known to Roswell Field in Windham County, although land suits had played an active part in Vermont's stormy early history, when "multiple charters and grants" during colonial days

1. Myron Leslie later became circuit attorney for St. Louis and a delegate to the state constitutional convention. He died in 1854, leaving a wife and two children. Bay, *Reminiscences,* 350; *St. Louis Directory for 1845.*
2. Hyde and Conard, *Encyclopedia of the History of St. Louis,* vol. 2, 741.

caused confusing title conflicts.[3] In St. Louis during the 1840s, however, it was a well-practiced field of law—and one that would certainly have attracted Field's attention soon after his arrival from Vermont.

As he became acquainted with the one hundred or so other lawyers in St. Louis, either at the courthouse or on the city streets, Field would have noticed that about a dozen of them had practices that focused on real estate law.[4] Field would also have noted that these lawyers seemed to be those who were most esteemed within the legal profession and whose names, when mentioned outside the bar, were likely to be well known among the city's prominent merchants and civic leaders. Many, if not all, of these same attorneys appeared to have achieved, as Field very likely expressed it, Yankee proof of success in life—that is, a thriving and financially successful legal practice. Real estate was, as Field probably noted, a profitable branch of law, and since he was a new attorney in town, strapped for money to pay even his weekly room and board, that advantage would have had a strong attraction.

Another attribute that probably appealed very much to him was the highly combative nature of real estate law. In this field of law, the emphasis was on the studious resolution of complicated and intricate legal questions rather than courtroom oratory, which had little appeal for Field. Field's intellectual skills and his proficiency in languages could be put to good use, giving him a decided advantage and serving as judicial weapons; for as one historian noted, the St. Louis real estate lawyers were like "legal gladiators" meeting for the fray in the courtrooms, and when they met "you found no child's play there."[5]

There was a good reason why the practice of real estate law during the 1800s was so esteemed in St. Louis and why it paid so well, and that was the craving for land. Americans arriving in St. Louis were "rapaciously opportunistic" when it came to land, viewing the new lands of Missouri "as a national treasure to be openly sold by land offices as expeditiously as possible." But long before the Americans arrived, much of Missouri's land, especially along the rivers, had already been claimed by French and Spanish settlers under grants not often fully understood by the Americans. As a result Missouri had "more different classes of land titles than any other state in the union," growing out of a history that was unique to the new state. Noted one early attorney, "There were not three perfect titles to land in the whole territory of the Upper Louisiana."[6]

3. *A New Fane in the Second Century,* 7.

4. There were several works published in the nineteenth century that contain lists of St. Louis lawyers, along with brief biographical information about them. Of these, Scharf's *History of St. Louis and St. Louis County,* vol. 2, 1449–1514, contains probably the most complete and detailed listing of St. Louis attorneys during the nineteenth century.

5. Stewart, ed., *Bench and Bar,* 361.

6. Dunne, *Missouri Supreme Court,* 24; Foley, *History of Missouri,* 174; Stewart, *Bench and Bar,* 360; John F. Darby, *Personal Recollections,* 14.

Settled first by the French, Missouri was part of the province of Louisiana and operated under the Customs of Paris and Roman Civil Law, which Louis XIV of France had decreed in 1712 would govern the "edicts, ordinances, customs, etc." of the French inhabitants living in the Valley of the Mississippi.[7] In 1763, after almost a century of settlement, France ceded all of Louisiana west of the Mississippi to Spain, which controlled the province until 1800 when it was re-ceded to France.

Then, in 1803, the province was sold to the United States and, in the treaties and cessions conveying the province, the French and Spanish inhabitants were assured by the United States that it would protect and confirm their rights to the land acquired under the French and Spanish governments.[8] The Customs of Paris and Roman Civil Law therefore remained in force until 1816, when they were superseded by English common law. The result was, as one legal historian has noted, the existence along the western banks of the Mississippi of the two great legal systems of Europe: the common law of England and the civil law of Rome.[9] These resulting conflicts in law would keep lawyers in St. Louis busy—and wealthy—for decades to come.

Legal conflicts frequently involved more than differences in the language of land titles and in the ways land was measured. French law reflected long-standing cultural traditions that differed from those of the English. Adding to the "turbulent conditions" were the many American legislative enactments during the early 1800s, which were intended to make the transition easier, but more often only added to the chaos.[10]

Before the territory was acquired by the United States, the law in St. Louis was administered by the French and Spanish governors, working together with the leading French families of St. Louis—the Chouteaus, the Chauvins, the Prattes, and the Soulards. In many instances, civil suits were simply taken before the local governor, who in turn selected arbiters to resolve the conflicts.[11] When Missouri became a territory and later a state, lawyers began arriving from the eastern states and new courts were established. In 1825 St. Louis had both a circuit court and a probate court. But the court calendar of the circuit court soon became so crowded that in 1839, the year Roswell Field arrived in St. Louis, three more courts were added: first the Court of Common Pleas, then the Criminal Court, and, a little later, the Land Commissioners' Court. Among those attorneys signing the register to practice before the new St. Louis Land Court

7. Stewart, *Bench and Bar*, 360.

8. Treaty with France, 1803, Article III.

9. Dunne, *Missouri Supreme Court*, 22.

10. Stewart, *Bench and Bar*, 109–10; The "turbulent conditions" in the Missouri territory involving land during this period are described in detail by historian William E. Foley in *The Genesis of Missouri from Wilderness Outpost to Statehood*, 170–74, 248–52.

11. Walter B. Stevens, ed., *St. Louis, the Fourth City*, 500.

was Roswell Field, whose signature, R. M. Field, confirms his decision to practice real estate law.[12]

Among real estate lawyers in St. Louis in the mid-1800s, Roswell Field was considered one of the best, ranked among the top three in Missouri according to A. J. D. Stewart, who compiled *The History of the Bench and Bar Of Missouri* in 1898. The other two attorneys were Abiel Leonard, who practiced at Fayette in central Missouri, and Hamilton R. Gamble, who practiced in St. Louis. Even Henry S. Geyer, whom Stewart considered the "greatest lawyer at the Missouri bar," was not equal, Stewart said, to Field, Gamble, and Leonard when it came to "knowledge of law relating to real estate."[13]

Among such an elite group of Missouri attorneys, all involved in land law, a rather intense competitiveness could have existed, but there is no evidence that it did. However, there probably did exist within the St. Louis bar rival factions, since the court records indicate that certain attorneys seemed to work together more frequently on behalf of common clients. For example, Henry Geyer and Roswell Field had many cases in the land court, but in none of them did they join together to represent a common client. When Geyer and Field were involved in the same suit, they were opposing counsels.[14] Between Roswell Field and Hamilton Gamble, on the other hand, there seems to have existed a rather amiable professional relationship, evidenced not only in cases where they represented a common client but also in their business correspondence wherein they discussed cases and gave advice to one another.

At the time of Field's arrival, Hamilton Gamble was in partnership with Edward Bates; the firm was located at 21 Chestnut Street, just a few doors east of Field's office. Gamble was a native of Virginia and about ten years older than Field. He had come to Missouri in 1818, twenty years before Field, and after serving as prosecuting attorney was appointed secretary of state for Missouri.[15]

Field's association with Hamilton Gamble indicates that Field, even with his New England background and his perhaps rather staid and reticent ways, could still form a professional relationship with a Southerner like Gamble who not only had been educated in the South but also owned slaves. Gamble's views concerning slavery were rather typical of many Missourians of the time. He favored some form of emancipation for slaves, but he could not countenance the thought of equality with blacks and thought African Americans should be colonized in Africa.[16]

---

12. Scharf, *History of St. Louis City and County,* 1450; Undated manuscript entitled "Register of the St. Louis Land Court," St. Louis Circuit Court Records, MHS.

13. Stewart, *Bench and Bar,* 113.

14. For example, *Milburn v. Corthron.* In 11 *Missouri Reports,* 369, MSC.

15. Bay, *Reminiscences,* 18, 19, 280; Jno. F. Philips, "Hamilton Rowan Gamble and the Provisional Government of Missouri," 2.

16. Hamilton Gamble was a contributor to the Missouri State Colonization Society, *Missouri Republican,* May 16, 1854; In 1847, Gamble purchased for $1,050 a slave woman named Sukey, age

Compared with the rather unpolished frontier-style judicial demeanor of Field's early partner, Myron Leslie, Hamilton Gamble would have seemed almost patrician by comparison. A talented lawyer with broad legal experience and knowledge, Gamble probably was impressive to Field, and Field may well have seen in Gamble some of the characteristics he had admired in his own father. Like General Martin Field, Gamble was also a man of noble presence, "of full height, and form, calm and grave in demeanor," and on horseback he had the martial appearance of one who might lead an army.[17]

A letter dated 1844, in which Gamble recommended Roswell Field for judge of the St. Louis Circuit Court, indicated that the association between the two men commenced shortly after Field began his practice of real estate law. Gamble stated in the letter to Governor John Marmaduke that he was not intimate with Field but recommended him based on Field's reputation among other St. Louis attorneys.

> If the principle on which appointments are to be made cuts off all hope of obtaining the appointment of any person who is a Whig, I venture to suggest to you that R. M. Field, Esq. who is represented to me to be a Democrat would accept the office if tendered to him. My personal acquaintance with Mr. Field has not been intimate, nor have I had much professional intercourse with him, but I rely very strongly on the representations of those members of the bar here who know him well and who say to one that he is a gentleman [*ms. damaged*] and high legal attainments for a man of his age [*damaged*] the members of the bar best acquainted with Mr. Field would be fully satisfied with him. He is here comparatively a stranger but this arises from his retiring manners and habits and not because of the shortness of his residence in the city. He has been here several years.[18]

Roswell Field did not receive the appointment from the governor, and this probably did not disappoint him. Field may even have been relieved and very possibly agreed to accept an appointment to the court only out of his respect for Gamble. Gamble's comment that Field "would accept the office if tendered to him" is most uncharacteristic of Roswell Field, whose lack of interest in public office was almost legendary among attorneys in St. Louis. If any one trait characterized Roswell Field during his twenty-five years of legal practice in St. Louis, it was his lack of ambition for public office. He neither sought nor seemed interested in any elected or appointed position and was said to be "utterly devoid of all ambition for power and place;" he "uniformly declined all offers of advancement to the highest

---

forty-two, and her three young daughters. Sales receipt dated September 10, 1847, Hamilton R. Gamble Papers, MHS; He also had an account at Lynch's slave pen where he sold in 1849 a negro and her two children for "$700 less commission and 25 cents per day board." Receipt from B. M. Lynch dated October 31, 1849, Hamilton R. Gamble Papers, MHS.

17. Daniel M. Grissom, "Personal Recollections of Distinguished Missourians," 662.

18. Manuscript letter, slightly damaged, from Hamilton Gamble to Governor Marmaduke dated March 1844. Hamilton R. Gamble Papers, MHS.

judicial honors of the State." His friend Montgomery Blair said that Roswell Field "never, during the fifteen years I have known him, manifested any interest in politics." Judge Alexander Hamilton shared this observation and said of Field that while he was "eminently qualified to serve . . . he shrank from offering himself" for public positions and was not in any way "covetous of gain and of fame."[19]

Whatever reasons prompted Field to avoid positions of leadership seem to have developed after his arrival in St. Louis. In Vermont, where he practiced law for almost fifteen years, there is no indication that he shunned public life. During these Vermont years, Field was elected and appointed to many offices: state representative, state's attorney, postmaster, even school board member.

When Roswell Field first became acquainted with Hamilton Gamble, Field's practice of real estate law was just commencing and Gamble's, after many years, was drawing to a close. Edward Bates, his partner, noted that Gamble was not in "good health and having an easy fortune" could retire "from the drudgery of attorney practice." His retirement came in 1851, but it would not take him out of public life, for before the year ended, Hamilton Gamble was elected a justice of the Missouri Supreme Court, where his presence would have far-reaching significance for both Dred Scott and Roswell Field.[20]

Before Gamble retired from law practice, however, and before he went on the Missouri high court, he and Roswell Field worked jointly on several lawsuits involving real estate. The most notable case in which they represented the same client was *Norman Cutter v. William Waddingham and others.* The suit commenced in the St. Louis Circuit Court in 1846 and reached the Missouri Supreme Court in 1855.[21]

The case deserves special attention, not only because both Field and Gamble worked together on it but also because *Cutter v. Waddingham,* of the many Missouri and Vermont lawsuits in which Roswell Field participated, most clearly reveals his brilliant legal mind and the broad scope of his knowledge.

A total of eighty-five printed pages are devoted to this case in volume 22 of the *Missouri Reports,* far more than any other case that, up to that time, had come before the Missouri Supreme Court. It was a case so unusual in the annals of the state supreme court that the court reporter wrote in a preface:

> The importance of this cause, both as regards the amount of value involved and also the principles established by the decision of the court, is such, that the Reporter has considered himself justified in giving an extended report of the views presented by

19. Pierce, *Field Genealogy,* 510; *National Intelligencer,* December 14, 1856; *Centennial Proceedings,* 49.

20. Edward Bates diary, March 10, 1851, Bates Family Papers, MHS; Stewart, *Bench and Bar,* 10.

21. *Norman Cutter v. William Waddingham and others,* October term, 1855, 22 *Missouri Reports,* 206, MSC.

counsel. The brief of Mr. R. M. Field, filed by him on motion for a rehearing, will, it is thought, be of interest to the profession, and it is accordingly printed at large.[22]

At issue in the suit was a large parcel of land in the heart of the city of St. Louis. Known as the *Prairie La Grange de Terre,* the parcel measured one arpent [a French measure] in width and forty arpents in length. The area was dominated by what St. Louisans then called *the barn of earth,* a large mound of earth painstakingly constructed centuries earlier by the Indians. Originally granted to Louis Lirette in 1769, the land was sold to John Baptiste Vifvarenne. Later it came into the hands of Pierre Chouteau and his wife, who in 1819 sold it to John Mullanphy, whose family in turn leased the land to William Waddingham.[23] It was the Mullanphy family, along with Waddingham, who were represented by Hamilton Gamble and Roswell Field. Among the opposing counsel was Henry S. Geyer, the most-often-mentioned contender with Hamilton Gamble for the position of titular head of the Missouri bar. Before the Missouri Supreme Court reached a decision in *Cutter v. Waddingham,* the three attorneys—Gamble, Geyer, and Field—would once again be involved together in still another famous lawsuit, this one pertaining not to wealthy landowners, but to two penniless slaves named Dred and Harriet Scott.

With the Mullanphys and the Chouteaus, *Cutter v. Waddingham* involved two of St. Louis's wealthiest and most prominent families. The Chouteau family had its roots in the very founding of the city, and John Mullanphy, an Irishman, came to St. Louis in 1814 and amassed, through business ventures and real estate investments, an immense fortune that was later used to build hospitals, orphanages, and convents, and to endow an Emigrant Relief Fund offering assistance to travelers coming into St. Louis on their way to the West.[24]

At issue in the controversy over the forty arpents of land was a title dispute going back to the early French owners, and more specifically, a marriage contract between John B. Vifvarenne and his wife, Genevieve Cardinal, dating from 1777. Both parties to the suit claimed title through the last surviving son of John and Genevieve Vifvarenne, Louis Vifvarenne, who died without issue. Norman Cutter claimed title through Louis's two paternal aunts, and William Waddingham claimed title from three of Louis's half-brothers who were born after Genevieve remarried, following John Vifvarenne's death. At issue in the litigation, along with several other minor points, was whether Spanish or French law applied to the marriage contract of John and Genevieve Vifvarenne. Under French law, Genevieve Vifvarenne

22. Ibid.

23. Ibid.; There were several Indian mounds in St. Louis. One at Mound and Broadway rose about fifty feet above the street, upon which the European settlers built a pavilion, two stories high, from which "there is a magnificent view up and down the river and over a portion of the city." *St. Louis Directory for 1845,* xix.

24. Darby, *Personal Recollections,* 52–55.

would be entitled to her share of the conjugal property even when she remarried, but by Spanish law, a widow who remarried forfeited "to the children of the first marriage all the property she may have acquired from her deceased husband."[25]

The Missouri Supreme Court was quite obviously uncertain as to how to apply the law, and, for that matter, what law—French or Spanish—to apply. The court said:

> We remark that the case involves a large amount of property, and that the questions discussed and to be decided depend on a foreign system of law quite different from that to which we are bred and with which, of course, we have very little familiarity. These questions, too, spring out of the transaction of a foreign race of men, the French inhabitants of this city, whose manners and customs as well as institutions, both legal and social, were very different from our own.[26]

The question before the court was what law prevailed in St. Louis in 1777 when John and Genevieve were married: "the customary law of Paris, which the French colonists brought with them to Louisiana," or the Spanish law of their new Spanish sovereign who had taken control of the territory from the French. In its opinion, the court decided that Spanish law prevailed in St. Louis in 1777, using as precedent an earlier decision made in 1816 by the supreme court of the state of Louisiana. In this decision the Louisiana Supreme Court held that Spanish law was introduced into the French province of Louisiana in 1769. This would have been eight years before the marriage of John and Genevieve Vifvarenne.[27]

Roswell Field took exception to this decision by the Missouri high court and filed a motion for a rehearing. This the Missouri Supreme Court denied, but in turning down the motion, the court apparently was impressed enough by Roswell Field's arguments that it took the unusual step of appending to its decision the "reasons for a rehearing presented by R. M. Field."[28] Therefore, what followed in the next twenty-six pages of the *Missouri Reports* were Roswell Field's arguments challenging the validity of the supreme court's decision. Roswell Field argued that French law, not Spanish, prevailed in St. Louis in 1777, and in making his arguments, Field lectured the Missouri Supreme Court on American history, the French and Spanish languages, and, most importantly, the law—French, Spanish, and English.

Field contended that while Spanish law may have been introduced into New Orleans in 1769, this did not mean it was also introduced at the same time into the northern part of Louisiana where St. Louis was located and where the marriage took place. Furthermore, Field argued, it also did not necessarily follow that

25. 22 *Missouri Reports*, 250, 207, MSC.
26. Ibid.
27. Ibid.
28. Ibid., 168.

Spanish law supplanted French law just because the territory came under control of Spain. Field contended that history showed Upper and Lower Louisiana to have been two distinct governmental units.

> The country of the Illinois, embracing the territory on both sides of the Mississippi river, north of the mouth of the Ohio, was originally settled by the Canadian French. Kaskaskia was said to have been founded in 1682 by LaSalle on his return from the discovery of the mouth of the Mississippi [and] this settlement and several others in Illinois existed in a flourishing condition a full twenty years before the foundations of New Orleans were laid. During the course of the French and Spanish dominations, this country was under a government distinct and separate from that of Lower Louisiana.[29]

Roswell Field reported that he had made a study of marriage contracts after the Spanish, under governors Pedro Piernas and Francisco Cruzat, took control of St. Louis.

> The practice and usage at St. Louis . . . appear in the archives in which many of the marriage contracts were deposited. An abstract shows that from the accession of Piernas, up to the date of the contract in dispute, nineteen marriage contracts were entered into before Piernas and Cruzat. Of these, eleven adopt precisely the formula of the one in dispute, and six of the others bear plain marks of their origin in French law. Only six are in the Spanish language. Four of these are verbal translations of the French formula of the contract in dispute . . . It is manifest, from this abstract, that, in the matter of contracts, there was not as early as 1777 any adoption of the Spanish law at St. Louis; but on the contrary, that, by consent of the governors and governed, it was excluded.[30]

Since these marriage contracts were written under the influence of French law, Field argued that it was important that they be understood as the French would have understood them.

> It is an established rule of interpretation that when technical words are used in an instrument, they must be construed according to the meaning which they have in the art or science from which they are borrowed. This rule is recognized by all courts and is applicable to all languages. Now the contract in question is full of these technical terms, borrowed from the French law. The words *conquets, douaire, prefix, preciput,* are of this description. To the ear of a judge of Spanish or English law alone, they are mere gibberish. By the light of the French law, their meaning is plain. He who, in expounding this contract, lays aside the French law as a sealed book, will put away the only interpreter by which the meaning of its terms can be known.[31]

29. Ibid., 270.
30. Ibid., 272.
31. Ibid., 276.

Field argued that not only the French words but also the clauses and, in fact, the whole marriage contract must be interpreted as the French would have interpreted them.

> What is true of particular words may be predicated of clauses. Take the clause *ameublissement*. In light of English law it has no sense. In the light of Spanish law it is nugatory. With the aid of French law, its meaning and force become apparent . . . but this rule of interpretation is not confined to words and clauses. It is applicable to the whole instrument.[32]

Field then chastised the Missouri Supreme Court for its comments that the early French laws of St. Louis were foreign laws and that the French people of early St. Louis represented a foreign race of men.

> It is proper to remark that there is an inaccuracy in calling the custom of Paris a foreign law. Strictly speaking, it is a domestic law repealed. In 1770, it had been in force in this place, as part of the Illinois district, a full three quarters of a century. Supposing it to be then repealed, it could not, in 1777, the date of the contract, be called a foreign law in any other sense than as our revised code of 1835 is a foreign law. And it is conceived that our courts are bound to know and take notice of the custom of Paris in the same manner and to the same extent as of any other of our repealed codes.[33]

Field then pointed out that even after the Spanish governors took control of St. Louis, the people, who were French, continued to rely on French law by custom and that the Spanish made no direct effort to replace French law with Spanish law.[34]

> When the Spanish officers succeeded the French authorities in the district of Illinois, in 1770, they found there a population entirely French, and acquainted with no other system of municipal law than the custom of Paris, which had been in use from the time of the first settlements, about four-score years before. The abstract of the marriage contracts in the hands of the court, shows that up to this date there were sixteen marriage contracts entered into at this place, which were deposited in the archives, and still remain there. Fifteen of these created a community in express terms, according to the custom of Paris *(suivant et au desir de la coutume de Paris)*. The other does not name the custom expressly, but it contains the clause of *ameublissement,* and is thoroughly French in character.[35]

Field told the court that during the first ten years under Spanish control, only one marriage contract written in St. Louis was written according to Spanish law.

32. Ibid.
33. Ibid., 277.
34. Ibid., 284.
35. Ibid.

During the first ten years of Spanish government, under the administrations of the royal governors, Piernas, Cruzat and Leyba, there were twenty-eight marriage contracts entered into that still remain in the archives . . . There are two that clearly do not adopt the custom. The one says nothing on the subject of community, and the other expressly adopts the Recopilacion of Castile.[36]

Field says that not only did John Vifvarenne and his wife clearly make their 1777 marriage contract according to French law, but that, since they were both illiterate, the Spanish authorities would have assisted them in understanding the marriage contract.

We see that the parties intended to adopt the community established by the custom of Paris. The governor advised them that the intention was lawful; and he drew up the contract in a form to effectuate that intention . . . Neither party could read or write. In Spanish practice, formal instruments were to be drawn up by or under the supervision of some public officer. It was the duty of the officer to explain to illiterate parties the legal effect of its particular clauses, and the officer himself was amenable to severe penalties if he inserted any stipulation contrary to laws.[37]

Under the Spanish constitution, the power of making and dispensing with the laws was vested with the King of Spain who, in turn, had the power to delegate another at his royal pleasure. The King thereby granted the Spanish governors at St. Louis authority to modify general laws to suit the conditions in distant colonies like America. In conclusion, Field pointed out that not only were such actions by the Spanish governors sanctioned by the King of Spain, but they were also sanctioned by the United States Supreme Court.

The Supreme Court of the United States, in speaking of the acts of the Spanish governors, holds this language: "No principle can be better established by the authority of this court, than that the acts of an officer, to whom a public duty is assigned by his king, within the sphere of that duty, are *prima facie* taken to be within his power. The principles on which it rests are believed to be too deeply founded in law and reason ever to be successfully assailed."[38]

After hearing these arguments, the Missouri Supreme Court held to its decision and did not grant Roswell Field's motion for a rehearing. However, the court quite clearly felt some uneasiness about its decision, admitting, as stated in its own words, a "distrust in the correctness" of what was decided. This uncertainty probably explains why Field's arguments were printed in full at the conclusion of the case and why the court felt it would be of interest to other attorneys.[39]

36. Ibid., 285.
37. Ibid., 286.
38. Ibid., 287.
39. Ibid., 251.

During the eight years the case was in litigation, Gamble and Field corresponded several times concerning the case. In one instance, Hamilton Gamble sent to Field five lengthy handwritten pages containing his observations on the John Vifvarenne marriage and asked for Field's thoughts. In another, Field asked for Gamble's opinion on the filing of amended declarations in the case.[40]

Since the case involved large sums of money, as the Missouri Supreme Court noted, the attorneys' fees were also probably equally large, although nothing in the records mentions compensation. In 1863, eight years after the decision, a letter to John Mullanphy's daughter Octavia notes, "I have seen Mr. R. M. Field and he seems satisfied with the payment of a part of his bill. His fees have not been paid for a number of years which accounts for the bill being so large, as it embraces several old land cases."[41]

In the years following Hamilton Gamble's retirement from the firm of Gamble and Bates in 1851, and before Edward Bates left St. Louis ten years later in 1861 to serve as attorney general under President Abraham Lincoln, Field also handled a number of cases jointly with Edward Bates and his son Barton.[42] It would appear that perhaps Field enjoyed the same close professional relationship with Edward and Barton Bates that he did with Hamilton Gamble.

It was also Edward Bates whom Roswell Field succeeded when Field was selected in the late 1840s to handle legal affairs for the St. Louis Board of Education. Serving as attorney for the school board was a natural adjunct for any St. Louis attorney specializing in real estate law, for the school board ranked among the largest landowners in the city and was active in the leasing and renting of lands it owned. School board involvement in real estate had its origins in a congressional act of 1812 during Missouri's territorial days. Under this act, all "village lots, out-lots or common-field lots" that were "not rightfully owned or claimed by any private individuals" were to be reserved "for the Support of schools." In 1833, St. Louis set up its first public school board, and the acquisition of unclaimed land soon became a major function of the board. By 1854, when the city's western limits extended no farther than Grand Avenue, the St. Louis School Board owned more than 170 acres of land, including many very valuable tracts, such as a lot with

40. Undated reply of R. M. Field to Judge (H. R.) Gamble, Hamilton R. Gamble Papers, MHS; Letter of R. M. Field to H. R. Gamble, March 19, 1855, Hamilton R. Gamble Papers, MHS.

41. James M. Carpenter in St. Louis to Mrs. Octavia Boyce in New York, January 29, 1863. Written during the Civil War, the letter states it was sent out of St. Louis "by flag of truce" through the soldiers blockading the city. Mullanphy Family Papers, MHS.

42. Among the cases were: *Blair v. Marks,* 27 *Missouri Reports,* 579, MSC, *Evans v. Green and others,* 21 *Missouri Reports,* 170, MSC, *James v. Christy,* 18 *Missouri Reports,* 162, MSC; Stewart, 113; "Being Attorney General in 1861 was not much of a job. The true Department of Justice was still ten years in the offing. Bates' functions were to give opinions as asked to the President and department heads, and to handle the government litigation in the Supreme Court." John P. Frank, "Edward Bates, Lincoln's Attorney General," 35.

150 front feet at the corner of Market and Fourth Streets. Court records show that the land cases in which Field represented the school board were many in number, and he probably devoted a good part of his time to this work in the late 1840s and early 1850s.[43]

In handling land cases such as these, Roswell Field acquired his reputation as one of the foremost land attorneys in Missouri. Among his fellow members of the St. Louis bar, Field's opinions and advice were highly valued, and after a few years in St. Louis his law office on Chestnut Street, like the one he left behind in Vermont, had become a frequent meeting place for those who shared his interests. A New Englander who frequently visited St. Louis in those years described Field's St. Louis law practice to Field's mother, Esther, who, in turn, passed the New Englander's report on to the family in Vermont.

> [Mr. Dyer] . . . is quite familiar with Roswell, spends his time in Roswell's office when in St. Louis, speaks much of his praise, says his health is good and his business prospects are flattering. He thinks him the best lawyer in St. Louis and says the junior members of the bar are more in the habit of applying to Roswell for aid rather than their books. He says Roswell mixes little with society, and is constantly in his office where he is surrounded by friends who express the greatest admiration for his talents.[44]

It would probably be a mistake, however, to assume that among the attorneys in St. Louis Roswell Field was universally respected and admired and had no detractors. Working in a competitive profession that often found itself deeply embroiled in politics, Field was almost certain to have attracted some animosity. Who exactly his detractors might have been is uncertain, although one St. Louis attorney, at least, appears to have defamed Field not so much by what he said about Field but what he left unsaid.

John F. Darby, a "beloved and esteemed" St. Louis attorney and mayor of the city for four terms from 1835 to 1840, was, like Field, primarily a real estate lawyer.[45] On at least two occasions, he and Field jointly represented the same client. Later Darby wrote a book entitled *Personal Recollections,* a rather colorful history of the Missouri bar during the last century. The book was written in 1880 and almost every attorney in St. Louis prior to the Civil War is mentioned: Gamble, Bates,

---

43. Gray, "Recollections," 128; Report of Charles L. Tucker, president of the school board, in its 1853 report. St. Louis (Mo.) Board of Education Records, MHS; Record book no. 4, August 24, 1858, St. Louis (Mo.) Board of Education Records, MHS; Among some of the land cases were: *Byrne v. the Board of President and Directors of the St. Louis Public Schools,* 12 *Missouri Reports,* 402, MSC, *Mary Pembridge and the Saint Louis Public Schools v. Francis H. Manter and Charles N. Hicks,* 13 *Missouri Reports,* 586, MSC, and *George Eberle v. The Board of President and Directors of the St. Louis Public Schools,* 11 *Missouri Reports,* 247, MSC.

44. Undated letter of Esther Field to Mereb Ann Kellogg, Kellogg Collection, VHS.

45. Stewart, *Bench and Bar,* 114.

Lawless, Gannt, and Barton, among others. Mentioned also is Henry S. Geyer, whom Darby says was "by common consent considered the head of the bar in St. Louis" and "whose great argument before the United States Supreme Court in the Dred Scott case . . . caused William H. Stewart and other Abolitionists to denounce Chief Justice Taney so severely."[46]

However, the name of one prominent St. Louis attorney is notably absent in the book—Roswell Field. Legal historians using this book—and many have, for it was reprinted in 1978—might view the omission as simply an oversight. And this would be a likely explanation were it not for a notation in the estate papers of Roswell Field. On July 2, 1861, Field made a loan of five thousand dollars to John Darby. Four years later Field wrote Darby.

> I fear you have misinterpreted a remark I made to you more than 2 years ago to the effect that I should dun you no more. I certainly did not mean to convey the idea that you are released from the debt, or that you were at liberty, as long as you pleased, to postpone my necessities to your convenience. I meant only that I should not spend more time in importuning you for payment, and that at the proper time I should turn this disagreeable business over to other hands.[47]

The loan remained unpaid during the remainder of Roswell Field's life. It was subsequently canceled in 1876 by default when John Darby went into bankruptcy.[48]

46. Darby, *Personal Recollections,* 234.

47. Letter dated June 24, 1865, from Roswell M. Field to John Darby, John F. Darby Papers, MHS.

48. Letter of M. L. Gray, executor of R. M. Field estate, to judge of the probate court, R. M. Field estate papers, SLPC.

11

Harriet and Dred

On Monday, April 6, 1846, attorney Francis B. Murdoch followed a path through the muddy streets of St. Louis and, pushing his way into the crowded courthouse and through the corridors, appeared before Judge John Krum of the St. Louis Circuit Court where he filed petitions for the freedom of his slave clients, Dred and Harriet Scott.[1]

The courthouse, which was located on Fourth Street along the brow of a hill some six hundred yards up from the banks of the Mississippi, was unusually busy and crowded that day. Not only had the steady rains, which had been falling for three days, driven many of the habitual loiterers inside, but it was also a local election day, and hundreds of American and Whig party supporters lingered around the government offices awaiting the closing of the polls at sundown.[2] Adding to the commotion, at noon on that day, twenty-three immigrants, accompanied by relatives, had been herded into the huge rotunda, given the oath of allegiance to the United States, and then marched to the polls to vote. An editor commented, "It takes 21 years to prepare Americans to vote, but the process of manufacturing voters out of foreigners is much shorter."[3]

1. The atmosphere was "anything but pleasant" and rendered the streets "muddy and disagreeable for walking." *St. Louis Reveille,* April 6, 1846.

2. On that day, Peter G. Camden, the American Party candidate, was elected mayor of St. Louis. The party advocated a government of native-born Americans against foreign-born. William Rufus Jackson, *Missouri Democracy,* vol. 1, 766; Scharf, *History of St. Louis City and County,* vol. 1, 676.

3. *St. Louis Daily New Era,* April 7, 1846.

But by far the largest number of those crowding into the courthouse were there in hopes of glimpsing Henry Clay—"Harry of the West," St. Louisans called him— who had arrived in the city the morning before and who was now visiting the courthouse to sell some St. Louis land he owned and to hear legal arguments being presented in one of the courtrooms by Hamilton R. Gamble. Clay, a noted Whig from Kentucky, proponent of American nationalism, and booster of the West, had arrived early on Sunday morning aboard two steamers that had been lashed together.[4] As cannons aboard the vessels boomed to announce his arrival, thousands of St. Louisans, forgetting breakfast, ran to the levee where Clay, "wishing to avoid a public demonstration, walked down from the deck with his brown box coat tightly buttoned," then disappeared into a "sea of heads" stretching out in all directions. Many who failed to see Clay on his arrival, now came to the courthouse on Monday hoping to meet him and, with luck, shake his hand.[5]

Whether Dred and Harriet Scott caught a glimpse of Henry Clay in the courthouse that day, or, for that matter, whether they were even in the courthouse when their petitions were filed, is not known. Francis Murdoch no doubt had the slaves' petitions in his pocket when he appeared in court, but it is not certain whether the slaves stood before Judge Krum along with their attorney. All that can be said with certainty is that on April 6 both Dred and Harriet signed their petitions with an "X" and swore, in the presence of Justice Of The Peace Mann Bullen, that the facts in their petitions were true.[6]

The petitions of Dred and Harriet Scott were prepared according to Missouri statute and were not unlike the one Francis Murdoch had prepared for Diana Cephas in her suit for freedom against Murry McConnell in 1841. Nor were they significantly different from the petitions Roswell Field had prepared for Martha Ann and her son James in 1843. In the Scotts' two petitions, both Dred and Harriet related that they had been slaves of Dr. John Emerson while he was stationed at Fort Snelling in free territory and that several years later they were brought to St.

4. Stella M. Drumm and Charles van Ravensswaay, "The Old Courthouse," 12; A steamboat was also named "Harry of the West." *St. Louis Weekly Union,* October 28, 1846; The "program of protective tariffs and internal improvements," designated by Clay as the American System, became "one of the most important statements of American nationalism to emerge from the nineteenth century." Mark E. Neely Jr., *The Last Best Hope of Earth,* 11; Clay was very much in the public eye, having been a three-time presidential candidate, narrowly losing to James K. Polk two years earlier.

5. *St. Louis Reveille,* April 6, 1846; Years later Colonel William F. Switzler would write, "I found the courthouse full of people. I was not in the courthouse that day to hear speeches, no difference by whom made or the subject of them, but to see Mr. Clay." Drumm and van Ravensswaay, "Old Courthouse," 14.

6. Petition of Harriet, a woman of color, dated April 6, 1846, to the Hon. John M. Krum, judge of the St. Louis Circuit Court, photocopy of original, Dred Scott file, U.S. District Court, eastern division, St. Louis (USDC); Petition of Dred Scott, dated April 6, 1846, to the Hon. John M. Krum, judge of the St. Louis Circuit Court, typescript of original, Dred Scott Collection, MHS.

Louis where Irene Emerson, the doctor's widow, now held them as slaves. On the basis of "this statement of facts" Dred and Harriet asked the court to allow them to sue and establish their "right to freedom." Since the petitions followed a course prescribed by Missouri statute and were, in most respects, similar to slave petitions for freedom filed previously with the court, Judge Krum, apparently having no reservations, immediately granted Dred and Harriet Scott "leave to sue." On the same day, Murdoch also filed charges of trespass for false imprisonment against Irene Emerson as required by statute, and, as a final step, generously posted bond for the two slaves, acknowledging himself "bound for all costs that may accrue."[7]

Historians have long speculated on what motivated Dred Scott to file suit for freedom, and, more importantly, whether his actions were of his own volition or whether he was encouraged by others who had motives of their own. At least initially, the suit attracted no attention, but in the years that followed, especially after the historic decision by the United State Supreme Court, there were those who claimed the Dred Scott case had been fictitious from its inception, contrived by leaders of political factions and designed to further either proslavery or antislavery interests. While these suspicions sometimes still surface today, historic research and the calming of North-South sectional rivalry has largely put them to rest, and modern-day historians generally agree that, at least initially, the Dred Scott case was simply a suit for freedom by a slave who wanted nothing more than to escape bondage.[8]

However, while disallowing political motivations, historians have been less willing to credit Dred Scott himself with the idea, permitting themselves, it seems, to be swayed by the common depiction of Scott in history books as a "stupid" and "shiftless" black slave and therefore incapable of sufficient initiative to seek his own freedom in the courts.

In the past, several historians have attributed the suit's origins to attorneys in St. Louis. One author said Scott was talked into filing the suit by lawyers whose "main objective was to pave the way for a suit against the Emerson estate for the twelve years' wages to which Scott would be entitled should the courts declare that he had been illegally held as a slave since 1834." Another writer implied that Roswell Field encouraged the suit "as an opportunity of making some money out of the man." Still another author said that Dred Scott "was approached by two attorneys,

7. Ibid.; Grant of privilege to sue, along with conditions. Signed by Judge Krum on the back side of both petitions and dated April 6, 1846. Dred Scott Collection, MHS; Photocopies of each individual Writ of Summons issued to Irene Emerson. On the bottom of each summons Murdoch agrees to be "bound for all costs that may accrue in the above cause." Dred Scott file, USDC; Some Dred Scott court papers have been destroyed, others badly damaged by fire, the result of having been accidentally thrown into a furnace a century ago. For details on this incident see Ehrlich, *They Have No Rights,* 187.

8. Ehrlich, *They Have No Rights,* 34; "There is no evidence of underlying political purposes, or an intent to contrive a test case." Fehrenbacher, *Dred Scott,* 251.

Burd and Risk, who were called the nigger lawyers, and that they urged Scott to sue for his freedom."[9] Such speculation is given little credence today: historians point out that any St. Louis attorney at the time who was familiar with legal precedents would have realized that a financial judgment against a slave-owner was most unlikely, and would furthermore have violated the *Revised Statutes of Missouri,* which forbade the recovery of damages in a freedom suit.

More numerous, however, have been those historians and writers who, during the past century, have attributed the motivation for the suit to "friends" of Dred Scott, most notably to members of the Blow family. Such speculation grows out of the fact that after the suit was filed, several members of the Blow family aided Dred Scott's legal efforts. The most frequently cited account claims that Dred Scott, after his sale to Dr. Emerson, was "sold but not well sold" and that he remained a burden on the Blow family. To rid themselves of this dependency, the Blows encouraged Scott's suit for freedom. "Quarters, half-dollars, and old clothes were the least of his demands," one family member was quoted as saying of Scott. A similar version claims the Blows encouraged the suit because they did not want "to continue supporting slaves belonging to someone else."[10] Another author attributes the suit to Taylor Blow, who, after arriving in St. Louis from Virginia, discarded his Southern sentiments and "instituted a suit in the lower courts of Missouri to secure the freedom of Scott . . . so that Dred could have the income from his labor." Yet another historian credits the suit to Henry Blow, who with "the worthless Dred Scott on his hands . . . felt that he was morally in duty bound to take care of his father's old slave."[11]

Today, more than a century and a half later, speculation on the suit's origins continues. Historian Don E. Fehrenbacher, one of the recent historians to write at length on the Dred Scott case, sums up the speculation with this comment:

> The possibility that Dred Scott himself conceived the idea of going to court should not be discounted entirely. From his travels, he had no doubt gained some measure of self-reliance, as well as a fund of practical knowledge, and suits for freedom occurred often enough to be common talk among St. Louis slaves. What seems most likely is that the decision to take legal action emerged from discussions with old friends like the Blows and new acquaintances whose sympathies he managed to enlist.[12]

While it will probably never be known for certain how the suit originated, it is surprising how much of the speculation over the years has focused solely on Dred Scott. Historians have usually ignored the motivations of the second party involved

9. Hill, *Decisive Battles,* 118; Field is not named in the report reading, "Scott worked about St. Louis at odd jobs, and found employment, among other places, with a young lawyer, who thought he saw the opportunity of making some money out of the man." *Springfield Republican,* February 12, 1903; T. W. Chamberlain Collection, MHS.

10. Drumm and van Ravenswaay, "Old Courthouse," 27; Bryan, *Blow Family,* pt. 2, 20.

11. Smith, *Blair Family,* 383; Holbrook, *Lost Men,* 161.

12. Fehrenbacher, *Dred Scott,* 252.

in this famous litigation, Dred Scott's wife, Harriet. Yet when Murdoch walked into the St. Louis Courthouse on April 6, 1846, he filed one suit for freedom for Dred Scott, and another for Dred's wife, Harriet.

Today, few American school history books mention Harriet, and in the more extensive works written about the case she receives, at most, casual mention and perhaps a few footnotes. The reason for such an omission is obvious, for very early in the suit's litigation it was decided by the court, with the agreement of the attorneys, that since the two cases were "identical," whatever was decided in Dred Scott's case would apply to Harriet's too. The result, perhaps unfortunately, was that Dred Scott's name would go down in American history while Harriet's would not. Yet when the United States Supreme Court ruled adversely on Dred Scott's bid for freedom in 1857, it also ruled adversely on Harriet's as well.[13]

If the Blow family encouraged Dred Scott to file suit for freedom, as many historians claim, did they likewise encourage Harriet Scott? The Blows very likely hardly knew Harriet. She had never been their slave, nor had she, like Dred, shared with the Blows in their journey from Virginia to Missouri. If the Blows knew Harriet, it was because Scott, proud of his new wife, had brought her around to the Blow family residence to meet—as Dred might have said—"them boys he was raised with."[14]

What seems more likely, and in some ways perhaps more logical, is that Harriet Scott was not talked into filing a suit for freedom by the Blow family nor by solicitous St. Louis attorneys, but that she made the decision herself, and that it was perhaps Harriet and not the Blows who persuaded Dred Scott to embark on his difficult and futile legal journey for freedom.[15]

Not only did Harriet, as a wife and mother, have some very good reasons for seeking freedom, but she also had some friends within the St. Louis African American community who could tell her how to go about it. Above all, it would not have been an unusual step for a black woman like Harriet, for there had been many others before her who had done likewise. In fact, of the approximately two hundred slave suits for freedom filed in the St. Louis Circuit Court prior to Harriet's, some 60 percent were filed by women.[16]

Unlike many white women of that period in St. Louis, who when it came to legal matters often had their husbands or attorneys act on their behalf, Harriet, as a slave, enjoyed no such immunity and had no one to shield her from the harsh

13. Agreement to combine the two suits made by Judge Alexander Hamilton and attorneys for the plaintiffs and defendant on February 12, 1850, Dred Scott Collection, MHS; *Proceedings of the United States Supreme Court,* February 11, 1856, 8262, archives, United States Supreme Court, Washington, D.C.

14. *Frank Leslie's Illustrated Newspaper,* June 27, 1857.

15. Historian Walter Ehrlich, in *They Have No Rights,* 37, discusses the possibility that Harriet Scott might have instigated her own suit for freedom.

16. A compilation of slave freedom cases in the St. Louis Circuit Court by Robert Moore Jr. and Melvina Conley.

realities of legal litigation. This was probably made very evident to her when John Rutland, clerk of the circuit court, wrote out a summons on April 6 after Harriet filed her petition for freedom. In writing her name, Rutland wrote "Harriet" and then started to add "Scott." But Rutland got no further than the capital "S" when, apparently realizing his mistake, he drew two slash marks through the "S" and in place of "Scott" wrote the words, "a woman of color."[17]

John Rutland knew, as did Harriet, that according to Missouri slave law there was no such thing as a marriage between two slaves, even if the marriage was performed by a justice of the peace, as was Harriet's at Fort Snelling. Marriage constituted a legal contract between two parties, and Missouri slave law prohibited slaves from entering into legal contracts. To have allowed Harriet to use her married name of "Scott" would have been an affront to the court and white society, and John Rutland obviously knew it. Even more to the point, nowhere in the petition itself is it mentioned that Harriet was married or that she had a husband named Dred Scott. Before the law in the St. Louis Courthouse that day, Harriet stood alone. She was simply a black female slave.

Also not mentioned in Harriet's petition were her two children: Eliza, who in 1846 was seven years old, and Lizzie, perhaps only an infant. Just why the children are omitted is unclear, although in all likelihood, Francis Murdoch, in drafting the petition, did not think they were important to the suit. But they most certainly would have been important to Harriet.

Historians have wondered why Dred and Harriet waited so long to file suits for freedom when they could have done so a decade earlier after first residing in free territory. Perhaps something happened in 1846 that made it seem, at least to Harriet, that filing a suit for freedom was worth the effort and the risk. Just what that might have been can only be speculated.

Certainly, the relationship between the Scotts and their master, Irene Emerson, would have been a major factor in any decision to sue for freedom since their desire for freedom had to outweigh any sense of obedience or loyalty they might have felt for her. A master was the single most important person in any slave's life. Slave law gave a master total legal dominion over a slave, which kept a slave in a constant state of dependency and uncertainty.[18] Did Dred and Harriet feel secure with Irene Emerson as their master? Did they feel that if they behaved well and worked hard she would look after them? More likely, they saw Irene Emerson too rarely to know how she felt about them. Dred and Harriet lived in the city and were hired out at random for wages while Mrs. Emerson lived on her father's farm

17. Summons to Irene Emerson dated April 6, 1846, photocopy, Dred Scott file, USDC; Slave marriages were never recognized by the law, consequently a [Missouri] statute was passed after the Civil War requiring former slaves to record their marriages. Trexler, *Missouri Slavery*, 88; Not only were slave marriages not recognized in law but "offspring became the property of the master, not children of the parents." Wade, *Slavery*, 117.

18. Mark V. Tushnet, *The American Law of Slavery*, 6.

outside the city. Even more unsettling for the slaves, they may have heard that Irene Emerson was planning to move to Massachusetts. Was Mrs. Emerson planning to take them along? If not, what was to become of them? It was a question whose possible answer would be certain to strike fear in any slave.

Another occurrence just prior to the filing of the Scott's suit for freedom in April 1846 was the hiring out of Dred and Harriet to Samuel and Adeline Russell, who owned a wholesale grocery called Russell and Bennett at 82 Water Street in St. Louis.[19] Did the Russells mistreat the slaves? Perhaps they objected to the hours Harriet devoted to her new infant child, hours she should have spent working. There is no way of knowing.

The birth of this child, however, may have influenced in another way the Scotts' decision to seek freedom. Once again the absence of documentation leaves room only for speculation, but the timing of the child's birth with the filing of the suit seems to indicate that the birth may have influenced the Scotts' decision to seek freedom.

For one thing, burdened with the care of two children—one an infant—Harriet's wages were probably reduced, and she would have been paid less than Dred. This, in turn, meant less money each month for Irene Emerson, increasing the possibility that Mrs. Emerson, looking out for her own short-term financial interests, might sell Harriet and the children and invest the money where she could receive a greater return. Such fears would not have been unfounded, for Harriet was well aware that Dred's first wife had been "sold from him," something that Dred and Harriet had no doubt discussed on numerous occasions. Harriet would also have been aware of the woman who lived at the corner of Morgan and Garrison Streets and "who bought up infants at the slave market and raised them to sell."[20]

A newspaper reporter who visited the Scott home in 1857 after they had been denied freedom by the Supreme Court and were still owned as slaves described Harriet as "neat, industrious, and devotedly attached to her husband and children." Harriet was also depicted as being protective of her husband, whom she seemed to fear might at any time be snatched away by white people. When the reporter inquired after Dred, Harriet wanted to know why he was seeking her husband, and told him to mind his own business and leave Dred alone. She confided in the reporter that she was even afraid that some day her husband would be stolen

19. *St. Louis Directory for 1845.*

20. In determining the value of a slave's labor, loss of time resulting from the birth and rearing of children was an item not overlooked. Young slave children were considered "an expense to the hirer" because they commanded a mother's time. Trexler, *Missouri Slavery,* 33; Dred Scott reported he had a wife prior to his marriage to Harriet Robinson, although he gives no details. *St. Louis Daily Evening News,* April 3, 1857; Van Ravenswaay, *Informal History,* 401; "Throughout the antebellum period, children were in great demand, and slaveholders in Little Dixie [Missouri] felt little remorse about separating them from their mothers and families." Records of slave sales of children as young as one or two years of age "were common." Hurt, *Agriculture and Slavery,* 260, 261.

away. As for her two daughters, Harriet apparently lived in such fear of their being taken from her that they "were hidden away" during the many years her suit was in litigation, their whereabouts "a mystery."[21]

One other important fact about Harriet Scott that is overlooked by most historians, but was mentioned by the reporter who visited the Scotts in 1857, was that Harriet was "an accepted member of the church." To what church Harriet belonged is uncertain, but in 1846 she was a Baptist and belonged to a Christian fellowship headed by a minister named John R. Anderson.[22]

In April 1846, when Harriet filed her petition for freedom, Rev. Anderson's flock of black Christians had just organized themselves the month before into what would later become known as the Second African Baptist Church. Before this the small band of African American Christians had been meeting in a hall adjacent to the Liberty Engine House at Third and Cherry Streets, and before that in small prayer groups at the homes of Brother Lewis and Sister Mary Scott and Deacon Patrick Sexton. Some members of this church were slaves and some were free.[23]

But perhaps more influential in the life of Harriet Scott than the church itself was the pastor, Rev. John R. Anderson, a free black and a towering man of more than two hundred pounds, whose mother came west from Virginia to St. Louis with the Edward Bates family. Self-made and self-taught, Anderson received his schooling from a blue-back spelling book and from friendly white playmates. As a young man he earned money as a newsboy and was taught to set type by John and Charles Knapp, later the publishers of the *Missouri Republican*. When Rev. Elijah P. Lovejoy set up his newspaper in Alton, Illinois, Anderson moved there and became Lovejoy's typesetter. He was in Alton the night proslavery mobs broke into Lovejoy's print shop, murdered the young editor, and destroyed his printing press. Grief-stricken by the event, Anderson later related that Lovejoy had a lasting spiritual influence on him. After returning to St. Louis, Anderson aided many slaves to achieve freedom and sometimes advanced money to keep them from being sold South. To the slaves, he said, "You are slaves. You belong to your masters. Now you have no money, but you can have as much religion as anybody else."[24]

---

21. *Frank Leslie's Illustrated Weekly,* June 26, 1857; According to the reporter, Harriet said, "What white man arter dad nigger for? why don't white man 'tend to his own business, and let dat nigger 'lone? Some of dese days dey'll steal dat nigger—dat are a fact." Ibid.; Harriet may have had good cause to worry for St. Louis had a reputation of being an exportation point for slave shipments South, and "the disproportionate number of female slaves in St. Louis" may "have been due in part to the shipment of males down river." March, *History of Missouri,* vol. 1, 816.

22. Ibid.; George E. Stevens, *History of the Central Baptist Church,* unnumbered pages; The first African American church in St. Louis was established in 1827 by John Berry Meachum, and was located at Third and Almond Streets; Separate religious instructions for black persons in St. Louis started as early as 1817 or 1818. Christensen, "Black St. Louis," 22.

23. Church organized March 22, 1846, George E. Stevens, *Central Baptist Church;* Richard Anderson was a highly respected black minister and his congregation totaled a thousand members, equally divided between whites and blacks. Perry McCandless, *A History of Missouri, Volume II: 1820 to 1860,* 213.

24. Ibid.

Whether Anderson encouraged or assisted Harriet in making the decision to sue for freedom is not known, though it seems doubtful, given her long residency in free territory, that he would have discouraged her from such action. What is perhaps less certain is whether Anderson, as a friend of Elijah P. Lovejoy's, helped bring about contact between Harriet and another Lovejoy acquaintance, attorney Francis Murdoch, who was also in Alton when Lovejoy was murdered and who might well have known Anderson as a typesetter in Lovejoy's print shop. If, indeed, Harriet, and not Dred, hatched the idea of suing for freedom, would Harriet have been able to convince her husband to join her in the action? Probably so; the New York reporter who interviewed Dred and Harriet quickly observed from his conversations with them, that, while Dred Scott had a master, "the legitimate owner of Dred" was *"his wife"* (reporter's italics).[25]

Once the idea of a suit for freedom had been agreed upon, Francis Murdoch would likely have told his slave clients that they had a very strong case, and that based on Missouri legal precedents there was no reason to doubt that they were entitled to freedom. Where Murdoch may perhaps have erred in his optimism, however, was in underestimating the mounting hostility in St. Louis to the presence of free blacks and the determination—the almost ardent fervor—of Irene Emerson and her family to keep the slaves in bondage.

Considering Irene Emerson's strong proslavery sentiments, it is not difficult to visualize her reaction on the morning of April 7, the day after Murdoch filed the petitions, when Deputy Sheriff Henry B. Belt arrived on horseback at the Sanford plantation in north St. Louis County and handed her the summonses to appear in court at the next term in November to answer charges of trespass and false imprisonment by her two slaves, Dred and Harriet. No immediate response was required, but apparently Irene Emerson or her father, Colonel Alexander Sanford, felt otherwise, for before the day ended they met with George W. Goode, an attorney and a "bit of a fox-hunting country squire of pro-slavery beliefs" who lived nearby, and decided a quick legal counterattack was appropriate. Accordingly, on the next day, April 8, individual notices were served on the slaves. "Take notice," the papers read, "that on the 9th day of April 1846, I shall move the Court to dismiss the suit of yourself against me for your freedom." Each notice was signed "Irene Emerson, by G. W. Goode, Atty." Irene Emerson claimed that the Scotts had failed to meet the court's condition requiring that bonds be posted to cover possible costs, although it was quite clearly stated on both summonses served to her that bond had indeed been posted by Francis Murdoch. Aware of this, Judge Krum properly refused to entertain the motions to dismiss the suits.[26]

25. *Frank Leslie's Illustrated Weekly,* June 26, 1857.

26. Photocopies of individual summonses to Irene Emerson signed by John Rutland, clerk of the St. Louis Circuit Court, April 6, 1846. Dred Scott file, USDC; Vincent C. Hopkins, S. J., *Dred Scott's Case,* 11; Notices of motion to dismiss filed April 8, 1846, by G. W. Goode, attorney for Irene Emerson, and served on Dred and Harriet Scott individually by Sheriff William Milburn. Photocopies. Dred Scott file, USDC.

Why then did Irene Emerson file these motions when her attorney probably knew full well that bonds for the slaves had already been posted? Most likely it was done with the malicious intent of striking terror into the hearts of Dred and Harriet. Irene Emerson may have envisioned the fear that would ensue when Sheriff William Milburn rode into the crowded slave alley where the Scotts lived, pounded on their door and handed them the papers. She may also have foreseen the slaves' reaction as they looked at the documents that they could not read, then raced through the streets of St. Louis to the law office of Francis Murdoch for a translation of the writing. Even after Murdoch read the words for them and assured them not to worry, they may have wondered what exactly a motion to dismiss meant.

Dred and Harriet may not have completely understood the legal term, but they probably understood the intent: their master, Irene Emerson, was not going to give them their freedom without a fight. And she made this clear some six months later, when, on November 13, 1846, she filed in court her pleas of not guilty to the charges brought by Dred and Harriet in their two suits.[27]

Like many court actions, the two suits soon took on lives of their own, with their individual foibles, bitterness, and passions, and as in so many court suits, soon expanded to include other parties not directly named in the litigation. One of those probably involved early on was Mrs. Emerson's father, Colonel Alexander Sanford, who, while advising and counseling his daughter, had his own personal reasons for wanting to keep Dred and Harriet Scott in bondage. That these reasons were both personal and political in nature adds credence to the likelihood that politics tainted the Dred Scott case much earlier than is generally believed by many historians.

During the same week in November 1846 that Irene Emerson filed her pleas of not guilty, her father attended a large gathering of fellow proslavery citizens in the rotunda of the St. Louis Courthouse, where he was elected to a select committee of a dozen men charged with the task of protecting slave property in St. Louis from the "evil designs of abolitionists and others." The gathering, described as "very numerous" in size, was sponsored by the Committee of One Hundred, who, on the night Sanford attended, established an Anti-Abolitionist Society in St. Louis and elected Sanford as one of the society's twelve vice presidents. The vice presidents, along with the president, John O'Fallon, were to constitute a select committee, which, meeting in secret, was authorized to employ agents "to aid in the execution of laws covering slaves." The names of these agents would be known only to Sanford, the other members of the committee, and the president.[28]

---

27. Pleas of not guilty filed by Irene Emerson's attorney, November 13, 1846, *Dred Scott v. Irene Emerson* and *Harriet, a woman of color v. Irene Emerson,* typescript copies, Dred Scott Collection, MHS.

28. *St. Louis Weekly Union,* November 13, 1846.

Colonel Sanford was not a large slave-owner by Southern standards. On his north St. Louis County planation—which he named California—he had four slaves: three black men and one black woman. Also, like Sanford, St. Louis had few blacks by Southern standards. St. Louis's total population in 1848 was 47,976, of whom 2,772 were "colored," and of these only 745 were free.[29] Yet to St. Louis slave-owners, the menace posed to the community by these 745 free blacks was great indeed. In fact, by 1846, when Dred and Harriet filed their suits, this fear had almost reached levels of paranoia.

This fear perhaps helps explain why one of the first actions of Colonel Sanford's Anti-Abolitionist Society was to inform the General Assembly of the State of Missouri "that a large number of free negroes and mulattoes reside among us and this number is constantly increasing, nearly all of whom are tainted with the poison of abolitionist principles, and who are constantly instilling into the minds of our slaves the most pernicious opinions, rendering them discontent with their present situation, and inciting them to escape from the service of their masters." It was the society's opinion that Missouri's "laws are so mild" that correction of the problem would not be possible without "proper laws against this mischief."[30]

The society also asked the state legislature to introduce stronger prohibitions against African American churches. Black attendance at these churches, the society urged, should only be permitted when the religious services were conducted by "a regularly ordained or licensed white minister or priest."[31]

Several of the more pronounced proslavery newspapers in St. Louis gave support to the new society and its resolutions, with the *Saint Louis Weekly Union* pointing out that the laws on free blacks were "stringent" enough but that "they have never been enforced."[32]

This laxness in law enforcement was soon corrected. Whether the credit should go to the Anti-Abolitionist Society, or to the secret agents hired by that society, or perhaps to coincidence alone, within two weeks after the establishment of the society, seven persons with dark skins were rounded up on the streets of the city, thrown in jail and charged with failure to show a license.[33]

Apparently the incident did not go unnoticed, either by slave-owners or by St. Louis's growing—but largely silent—antislavery faction. While the seven persons with dark skin were being held in jail, a case was quickly put together to test the "legality" of Missouri's laws on the licensing of free blacks. Entitled *The State v. Charles Lyons,* the case was brought quickly before the court of Judge Krum,

29. Sanford's plantation was located in St. Ferdinand Township, not far from the present-day city of Bridgeton; Alexander Sanford estate, no. 2486, SLPC; *St. Louis Weekly Union,* March 5, 1848.
30. *St. Louis Weekly Union,* November 13, 1846.
31. Ibid.
32. Ibid.
33. *St. Louis New Era,* December 8, 1846.

where Dred and Harriet's cases were also pending. One of the legal issues in the case—perhaps the major issue—was "negro citizenship," an issue that the Dred Scott case would raise before the United States Supreme Court almost a decade later.[34]

Charles Lyons, the defendant in the suit, had come to St. Louis from Tennessee. Lyons's mother was a free mulatto and his father a Seneca Indian. He was therefore born of two free parents, but being of dark complexion and unable to produce "a certificate from any state" proving freedom, he was arrested by the city marshall and charged with "living in the State without license."[35]

Attorney Uriel Wright served as counsel for Lyons. In his statement before the court he contended that Lyons was arrested without a warrant or other judicial process and was deprived of his liberty without any authority of law or judgment of his peers. Furthermore, Wright declared, "the act of the Missouri General Assembly" requiring licenses for free blacks "is inconsistent with the Constitution of the United States."[36]

The case for the state—and likely the St. Louis proslavery forces—was argued by three attorneys, one of whom was Henry S. Geyer; a decade later he would again argue the question of black citizenship, this time before the United States Supreme Court and against another person of dark complexion—Dred Scott.[37]

The decision of Judge Krum, according to local newspapers, was on the "constitutionality" of Missouri's laws on free blacks and was quite lengthy. It was also totally favorable to proslavery interests. Judge Krum held that "negroes or mulattoes were not citizens of the United States in the meaning of the word as expressed in the Constitution," and that the laws governing blacks in Missouri were constitutional. The judge held that only free white persons "could enjoy the rights of citizenship," with blacks and Indians excluded. As for Missouri and the matter of interstate comity, Judge Krum said, "I maintain that the State of Missouri has jurisdiction and control over all persons and things within its territorial limits in all respects as a sovereign and independent government."[38]

Charles Lyons was sent back to jail, where he joined the six other free blacks who had been arrested. His penalty was, Judge Krum decreed, a "$10 fine and leaving the state forthwith, committed until the fine is paid and if not paid to receive ten to twenty lashes and hired out by the sheriff until he earns enough to pay his fine and costs of imprisonment and then made to leave the state."[39]

34. Ibid., December 7, 1846.
35. *St. Louis Weekly Union,* December 9, 1846.
36. *St. Louis Weekly Union,* December 16, 1846.
37. Ibid.
38. *St. Louis Weekly Union,* December 9, 1846. Copies of the *Missouri Reports* for the decade following Judge Krum's decision do not indicate that it was reviewed by the Missouri Supreme Court.
39. *St. Louis Weekly Union,* December 15, 1846.

The *Saint Louis Weekly Union* welcomed the decision, considering it "an important one as it permits the officers of the law to rid this city of an evil which has been increasing for some time."[40]

Meanwhile, within the city there were other less strident voices suggesting solutions to the problem of the free blacks in St. Louis. While the editorial columns of the city's newspapers were reporting the "important decision" of Judge Krum, an advertisement appeared in the *St. Louis New Era*.

AN APPEAL TO THE PATRIOTIC AND BENEVOLENT - A family of free persons of color have arrived in this city on their way to Liberia. They expect to embark at New Orleans about the 15th inst. in a vessel to be chartered for that purpose by the American Colonization Society.... They have not the means of paying their passage to Liberia which will be about one hundred dollars. They will also need provisions to sustain them for some time after their arrival in Liberia—say three or four barrels of flour, and one or two barrels of pork, and some utensils of husbandry, etc. etc. Money can be left with the office of the Missouri Colonization Society at Keith & Woods Bookstore or Gen. Ransey on the levee. R. S. Finley, agent, Mo. Col. Soc.[41]

For several decades before Dred and Harriet Scott filed their suits for freedom, Missouri slave law had been guided "by liberal-minded judges who were predisposed to favor freedom and whose opinions seemed to reflect the older view of enlightened southerners that slavery was, at best, a necessary evil." But this liberal attitude was quickly changing in Missouri, and Judge Krum's decision in the 1846 case of Charles Lyons was typical of a new, more conservative, and more restrictive policy toward slavery, and especially toward free blacks.[42] The change could not help but bode evil for Dred and Harriet's suits for freedom.

In fact, though Francis Murdoch's likely earlier encouragement to the Scotts that Missouri law was on their side was perhaps an accurate reading of Missouri legal precedent in the early 1840s, by 1846 it was no longer reflective of the dominant slavery attitudes in St. Louis. By 1846, unfortunately for the Scotts, the legal signposts were pointing in the opposite direction and had been for some time. During the two years prior to April 1846, when Dred and Harriet filed their suits,

40. Ibid., December 9, 1846.
41. *St. Louis New Era,* December 8, 1846.
42. The quote is from Fehrenbacher, *Dred Scott,* 262; There existed in St. Louis, as in most large Southern cities, a black aristocracy whose wealth and position protected it from much of the restrictive abuse directed toward free black persons. In St. Louis this aristocratic society was described in a small volume entitled *The Colored Aristocracy in St. Louis,* authored in 1858 by Cyprian Clamorgan, a free black. Not only did members of this elite group own property, but some operated taverns, and a few sent their children out of state to be educated. Clamorgan claimed free blacks "commanded several millions of dollars" in St. Louis, and had "influence proportionated to its amount." Lawrence O. Christensen, "Cyprian Clamorgan, The Colored Aristocracy of St. Louis (1858)," 3–31.

some twenty-five freedom suits had been filed by slaves in the St. Louis Circuit Court. And only one, that of *Sarah v. William Waddingham* in March 1845, had resulted in freedom.[43]

43. Based on research by Moore and Conley.

12

Frances and Roswell

Sometime early in the spring of 1848, Esther Field received word from her son Roswell in St. Louis that he planned to marry. It was likely welcome news to the matron of the Field family, something she had probably long hoped for and awaited, for Roswell was forty-one years old and, like any mother, Esther probably fretted that her son was living alone in a boardinghouse far away in St. Louis without benefit of wife, home, or family. The news also probably relieved Esther of some concerns she may have secretly harbored that the "unhappy incident" with Mary Almira Phelps a decade earlier had so emotionally scarred Roswell that he had given up any thought of matrimony and had committed himself instead to a life of bachelorhood.

Equally pleasing to Esther Field was the news that the young woman Roswell was to wed in St. Louis was named Frances Maria Reed, that she was from Vermont, and that she had been born in—of all places—Newfane. If Esther had known Roswell's fiancée it was probably when Frances was an infant, although she would certainly have known Frances's parents, who not only had once lived in the same village but also had been members of the church on Newfane Hill before moving west.[1]

At the time of her marriage to Field, Frances Reed was nineteen years his junior, having been born June 2, 1826, at Newfane. According to those who knew her, she was said to be "a very bright and attractive woman" and a woman "of unusual personal charm." A portrait of Frances Reed shows her having a very pleasant face with excellent, well-proportioned features. Her hair and eyes were dark. When

1. Newfane church record book, Newfane Collection, WCHS.

the portrait was made in 1851, shortly after her marriage, she had an ever-so-slight smile that gave her a certain warmth and friendliness, reflective, perhaps, of a cheerful disposition.[2]

Frances was the daughter of Merrill and Sarah Reed, who were married at Newfane on May 18, 1823. Little is known of Merrill Reed. A family genealogy says he was a "professional musician," although a newspaper account says that he made his living as a shoemaker and described him as being "always drunk but smart." On the day of his wedding, according to the newspaper, Reed was being held in the county jail on Newfane Hill for debt, which required the marriage ceremony to be performed within the limits of the jail yard. Merrill's father may have been David S. Reed, who opened a public house in Williamsville in 1815 or 1816.[3]

Of Sarah Reed somewhat more is known. Her maiden name was Townsley, and at the time of her marriage to Reed she was living at Newfane in the home of her brother, Colonel Calvin Townsley, who kept a public house there. Her brother had been born in 1796 at Walpole, New Hampshire, and after coming to Newfane married Maria Pomeroy, daughter of Chester Pomeroy.[4]

Of Merrill and Sarah Reed's life in Newfane little is remembered or recorded, except that the town records list the births of two daughters: Caroline on April 17, 1824; and Frances in 1826. At a later date, the Reeds had another daughter, Arabella.[5] How or when Frances Reed got to St. Louis is not known. During the 1830s and 1840s there was a large migration of Vermonters to the West, and Frances and members of her family were probably part of it. By 1848, when she married, Frances Reed was living in St. Louis along with her sister Arabella, members of the Chester Pomeroy family, and, a little later, Calvin Townsley and his family, who came in 1855 and opened a tavern.[6]

When Esther Field received the news of the impending marriage from her son, the Vermont snows had melted and the daffodils along the path leading to the front door of the house were in bloom; therefore, without concerns about the weather, she made immediate plans to travel to St. Louis for the wedding ceremony, which was planned for late May. At age sixty-eight, Esther would not have found the

2. Roswell M. Field family record, Ludlow-Field-Maury Family Papers, MHS; *Vermont Reformer,* January 24, 1902; Slason Thompson, *Life of Eugene Field,* 49; Portrait, Eugene Field House and Toy Museum.

3. Newfane church record book, Newfane Collection, WCHS; Slason Thompson, *Life of Eugene Field,* 14; *Vermont Reformer,* January 24, 1902.

4. Cabot, *Brattleboro,* 506.

5. A notation on an old photograph indicates Frances may also have had a brother named Edward. Collections, Eugene Field House and Toy Museum; Will of Roswell Field: "I give to Mrs. Arabella Angier, sister of my deceased wife, my land in Minnesota consisting of 206 acres about seven miles from St. Paul." Estate of Roswell M. Field, SLPC.

6. Cabot, *Brattleboro,* 506; Slason Thompson, *Life of Eugene Field,* 50.

journey from Vermont to Missouri an easy one. It was probably for this reason—and maybe her wish to make this second marriage of Roswell's, unlike his first at Putney, a family affair—that prompted her to take other members of the Field family along with her to Missouri. Her oldest son, Charles, and his eighteen-year-old daughter, Julia, agreed to make the trip, as did Mary Field French, the twenty-two-year-old unmarried daughter of Roswell's sister, Mary.[7]

The four travelers left Vermont in late April 1848 and made the journey to St. Louis in two weeks. A coach took them to Wheeling, where the water was high enough on the Monongahela to permit a boat trip to Pittsburgh, where they took passage on a steamboat bound for Cincinnati on the Ohio River. Here they boarded still another steamboat that took them on the final leg of the journey to St. Louis. There were no mishaps on the trip, but Esther found the drinking water, which was "drawn out of the river," quite disagreeable; on being assured that the milkiness was derived from clay in the water and not "filth and offal," she eventually came to consider it sweet in taste. Of greater concern to Esther was the presence on the boat of a Roman Catholic nun, who boarded in Cincinnati and was also going to St. Louis. Charles noted that his mother "kept a sharp eye upon" the nun the whole trip, "afraid she will make Catholicks of the girls."[8]

The travelers arrived in St. Louis on May 19, more than a week before the wedding day, and Roswell Field found lodgings for them in his boardinghouse. Charles Field noted that his mother spent the first part of every morning "ordering the girls about picking up things, putting the room in order" while she sat in a rocking chair "with her fan in her hand and talked about propriety."[9]

There were, according to Charles, "a world of friends" who called upon them during the family's stay in St. Louis, including two daily visits from Roswell's fiancée, Frances. Charles found her to be a very pleasant and "sweet-looking girl" while Esther Field, it was said, "was perfectly delighted with her."[10]

The late May days in St. Louis were "quite sultry," but Frances, serving as hostess, kept Esther, Julia, and Mary busy visiting the shops. A. S. Rutherford and Company, one of the larger dry goods stores in the city, was featuring that month the latest in "white straw bonnets just 10 days out of New York." Edwin Chaffin, another merchant, had "just received direct from Paris" a new beautiful assortment of kid gloves "made expressly for his shop." Evenings were given to dinners at the city's finer restaurants, including one that specialized in "fried frogs," which the visitors from Vermont found not only unusual, but delicious. Finally, after ten days

7. Series of seven letters from Charles K. Field to his wife, Julia, May 1848, Field Collection, JL.
8. Ibid.
9. Charles K. Field letter to his wife, Julia, May 19, 1848, Field Collection, JL.
10. Ibid.

spent entertaining relatives, Roswell Field and Frances Reed were married on May 30, 1848.[11]

A small frame row house at 28 Collins Street became home to the couple after their marriage. Collins was located immediately north of the city's commercial area and just two blocks from the river. The location was probably selected by Frances, for directly across the street was the home of her Vermont relatives, the Pomeroys. Roswell did not buy the house on Collins Street, but rented it. To help around the house, Frances had her sister Arabella, and also an eleven-year-old girl named Temperance Moon as a live-in servant.[12]

A Vermont newspaper account, written years later, said that Roswell Field "educated" his wife after their marriage, an observation that seems to imply Frances was unschooled and may have had to endure a sort of obligatory spousal training regimen administered by her more highly educated husband.[13] Frances's education was probably typical for a woman of her time, and while it no doubt fell far short of Roswell's, she was no dullard, nor for that matter did she probably require educating. What seems more likely is that Frances, a bright and intelligent young woman, admired and respected her husband's intellectual qualities and welcomed opportunities after their marriage to share in his interests, enhance her own knowledge, and show something more than simple curiosity about the new books her husband added with almost calendar-like regularity to the volumes already bulging from the shelves in their parlor.

On such an occasion Roswell may have first acquainted his wife with the poet Horace, for whom he had "a special love and admiration."[14] Perhaps Field read from one of his volumes of Horace in Latin, and then, for Frances's benefit, made the translation into English, maybe selecting one of Horace's *Odes* in which the poet spoke frequently of love and friendship.

Roswell may have told Frances how as a young boy of nine, studying Latin under the Rev. Whitcomb in Vermont, he had first become acquainted with the Latin poet. He may also have confided to Frances that as he grew older he admired Horace even more. Horace shunned the fame of public life, focusing instead on a life of rational contemplation—attributes that Field admired and respected. Field may also have told Frances that Horace, even though he had written two thousand years ago, understood the tensions between city and country life and the age-old futile striving for political power and wealth. Field might have read to Frances what

11. Ibid.; *St. Louis Daily Union,* May 19, 1848; Charles K. Field letter to his wife, May 19, 1848, Field Collection, JL; Roswell Field family record, Ludlow-Field-Maury Family Papers, MHS.

12. J. H. Sloss, *St. Louis Directory for the Year 1848*; Plat of subdivision showing Collins Street, Bates Family Papers, MHS; Chester Pomeroy residence at 29 Collins Street, *St. Louis Directory for the Year 1848*; Charles K. Field letter to his wife, May 19, 1848, Field Collection, JL; Slason Thompson, *Study in Heredity,* 50.

13. *Vermont Reformer,* January 24, 1902.

14. Gray, "Recollections," 128; Inventory, Roswell M. Field, SLPC.

Horace wrote about the beauty of a simple life, a life of tranquility—the kind of life, perhaps, that Field hoped one day for himself and for Frances.

However, the time the young couple had for the sharing of such interests was soon to be reduced, and the occasions for literary chats were to become less frequent, for within a few months of their marriage, Frances announced she was expecting a child. Before the Fields celebrated their first wedding anniversary, Frances gave birth to a son whom they named Theodore French Field.[15] Theodore was born on April 18, 1849, and while his birth was no doubt a joyful occasion for Frances and Roswell, it could not have come at a more inauspicious time in the history of St. Louis.

The year of Theodore's birth came to be known as The Year of the Cholera, and before 1849 ended, one in every ten people in St. Louis would be dead of the dreaded disease, the exact cause of which was then unknown. The epidemic had started in New Orleans, first arriving in St. Louis aboard the steamboat *Amaranth* on December 28, 1848, some four months before Theodore's birth. With the arrival of warm weather, the disease had established itself throughout St. Louis, and hundreds were dying each week.[16]

Roswell and Frances were fortunate, for they, along with young Theodore, not only survived the initial onslaught of the cholera but also—and just barely—escaped a second catastrophe that devastated St. Louis in the spring of 1849.

On the evening of May 17, 1849, fire broke out on the steamboat *White Cloud,* moored at the foot of Cherry Street only two blocks from the Field home. Fortunately for the Fields, but unfortunately for St. Louis, the winds were from the northwest that evening; as the burning ship broke loose from its moorings, it drifted south in the river current, brushing up against other boats docked along the levee and setting fire to some twenty-three vessels. As the flames leaped into the sky, they were fanned into nearby warehouses, and within hours the whole central commercial section of the city was in flames. The fire swept from block to block, and at midnight, with the flames approaching the St. Louis Cathedral, firemen were forced to use dynamite to blow up entire blocks of buildings to halt the fire from its southward path across the city.[17]

When dawn arrived, Roswell and Frances Field must have seen that the fire had come within one block of their home on Collins Street. Southward all the way to Market Street, the heart of the city was a smoldering pile of bricks and rubble. Gone were most of the banks, the newspapers and printing establishments, the

15. Roswell Field family record, Ludlow-Field-Maury Family Papers, MHS.

16. *St. Louis Globe-Democrat,* January 5, 1939; Stella M. Drumm, "The Year of the Cholera—1849," 56–57.

17. *St. Louis Daily Union,* May 18 and 19, 1849; "The streets of our city, laid out originally very narrow, are literally choked up with fallen walls of houses and destroyed property of various kinds," *St. Louis Daily Union,* May 19, 1849.

warehouses, and the original French section. Gone also were most of the lawyers' offices—including that of Roswell Field on Chestnut Street.[18]

Meanwhile, the cholera epidemic continued and was particularly severe in certain "unhealthy localities" on the near north side: Washington Avenue, St. Charles Street, and the area where the Fields lived. Probably even more frightening to Roswell and Frances was the recognition that "one third of the persons dying were reported to be children of five years or less." So-called remedies for the prevention and cure of cholera varied by doctor. Dr. William M. McPheeters, who was in charge of the St. Louis Hospital run by the Sisters of Charity, recommended large amounts of sauerkraut, and bloodletting until the blood assumed "a brighter hue." As the summer wore on, the deaths mounted—589 during the last week in June and 722 in the last week of July. Many residents fled the city in terror.[19]

After the record number of deaths during the last week in July, the epidemic seemed to subside, due in part to a quarantine but also to cooler fall temperatures. It was probably at about this time that Roswell Field, in his new role as husband and father, made what amounted to three resolutions on behalf of the welfare and health of his family. If the cholera continued, he decided, his wife and children would be sent back to Vermont for safety. He would also move his family away from the "unhealthy" north-side section of the city and find a new house somewhere else in St. Louis. Lastly, and this was probably as much a wish as a resolution, he would begin looking for land outside St. Louis as a rural estate for his family: a place away from the smoking chimneys, filthy dusty streets, and open sewers; a place where the air was clean, cooled by summer breezes; in short, a place probably not too unlike the one Roswell and Frances remembered as children—Newfane Hill.

Unfortunately, little Theodore would never see Vermont, nor a rural place outside St. Louis, and not even a new house in another part of the city. Theodore died in the Collins Street house on December 1, 1849, at eight months of age. By then Frances Field was already expecting the couple's second child. He was born on September 2, 1850, and named Eugene.[20]

However, as the cholera deaths in St. Louis once again began to increase in 1851 with the advent of warm weather, Roswell Field kept the first of his three promises: Frances and Eugene were sent back to Vermont, where they remained throughout

18. Letter from Willis L. Williams dated June 23, 1849, Hamilton R. Gamble Papers, MHS; Hand-drawn map showing fire-devastated areas, MHS.

19. Drumm, "Cholera," 57, 69; Undated letter from Edward Bates to R. B. Frazer, Bates Family Papers, MHS.

20. Roswell Field genealogy, Ludlow-Field-Maury Family Papers, MHS; September 3 is sometimes given as Eugene Field's birth date; Slason Thompson in *The Life of Eugene Field,* 15, wrote, "Eugene Field undoubtedly fostered the conflict of dates, for he was a stickler for the interchange of tokens on such anniversaries, and surely two anniversaries were better than one. If any of his friends forgot September 2nd, their consciences would prick them to make amends on September 3rd"; September 2, the date written by Eugene's father in the family record, is used here. Ludlow-Field-Maury Family Papers, MHS.

the summer. When they returned in the fall, after the cholera had subsided in St. Louis, Frances brought home with her a new son. Born in Vermont on September 4, 1851, he was named Roswell Martin Field after his father.[21]

Harriet and Dred Scott's suits for freedom came to trial on June 30, 1847, more than a year after the two slaves had filed their petitions for freedom; the delay had been caused by a crowded court docket. The proceedings were held in a courtroom on the west side of the first floor of the St. Louis Courthouse.[22]

However, before the trial occurred, two events took place that would significantly influence Dred and Harriet Scott's efforts to obtain freedom. Fortunately for the Scotts, both were favorable.

One event was the appointment early in 1847 of Alexander Hamilton as judge for the St. Louis Circuit Court. Hamilton was a young attorney from Pennsylvania with a scholarly background and an acquaintance of Roswell Field who later became one of Field's closest friends.[23] Hamilton replaced Judge John Krum, before whom Dred and Harriet Scott had earlier filed their petitions for freedom. While Krum was probably a competent judge, his proslavery sentiments were quite pronounced. Krum had achieved a rather tainted reputation not only by his indecisive handling of the Elijah Lovejoy murder while he was mayor of Alton but also by his 1846 decision in the Charles Lyons case, which had revealed both his proslavery attitudes and also the depth and bitterness of his racism.[24] It would be Dred and Harriet Scott's good fortune that Judge Hamilton would preside over both their trials in Missouri's lower courts, for on several occasions he would reveal his own personal compassion for the plight of the two slaves.

The other event that occurred prior to the trial that would have both immediate and future impact on the Scotts' efforts to secure freedom was the unexpected resignation of their attorney, Francis B. Murdoch. By the time the Scotts' case came up for trial on June 30, Murdoch had left St. Louis and was somewhere on

21. Field family record, Ludlow-Field-Maury Family Papers, MHS; Temperance Moon, who worked and lived in the Field home, in a letter dated February 25, 1901, to Slason Thompson, author of the book *Eugene Field, A Study in Heredity and Contradictions,* wrote that Eugene was born in a house near Cherry Street, that the family "went east for the summer," and when they returned "Roswell was a few months old." Slason Thompson, *Study in Heredity,* 51.

22. Record book 18, 10, SLCC; When the west wing of the courthouse was renovated in 1855, the courtroom underwent drastic modification. A wide corridor leading to the west entrance to the building was constructed and the remaining space divided into two courtrooms. Tom Richter, "If Walls Could Talk: A Courtroom's Story."

23. At Roswell Field's death, Judge Hamilton gave the eulogy in the courtroom of the circuit court before members of the St. Louis bar. *St. Louis Daily Democrat,* July 15, 1869.

24. Among the many racial comments in his decision, Judge Krum held that even though blacks were born free, that "does not transform them into another and different race of men. They are Africans, and descendants of Africans still. The fact that they are not held to service is evidence only of a change in condition of a portion of the same race of people." *St. Louis Daily Union,* December 16, 1846.

the western prairies on his way to California.[25] His sudden departure left Dred and Harriet lost within the labyrinth of a legal system that probably neither one understood, and the uncertainty this created must have filled them with great fear.

It is clear from the court records, however, that Dred and Harriet quickly found a way out of their predicament, for within weeks after Murdoch departed, an attorney named Charles Daniel Drake was busy taking depositions for the Scotts, and another attorney named Samuel M. Bay was preparing for the court trial. When Bay, two years later, fell victim to cholera, the noted law firm of Alexander P. Field and David N. Hall was retained to represent Dred and Harriet.[26] All four of these lawyers had in common professional reputations that placed them among the city's most respected attorneys, and that prompts the question: how did such an array of legal talent became available to two poor slaves such as Dred and Harriet Scott?

At this point facts leave off and speculation begins. According to most historians, members of the Blow family became involved in the Dred Scott case and became active—though often unnamed—supporters of Dred and Harriet's efforts to obtain freedom.

According to court records, at least seven members or relatives of the Blow family became involved in the Scott cases during the ensuing decade of litigation. The first of these supporters was the Scotts' new attorney, Charles Drake, who had married Martha Ella Blow, daughter of Dred Scott's old master. Another supporter was Joseph Charless, who on occasion put up bond for the Scotts and whose wife was Charlotte Blow. Still other Blow family supporters were Taylor Blow and Henry Blow, sons of Dred's old master, and Charles Edmund LaBeaume and Louis T. LaBeaume, brothers-in-law of Peter E. Blow, also one of the Blow sons.[27]

Of these supporters, Taylor Blow, the second-youngest child in the Blow family, is most often cited by historians as being Dred Scott's strongest ally.[28] If there is any weakness in this observation, it is that Taylor Blow, along with the other named supporters, were all males and were thus more likely to have had their names listed on court documents. Were none of the daughters in the Blow family friends of Dred Scott? Quite obviously they were, for it would seem unlikely that the Blow family's affection for a former slave would have been limited to those of one gender.

It was likely that when Dred Scott found himself in desperate need of a lawyer to replace Francis Murdoch, he turned for help to one of his old master's daughters, Charlotte. For if the stories about the Blow family are correct, it was Charlotte

---

25. *History of Madison County,* 188.

26. The names of Scott's attorneys are listed in not only records of the St. Louis Circuit Court but also Lawson's *State Trials,* vol. 13, 221–41.

27. Bryan, "Blow Family," pt. 1, 223–31.

28. "It was Taylor Blow who later became Dred Scott's most loyal sponsor in the long fight for freedom." Fehrenbacher, *Dred Scott,* 241.

Blow, one of the oldest children, who assumed the role of family matron when the parents died soon after the family's arrival in St. Louis, leaving behind four young sons and a stack of unpaid bills. It was Charlotte who, at age twenty, would have remembered when Dred Scott was sold by her father for badly needed money and who, along with her new husband, Joseph Charless, handled her father's meager estate and paid off the family debts. It was also Charlotte who, wishing an education for her two youngest brothers, Taylor and William, had her husband enroll them in Elihu H. Shephard's subscription school located on Fourth Street opposite the courthouse. When they completed their studies there, Charlotte and her husband had them, along with older brother Henry, enrolled at St. Louis College—the tuition for all three probably paid by Charlotte and her husband. After their graduation from the college, it was probably Charlotte who urged her husband to take all three of her brothers into his thriving drug and paint business known as Charless and Company. Within a few years, all three Blow brothers became partners and the name of the firm was changed to Charless, Blow and Company.[29]

Historians have frequently observed that the Blows were a closely knit family, and probably no member of the family better personified that unity than Charlotte. If indeed Dred Scott, as their slave, was made part of that bond, there seems little doubt that Scott had a true friend and supporter in Charlotte Blow. It is likely, therefore, that when Francis Murdoch left the Scotts without legal counsel, Dred fled for help to the Charless home at 123 Market Street; there his pleas may have prompted Charlotte to ask her brother-in-law, attorney Charles Drake, to help out the Blow family's old slave. It is also likely that from this same address on Market Street, Charlotte, as matron of the Blow family, directed how best, and by whom, the needs of Dred and Harriet Scott would be met in their long struggle for freedom.

Just why Charlotte and other members of the Blow family should have felt affection and concern for a slave, while others, like Irene Emerson and her family, felt little more than aversion, can perhaps be explained best by a Southerner of that period who lived in Missouri. William B. Napton, justice of the Missouri Supreme Court and a slave-owner, wrote in an opinion handed down by that court:

> The relation between master and slave is regulated by a variety of laws, all having in view to enforce their reciprocal rights and duties, obedience and submission on the one hand, and protection and kindness on the other; and although these rights and duties, to some extent, like those of parent and child, can, from their very nature, be enforced but imperfectly, yet their existence and validity is recognized,

29. Bryan, "Blow Family," pt. 1, 227–30; Bryan noted, "There is one source of information concerning a person that is most revealing—the file room of the Probate Court. The way in which a man or woman acts toward relatives when money is involved tells more of the true character than does anything else. When we apply this acid test to the various members of the Blow family, Charlotte (Mrs. Charless) emerges as the most admirable one."

and any deviation from them is punished in the same way and to the same extent as a dereliction of other moral obligations.[30]

Dred and Harriet Scott's trial in Judge Hamilton's court on June 30 took only one day, and, as with their previous appearance in the court more than a year earlier, went unnoticed by the St. Louis press.[31] What dominated the pages of the city's newspapers that day was not a case in the circuit court, but the excitement created by the return of the Missouri state militia from its victories in the Mexican War.

Over the past several days incoming steamboats had brought to the city Colonel A. W. Doniphan's regiment of Missouri troops, and civic leaders met in the courthouse to plan the welcoming festivities. There was a great parade with marching units of firemen and policemen and numerous bands, as well as a speech by Senator Thomas Hart Benton before an assembly of citizens in front of the Planters House Hotel on Fourth Street. Opening the festivities was a thirty-one-gun salute from Camp Lucas, the ringing of the city's church bells, and a prolonged blast of whistles by steamboats on the levee. New Orleans had gone all out to fete the returning soldiers, and St. Louis was not going to be outdone by its rival river city to the south.[32]

In court that day, Attorney Samuel M. Bay, who was representing the Scotts, was likely also jovial, for he was probably expecting little difficulty in gaining a verdict for his clients.[33] The facts were definitely on the side of the Scotts, and the preliminary work had been well prepared by Attorney Charles Drake.

After the jury was sworn in, Bay presented his witnesses, commencing with Henry T. Blow, who testified that Dred Scott had been sold by his father to Dr. Emerson. Later Miles H. Clark, who had been with the U.S. Army at Rock Island, testified that he knew Dred Scott as a slave of Dr. Emerson in Illinois. Miles was followed by Catherine A. Anderson, wife of a military officer at Fort Snelling, who testified that she knew Dred Scott, along with Harriet, as slaves at Fort Snelling, and that Emerson used Scott "entirely as a slave" and hired Harriet out to her for some two months.[34]

After establishing that the Scotts had been slaves of Dr. Emerson and had been taken by Emerson to live in territory declared free of slavery, Bay then called on Samuel Russell to establish that Scott and Harriet, after residence on free soil, were still being held as slaves by the doctor's widow, Irene Emerson. Russell told the

---

30. *Beaupied, Plaintiff in Error v. Jennings, Defendant in Error,* 28 *Missouri Reports,* 254, MSC.

31. Lawson, *State Trials,* 227–29.

32. *St. Louis Daily Union,* June 10, 1847.

33. Historians differ on which attorney or attorneys represented the Scotts at this trial. The court records often do not give an attorney's name. Lawson says the firm of Field and Hall represented the Scotts, Ehrlich gives Bay as the attorney, and Fehrenbacher says it "seems most likely" to have been Bay.

34. Typescript copies of depositions of Henry T. Blow, Miles H. Clark, and Catherine A. Anderson, Dred Scott Collection, MHS; Lawson, *State Trials,* 228.

court that he "hired Dred and his wife in March, 1846, from Mrs. Emerson" and "paid the hire of the servants to Colonel Sanford, the father of Mrs. Emerson." With this final piece of testimony, Bay was likely satisfied that he had clearly shown to the jury that Scott and Harriet had resided in free territory and that they were now being held as slaves by Irene Emerson. However, Bay did not anticipate Russell's testimony during cross-examination by Mrs. Emerson's attorney. To the surprise of the Scotts and their attorney, Russell stated that he "did not hire the negroes" and that it was his "wife who made the arrangements with Mrs. Emerson about them." He added that he knew "nothing of the hiring but what I have been told by my wife." Russell's testimony, therefore, was nothing more than hearsay evidence, and the Scotts had failed to give evidence that Mrs. Emerson was currently holding them in slavery. As a result, the jury found for the defendant, producing, as one historian noted, "the absurd effect of allowing Mrs. Emerson to keep her slaves simply because no one had proved that they *were* her slaves."[35]

Scott's counsel immediately moved for a new trial; Dred Scott in an affidavit told Judge Hamilton "he was surprised in the testimony" of Samuel Russell and assured Judge Hamilton that if granted a new trial "he expects to prove by the testimony of the wife of said Russell" that he is held in slavery by Irene Emerson. Judge Hamilton was unable to rule on Scott's request for a new trial during that term of the court, but on December 2, 1847, he granted the request, and in the first of several instances in which he would reveal his sympathy for the two slaves, he said that the Scotts were by Missouri statute entitled to their freedom, and that a legal technicality should not be allowed to bar them from obtaining the freedom to which they were entitled.[36]

No doubt Mrs. Emerson was not at all dismayed that a legal technicality had denied the slaves their freedom, and her attorney wasted no time in filing an exception to Judge Hamilton's decision to grant the slaves a new trial. This action by Irene Emerson's attorney meant that the case would move to the Missouri Supreme Court. As a legal tactic it achieved very little for Irene Emerson except to delay Dred and Harriet's chances for a new trial for two years, for the Missouri

35. Typescript letter from J. R. Lackland to S. Russell and reply from Russell to Lackland, both dated June 2, 1847, Dred Scott Collection, MHS; Typescript copy of court proceedings, Dred Scott Collection, MHS; Lawson, *State Trials,* 228; Fehrenbacher, *Dred Scott,* 254.

36. Typescript copy of affidavit dated July 2, 1847, and signed with an "X" by Dred Scott, Dred Scott Collection, MHS; Lawson, *State Trials,* 330; The day before, on July 1, 1847, Scott's counsel instituted new suits in the circuit court duplicating the initial suits and this time naming as defendants not only Irene Emerson but also Alexander Sanford and Samuel Russell. The suits were an obvious attempt to close any possible loophole through which those holding Dred and Harriet in slavery might escape. A month later Judge Hamilton asked the plaintiffs to decide which set of suits they wanted to litigate, and the Scotts decided in November 1847 to stay with their original suits. Dred Scott Collection, MHS; Record book 18, 74, SLCC; Ehrlich, *They Have No Rights,* 47.

Supreme Court, after numerous delays, denied Emerson's writ of error, noting that a final judgment had never been made in Judge Hamilton's court.[37]

On January 12, 1850, two-and-a-half years after the first trial and almost four years after the slaves had filed their petitions for freedom, the case once again came to trial in the St. Louis Circuit Court.[38]

In the interval between the first and second circuit court trials, Irene Emerson obtained new counsel, Hugh A. Garland and Lyman D. Norris, and, putting the case in their hands, departed from St. Louis for Massachusetts. Before leaving, however, she placed Dred, Harriet, and the two children in the custody of the St. Louis County sheriff to be hired out for wages. This was permitted by law and made it possible for Irene Emerson to maintain ownership of the slaves while freeing herself of any responsibility for their care and welfare. The wages earned by the Scotts would be held by the sheriff and later distributed to those who, after the litigation was over, had won the suit. Slaves placed under such court custody were often overworked and mistreated since both the sheriff and the person hiring lacked any long-range interest in the slaves' condition. It was probably out of such concern for the welfare of the Scott family that the Blows, on learning that Dred and Harriet had been placed in the custody of the sheriff, had C. Edmund LeBeaume, brother of Eugenie LaBeaume, Peter Blow's wife, go to the sheriff's office, post bond, and hire Dred and Harriet himself.[39]

When Judge Hamilton convened the court on the morning of January 12, 1850, Dred and Harriet Scott also had new counsel, the firm of Alexander P. Field and David N. Hall. They were prepared this time with testimony not only from Samuel Russell, but also from his wife, Adeline. In fact, Mrs. Russell's testimony was the only new evidence presented in the case; all of the other witnesses for the Scotts presented the same testimony as in the previous trial.[40]

Adeline Russell did not appear in the courtroom for the trial, but her deposition was read. She related to the jury that it was Mrs. Emerson who owned the slaves and who "hired them to me." And then added for emphasis, "I heard Mrs. Emerson say they were her slaves."[41]

Irene Emerson's attorney Lyman Norris presented no witnesses, but in his closing statement made a feeble effort to argue that the slaves were taken into free territory by Dr. Emerson on orders of the military and therefore the case did not come under

37. March 4, 1848, record book 18, 192, SLCC; 11 *Missouri Reports,* 413, MSC.

38. Record book 19, 295, SLCC.

39. Motion to hire out plaintiffs during the pendency of the suit, March 14, 1848, record book 18, 205, SLCC, and motion granted March 17, 1848, record book 18, 213, SLCC; Oberholzer, "Legal Aspects," 14; Lawson, *State Trials,* 232.

40. Alexander P. Field (1801–1876), who served as secretary of state for Illinois from 1828 to 1840, was not related to Roswell M. Field. Several historians in the past, in writing of the Dred Scott case, have assumed that both Fields were the same person, most notably Slason Thompson, who wrote two biographies on Eugene Field; Lawson, *State Trials,* 234.

41. Ibid.

civil law. The Scotts' attorney, David Hall, rebutted that point, however, calling the jury's attention to the fact that the slaves were left at Fort Snelling and hired out for money long after Emerson had been ordered to another post by the military.[42]

After Judge Hamilton gave instructions to the jury, the verdict was a decision for Dred and Harriet Scott, both of whom now, for the first time in their lives, enjoyed the taste of freedom. Irene Emerson's attorney, Hugh Garland, called for a new trial but it was promptly denied by Judge Hamilton.[43]

What the Scotts now believed to be freedom was not like that enjoyed by white people, but rather like that of a free African American named Stephen Lee, who, according to the *St. Louis Intelligencer,* was found walking around the city on the morning of the Scott trial without a license. The newspaper reported he was fined ten dollars and "ordered to leave the state."[44]

However, not even Stephen Lee's limited and fettered type of freedom was to come easily for the Scotts. While Dred and Harriet were giving thanks for their favorable court verdict, Irene Emerson and her attorneys were planning their next legal move to keep the Scotts in slavery. That would come thirty days later on February 14, 1850, when Irene Emerson filed a bill of exceptions moving the Scotts' case once again to the Missouri Supreme Court.[45]

42. Ibid., 237.
43. Ibid.
44. [St. Louis] *Intelligencer,* January 12, 1850.
45. Record book 19, 340, SLCC.

13

Politics

It was sometime early in the spring of 1850, shortly after Irene Emerson filed her bill of exceptions taking the Dred Scott case once again to the Missouri Supreme Court, that Roswell M. Field first heard of Dred and Harriet Scott and their legal pursuit of freedom.

The St. Louis newspapers still had not commented on the suits in their news columns and the cases were still unknown to the public, but among those in the local legal profession, Mrs. Emerson's action would have attracted notice, for her appeal to the state's highest court bestowed a certain element of notability upon what otherwise might have been a commonplace legal action. Only a few dozen or so cases each year were destined to receive the Missouri Supreme Court's attention.

Just exactly how Roswell Field was told of the case is unknown. He could have heard about it from his friend Judge Alexander Hamilton, who, during one of his social visits to Field's home or office, might have casually mentioned it. Field might also have learned of it from fellow attorneys in the St. Louis Law Library, located on the second floor of the courthouse. Field visited there daily and friends noted, he "would walk up and down the room for hours, with his hands behind him, and each step would take about four feet."[1] And Field could have learned of the case from Dred Scott himself, who, now in the employ of the

---

1. Bay, *Reminiscences,* 241; Scott's attorney, Charles Drake, a member of the Blow family, is credited with bringing about a law library for St. Louis. In 1847, the library had sixty-nine members and a collection of 1,285 volumes. Scharf, *History of St. Louis City and County,* vol. 2, 1490.

Blow family, may have been working as early as 1850 as an occasional janitor in Field's law office.[2]

Since the Dred Scott case involved no locally prominent clients, large sums of money, or complex legal issues, it is unlikely that it made much impression on Field when he learned of it. Also, the case was not in the St. Louis Land Court where Field was most active, nor did it relate to real estate. Furthermore, in 1850, as a husband and father, Field now had family matters on his mind. The cholera that killed so many in St. Louis the year before returned with the warmer spring temperatures, and the Fields wanted to move out of the cholera-prone, north-side section of the city.

The house that Roswell and Frances Field rented to replace their home on Collins Street was on the opposite side of the city, to the south of the commercial area. Here the family moved in the fall of 1851 not long after Frances returned from Vermont with their infant son, Roswell.[3]

Located on the east side of South Fifth Street, just one door north of Cerré, the house was on land owned by the St. Louis School Board. Although it was only an eight-block walk from Field's law office on Chestnut Street, it was on the outskirts of the city. Two blocks beyond it, Fifth Street became a rural road leading to the small Village of Carondelet, some five miles distant.[4] Compared with Collins Street, where the houses were being encroached upon by warehouses and factories, South Fifth Street in 1851 was a pleasant, tree-shaded residential street of individual family homes, and was dominated by two imposing churches: Second Presbyterian and St. John's Episcopal.

It is unlikely, however, that Roswell and Frances attended either of these two neighborhood churches, or, for that matter, attended any church in St. Louis. When they married in 1848, there was no Congregational church in the city, and most New Englanders found a home in the Third Presbyterian Church, whose pastor, Truman Marcellus Post, was an outspoken critic of slavery. Like Field, the Rev. Post was a graduate of Middlebury College, and his son later related that although Roswell Field's "opinions on religious subjects were such that he had little to do with the clergy," Field did enjoy a warm friendship with Truman Post that terminated only upon Field's death. In 1852, shortly after the Fields moved to the house on South Fifth Street, Pastor Post and a group of thirty-five members

---

2. Just when Scott started working in Field's office is uncertain. Arba Crane, an attorney in Field's office, said Scott worked for Field when the first suit was filed, but this is obviously incorrect. Letter John F. Lee to Mary L. Dalton, February 15, 1907, Dred Scott Collection, MHS.

3. Slason Thompson, *Study in Heredity,* 50.

4. Located today at 634 Broadway, the house on South Fifth Street was to be demolished in 1934 when a group of public-spirited citizens raised funds to buy and restore it. McCune Gill, *The St. Louis Story,* 70; Field's daily walk to and from his office was easily recognizable "at the distance of several squares by his peculiar long stride." Bay, *Reminiscences,* 241; *Directory for 1848.*

left Third Presbyterian and founded the First Trinitarian Congregational Church. One of Frances Field's Vermont relatives, Augustus Pomeroy, was a member of that founding group, but the early church records do not mention the names of Roswell or Frances Field.[5]

For Frances and Roswell, the house on South Fifth must have seemed very large and spacious compared with their first home. Although far from a fashionable mansion, even by St. Louis standards of the 1850s, it was of brick and three stories high with two large rooms on each floor.

The years that Roswell Field spent in the house on South Fifth Street were probably his happiest and most enjoyable in St. Louis. Long before 1850, he had finally overcome the bouts with melancholy that he had suffered during his early years in St. Louis. Also, long forgotten were his financial worries, for Field's law practice was thriving and he had no need to write home to Vermont for money to pay for food and lodging. He was also no longer confined to a room in a boardinghouse and meals with strangers around a public table. Field now had a comfortable home of his own, one he shared with his wife and growing family. Also, for the first time since leaving Vermont a decade earlier, Field probably now had space for his books, and the Fields' parlor in all likelihood bore a closer resemblance to a library, with its bookcases, easy chair, and fireplace.

Most of what is known of Roswell Field's life in St. Louis relates to his practice of the law, and from this perspective Field is often viewed as a rather reserved and dignified man who avoided friendships and casual conversations and preferred instead the company of law books and legal treatises. However, those who remember Field as a resident of South Fifth Street recall a different man. This Roswell Field was not serious and stern but warm and friendly, and rather than being withdrawn from society he was seen as "very social and entertaining."[6]

Neighbors also said that Field's "fondness for children was notable." They recalled that on warm summer evenings, when residents sought relief from the heat in the shade of trees along the street, Roswell Field—his young sons Eugene and Roswell at his side—sat on the front steps of his house playing his violin and collecting "a lot of boys around him."[7]

It was also said that during Field's walks to and from his law office, he often stopped to watch the neighborhood boys playing ball or marbles. "The children in

---

5. The Rev. Truman Post came to Third Presbyterian from Jacksonville, Illinois, in 1847, assured by a church elder that "though we have three or four families who own slaves, they are mostly as much antislavery as you or I, and long to see the curse removed." T. A. Post, *Truman Marcellus Post, D.D., A Biography,* 193–94; Scharf, *History of St. Louis City and County,* vol. 2, 1743; In 1859 another relative of Frances Field, Mrs. Maria Townsley of Brattleboro, joined the church. Many early records were destroyed when the church burned in 1856. First Trinitarian Congregational Church of St. Louis Minute Book, MHS; Field's funeral service was held at this church in 1869, the building then located at Tenth and Locust Streets. R. M. Field estate, SLPC.

6. Bay, *Reminiscences,* 240.

7. Ibid.

the neighborhood knew him well," friends said, "and he would let them approach him on terms of the utmost familiarity."[8]

Perhaps this fondness for children prompted Roswell Field to seek to fill his home on South Fifth Street with a large number of his own children. In fact, the Fields were not in the house very long before Frances was expecting another child. On November 6, 1853, she gave birth to the Fields' fourth son, whom they named William Bradley, probably after Roswell's good friend in Vermont, Jonathan Door Bradley, who along with Roswell had appeared before the court on Newfane Hill in 1825 for admittance to the bar. Fourteen months later, on January 7, 1855, a fifth son was born, whom they named Charles James, followed by the Fields' only daughter, Frances Victoria, on September 13, 1856. After giving birth to five sons, Frances probably decided that a daughter deserved her own name.[9]

During those years on South Fifth Street, the threat of cholera was never far removed, and the "mischief," as it was often described, returned again and again to St. Louis during the 1850s to alarm the city. During the major outbreak in 1849, civic leader and attorney Wilson Primm fled with his family to live in the Village of Carondelet, south of St. Louis. The Primms were soon followed by Henry T. Blow, one of Dred Scott's benefactors, who, with his family, also moved to Carondelet to escape the cholera, and who in 1850, having achieved a small fortune in the drug and paint firm of Charless, Blow and Company, built a Greek revival-style mansion in Carondelet equal to any in Blow's native Virginia. Soon Roswell Field followed in the footsteps of the Primm and Blow families and began buying land for a family estate in Carondelet. While the primary reason for Field's decision was probably his family's health, one historian noted that "it was quite the custom for judges and lawyers in the early history of St. Louis to resort to country life for recreation." Like St. Louis, Carondelet was also founded by the French, but unlike St. Louis, which grew and prospered as a fur-trading post for the upper Missouri, Carondelet remained a quaint and picturesque village of only a few hundred inhabitants well into the nineteenth century.[10]

In 1850 Roswell Field purchased his first land in Carondelet from Francois X. Pequiquot for four hundred dollars. Before the year ended, Field purchased five more parcels of land in the Carondelet Commons, and, as he became acquainted with his rural neighbors and the officials of the village, he served as counsel for the Village of Carondelet in several lawsuits. Additional purchases of land by Roswell Field followed in subsequent years—all parcels in Carondelet adjacent to one another.[11]

8. Ibid.

9. Field family record, Ludlow-Field-Maury Family Papers, MHS.

10. NiNi Harris, *History of Carondelet*, 25; Stevens, ed., *Fourth City*, vol. 1, 369; Scharf, *History of St. Louis City and County*, vol. 2, 1863.

11. Deed book I-5, 101, Recorder of Deeds, St. Louis. (When Carondelet was annexed in 1870 by St. Louis, the deed records for the two communities were combined.); Field's land

Just exactly what Roswell and Frances planned to do with this property is uncertain. Field may have purchased the land for speculation, since the St. Louis newspapers in those years were touting Carondelet as a "fresh young sister of St. Louis" that was both beautiful and healthy and had "one of the best harbors on the Mississippi River." Most likely, however, Roswell and Frances planned to use their land for a rural estate. Located adjacent to the impressive estate of Henry Blow, the Fields' property would have provided a beautiful building site, comprising a gently sloping hillside on the north bank of the River des Peres and affording a sweeping view not only of the River des Peres but also of the Mississippi River.[12]

Roswell and Frances Field would never build a home in Carondelet. For them, their plans for a rural estate would remain simply that—plans. If the land had any immediate benefit for them it was simply to serve as an excuse to escape from the city and to enjoy visits to the countryside. In a carriage, along with the children and a picnic basket of food, the ride from the Field home on South Fifth Street to Carondelet made for a beautiful and pleasant day, and it was very likely a trip they often took.

Irene Emerson's appeal of the Dred Scott case to the Missouri Supreme Court on February 14, 1850, signaled the case's entry into Missouri state and local politics. During the months that followed, individuals totally unknown to Dred and Harriet Scott, for various personal and political reasons, decided that they, too, had a stake in the outcome of the slaves' efforts to seek freedom.

Even stranger than the new participants who moved to center stage in the Dred Scott drama were those like Irene Emerson who exited through the side wings. In 1849 or 1850, Mrs. Emerson, experienced in the art of short engagements, moved to Springfield, Massachusetts, and married a local physician named Dr. Calvin

---

purchases can be found in deed books Q-5, 11; R-5, 124; S-5, 45; S-5, 338; and T-5, 37, Recorder of Deeds, St. Louis; Among Field's Carondelet court cases were: *Barada v. Inhabitants of Carondelet*, 16 *Missouri Reports*, 323 (March term, 1853); *The Town of Carondelet v. Beverly Allen's Executors*, 13 *Missouri Reports*, 556 (October term, 1850); and *Taylor v. City of Carondelet*, 22 *Missouri Reports*, 105 (October term, 1855), MSC; In 1873, five years after Field's death, the value of his land in the Carondelet Commons was appraised by Maj. Julius Pitzman, surveyor, at $129,477. The Carondelet estate of Field's neighbor, Henry Blow, was appraised at $302,720. *Glimpses of the Past*, vol. 4 (1937), 162; Henry Blow's daughter, Susan, born in 1853, established America's first kindergarten in a Carondelet school.

12. The quote is from the *St. Louis Daily Evening News*, May 15, 1854; A St. Louis newspaper asked, where would a person "sooner sojourn of warm nights and pleasant Sundays than in Carondelet?" *St. Louis Leader*, May 11, 1857; In 1875, the City of St. Louis purchased from Roswell Field's heirs about ten acres of the Field property, and combining that with a portion of the adjacent Henry Blow estate, created what today is known as Carondelet Park. The remaining portion of the Field property was later subdivided and sold as residential lots. The area today contains streets named after members of the Field family—Eugene, Roswell, Field, and French. Carondelet (Mo.) Collection, MHS; Roswell M. Field estate, SLPC.

Clifford Chaffee on November 21, 1850.[13] Irene Emerson was also experienced in the art of marital deception; if later newspaper accounts are correct, she kept secret from her Yankee husband the information that she had left behind in Missouri a group of slaves named Dred, Harriet, Lizzie, and Eliza. Dr. Chaffee, a devout abolitionist who was elected a U.S. Congressman for Massachusetts soon after the wedding, had innocently marched up the aisle with his Southern bride, unaware that his betrothed was soon to be unmasked as one of the most famous slave masters on the continent.

Also leaving the cast was Irene Emerson's father, Colonel Alexander Sanford, who died in 1848.[14] As a member of the secret committee of twelve, charged with ridding the St. Louis streets of free blacks, Colonel Sanford's influence on his daughter's legal decisions was probably great, and he no doubt discouraged her from any inclination to relax her efforts to keep the slaves in bondage.

The removal of Irene Emerson and her father from the case prior to 1850 leaves unanswered two questions: first, who decided to appeal the case to the Missouri Supreme Court; and, second, why was the appeal made when the evidence so clearly supported the Scotts? Of the two questions, the latter is easier to answer.

A clue comes from one of Mrs. Emerson's attorneys, Lyman D. Norris, who, in his closing arguments in Judge Hamilton's court on January 12, argued that the time had come to change Missouri's laws on slave freedom. Disavowing thirty years of Missouri legal precedent, Norris argued that when a slave who had been taken to reside in free territory returned to Missouri, that slave came once again "under the operation of our local laws and the rights of his master." Also, said Norris, this time quoting the "wisdom" of Missouri Supreme Court Justice William B. Napton, the slave state of Missouri should not encourage "the multiplication of a race whose condition could be neither that of freemen, nor slaves" and whose presence tended to "corrupt those of their own race and color remaining in a state of servitude."[15] Norris argued political issues in support of those who sought to restrict the increasing number of free black persons in Missouri. Under attack by Mrs. Emerson's attorney was interstate comity, the very foundation of the nation's federal system, along with Missouri's long-established statutes on slave freedom. Furthermore, the appeal to the state supreme court, if it achieved nothing else, kept the Scotts in slavery two years longer, and sent a clear message to other slaves that obtaining freedom in Missouri would not be easy or quick.

With political issues like these now part of the Dred Scott case, and with Colonel Sanford dead and Irene Emerson in Massachusetts, who in the defendant's camp made the decision to appeal the Scotts' favorable verdict to the Missouri Supreme Court? Quite likely it was someone attuned to Missouri politics who could sense

13. Ehrlich, *They Have No Rights,* 55.
14. Estate of Alexander Sanford, no. 2486, SLPC.
15. Lawson, *State Trials,* 236–37.

that the state's highest court might be receptive to voiding Missouri's laws on slave freedom. That person was most probably John F. A. Sanford, Irene Emerson's brother, who now moved to center stage and assumed the lead role in opposing the Scotts' efforts to obtain freedom, even though his sister remained the named defendant in the case.[16]

Historians have tended to depict Sanford as a protective older brother, whose primary concern was his widowed sister's financial welfare. Some have even stated incorrectly that Sanford's role in the Dred Scott case was simply an extension of his role as executor of Dr. Emerson's estate. As a resident of New York, Sanford periodically visited St. Louis on business, and these visits gave him an opportunity to assist his sister in her two pending slave suits, which had by 1850 been combined into a single suit.[17]

Little has been reported about John Sanford. One historian describes him simply as a "wealthy businessman" and another as "a businessman of some prominence."[18] Both descriptions are accurate as far as they go, but they reveal little about Sanford's life and even less about his involvement in the Dred Scott case.

John Sanford was a Virginia native who, after graduation from West Point, found his way to St. Louis. On November 22, 1832, he married Emilie Chouteau in the Cathedral of St. Louis, likely one of the major social events of the year for prominent St. Louisans. The marriage only lasted four years, since Emilie died in 1836 after giving birth to a son. It was sufficient, however, to ally Sanford with Emilie's father, Pierre Chouteau Jr., grandson of St. Louis's founder, Pierre Laclede, and the wealthiest, most influential man in the city. As son-in-law and member of the Chouteau clan, which comprised favored kinsmen and near relatives by blood or marriage, Sanford became an active partner in Chouteau's business ventures, not only throughout the West, but also in the East and in Europe; he also shared in Pierre Chouteau's fortunes, estimated in the millions of dollars.[19]

16. John F. A. Sanford's name does not appear in Dred Scott records until November 2, 1853, when suit was filed against him in the United States Circuit Court. Just when John Sanford first became involved in the case is unknown, but most likely his sister made him aware of the case from its very inception, and he may well have been involved from the start.

17. In this agreement dated February 12, 1850, the decision or outcome in Dred Scott's case would apply also to Harriet's case. *Harriet, a woman of color v. Emerson,* SLCC.

18. Ehrlich states that to attribute to Sanford "ulterior political motives . . . is totally unjustified." Ehrlich, *They Have No Rights,* 39–40; Fehrenbacher, *Dred Scott,* 248.

19. Oscar W. Collet, *Index to St. Louis Cathedral and Carondelet Church Records,* vol. 1, typescript volume compiled by the Missouri Historical Society, 1918, 76; Mary B. Cunningham and Jeanne C. Blythe, *The Founding Family of St. Louis,* 7; The Chouteaus also played a significant role in the Lewis and Clark Expedition. William E. Foley, "The Lewis and Clark Expedition's Silent Partners: the Chouteau Brothers of St. Louis," 132; Van Ravenswaay, *Informal History,* 101; Pierre Chouteau Jr. married his first cousin, Emilie Anne Gratiot, which to historian James Primm illustrated "the nature and complex interrelationships of St. Louis's ruling elite." Wrote Primm, "In 1814 when the revered *grande dame,* Madame Chouteau, died in her eighty-second year,

Chouteau described himself as being in "the Indian and fur business," but actually his financial interests were far larger and more varied than that. Chouteau owned forts and posts throughout the West, and sizable landholdings in the Mississippi Valley from Minnesota to Louisiana. He acquired large deposits of iron ore and lead, a flour mill, railroads, banks; in the East and in Europe, where he traveled from time to time, he also earned a reputation as one of America's leading financiers.[20]

Pierre Chouteau had spent much of his youth in the untamed West in company with trappers and Indians, and, as son-in-law, John Sanford was expected to follow in such ventures. In 1832 he was named Indian agent at St. Louis, and during his early years in the Chouteau family, Sanford spent most of his time in the West as a trader, working as far south as Santa Fe and Chihuahua and as far west as California. In 1836, following the death of his wife, he moved to New York as the eastern representative of the American Fur Company, which his father-in-law had acquired a year or so earlier from John Jacob Astor. By the 1850s, when Sanford became active in the Dred Scott case, he was one of three partners, along with John B. Sarpy and Joseph A. Sire, in the mercantile house that was known as Pierre Chouteau Jr. and Company. At the same time Sanford headed another Chouteau subsidiary, a steel-rolling business, known as Chouteau, Sanford and Company. During the 1850s Sanford was also a leading director of the Illinois Central Railroad, in which he had personally invested "a fortune" and for whom he had served as a negotiator in raising funds abroad.[21]

However, the Chouteau family also heavily invested in yet another American enterprise—slavery. How many slaves the Chouteaus owned within their vast business empire is impossible to determine. In St. Louis alone, Pierre Chouteau had fifteen slaves—eight men and seven women—and was probably the largest slave-owner in the city at the time.[22]

John Sanford enjoyed a close family relationship with his Chouteau relatives.

most of the many mourners at her funeral had familial reasons for weeping, some of them several times over." James Neal Primm, *Lion of the Valley, St. Louis, Missouri,* 55.

20. Will of Pierre Chouteau Jr., August 17, 1865, Wills Collection, MHS; Scharf, *History of St. Louis City and County,* vol. 1, 183; Nicknamed Cadet, Pierre Chouteau Jr. eventually "branched out into other enterprises and acquired substantial holdings in railroads, iron, and real estate" and "was a multimillionaire at the time of his death." William E. Foley and C. David Rice, *The First Chouteaus, River Barons of Early St. Louis,* 1189.

21. Sanford correspondence, Chouteau Family Papers, MHS; Paul Beckwith, *Creoles of St. Louis,* 56; *New York Times,* May 4, 1857; [St. Louis] *Intelligencer,* May 11, 1857; John Sanford later in life married Isabella, daughter of Thomas C. Davis of New York, by whom he had two children. Beckwith, *Creoles,* 56.

22. U.S. Census of 1850 for Missouri, St. Louis Third Ward, Slave Schedule; "Auguste and Pierre owned slaves in proportion to their wealth, and no doubt used them for a variety of tasks. It is quite likely that the slaves labored in the Chouteau milling and distillery operations, and on occasion the family probably farmed some of them out to other enterpreneurs for a fee." Foley and Rice, *First Chouteaus,* 192.

When in St. Louis he entertained his friends in the Chouteau home, and he referred to the wife of Pierre Chouteau as "my good mother." He was also a man of expensive tastes, traveling in luxury in America and Europe. In a letter to John Darby, mayor of St. Louis, for whose St. Louis home Sanford had purchased carpets and mirrors, he wrote from New York, "I hope you will not find them in cost beyond your expectation. I am always happy to favor my friends in anything, but as my good mother (Mrs. Chouteau) can tell you, I never select poor articles of any kind, nor am I influenced by cheapness—I select the best and, of course, I pay good prices."[23]

When John Sanford's father died in 1848, his entire estate was disposed of in a "private auction" to John Sanford in payment for an earlier loan the son had made to his father for $8,220, which along with the interest amounting to $3,082, took almost all of his father's estate. Of Alexander Sanford's four slaves—Solomon, John, Isaac, and Mary—three were later sold by John Sanford, along with the plantation called California, to James H. Lucas, a neighbor and ardent foe of Missouri Senator Thomas Hart Benton.[24] Irene Emerson, the daughter, appears to have gotten nothing.

The manner in which John Sanford settled his father's estate apparently caused concern to Pierre Chouteau, for in a letter dated July 6, 1848, Chouteau wrote to the administrator of St. Louis County:

> Sir—You will please to take charge of and administrate upon the estate of Alexander Sanford, deceased, and I will pay you all costs and expenses which may be incurred while so doing. Yours S—Pierre Chouteau, Jr.[25]

John Sanford was probably already involved in the Dred Scott case when he settled his father's estate in 1849, and it can be assumed as almost certain that Sanford's involvement in his sister's slave suit would not have escaped Pierre Chouteau's attention. From his offices on Washington Avenue near Main, Chouteau closely observed with great detail every event and movement involving his family and investments. Just what Pierre Chouteau might have thought of the Dred Scott case can only be speculated.

---

23. John Francis McDermott, "Americo Vespucci or Abroad in America," 376; Letter from John Sanford to John Darby, May 31, 1849, John F. Darby Papers, MHS.

24. Estate of Alexander Sanford, no. 2486, SLPC; Bill of sale dated February 1, 1849, between John Sanford and James H. Lucas, John B. C. Lucas Family Papers, MHS; James Lucas's brother, Charles, was killed by Benton in a duel on Bloody Island in the Mississippi River opposite St. Louis in 1817. Lucas had charged Benton with failing to pay taxes on his slaves. Benton responded by calling Charles Lucas "a scoundrel and a puppy." The duel involved two encounters. In the first, Lucas suffered a severed neck vein, from which he recovered. In the second encounter, Benton shot Lucas in the left breast, causing death. Darby, *Personal Recollections,* 180; Bay, *Reminiscences,* 10–13.

25. Letter of Pierre Chouteau to John Darby, administrator for St. Louis County, Alexander Sanford estate, SLPC.

Legal actions by slaves, however, would not have been unfamiliar to Pierre Chouteau, for he had been named a defendant in at least two different suits for freedom brought in earlier years by his own slaves, and the records of the St. Louis Circuit Court show numerous cases for slave freedom involving members of the Chouteau family, including his own father.[26] Of these Chouteau cases, two involving a cousin, Gabriel Chouteau, attracted widespread attention because of the unusual hostility they engendered. The suits involved two slaves, Pierre and Mary Charlotte of Canada, who were brought to St. Louis where they were sold to a Catholic priest, Father Didler, who in turn sold them, apparently without warranty, to the Chouteau family. On the basis of their residence in Canada, the two sued for freedom, and their actions sparked such a violent reaction from Gabriel Chouteau that they had to be placed in jail under the custody of the sheriff for protection. Their cases began in the St. Louis Circuit Court only a couple of years before Dred and Harriet filed their suits for freedom, but the Chouteaus and their attorneys fought so tenaciously to keep the blacks in bondage, using every legal device available, that it was not until 1863—some twenty years after the litigation started—that the cases were finally adjudicated. By then Pierre, who had been a man of "Herculean frame and unusual talent," had died in jail—"a physical wreck and a mental imbecile"—and Mary Charlotte had become an old woman.[27]

It was said of the Chouteau family that their confidential relations with the Indian tribes in the West were so extensive and reliable that the United States Government depended upon them for direction and guidance in Indian affairs.[28] A family capable of offering this kind of service to the government would seem equally qualified to provide to their kinsman, John Sanford, reliable information and direction concerning Missouri politics in what the Chouteaus probably considered a nasty legal matter involving slaves belonging to the sister of a Chouteau family member.

⊰⊱ ⊰⊱

26. The two cases were *Ellen Chevalier, deceased v. Pierre Chouteau* (April, 10, 1821) and *Charles v. Pierre Chouteau* (February 11, 1821), SLCC. Records of slave cases compiled by Moore and Conley; In a noted Missouri slave suit, Pierre's father was sued for freedom by Marie Jean Scypion, who claimed Indian and black ancestry. Filed in 1806, the legal efforts to obtain freedom were continued after Marie's death by her descendants. The cases spanned some thirty years of bitter litigation in Missouri courts. William E. Foley, "Slave Freedom Suits before Dred Scott: The Case of Marie Jean Scypion's Descendants," 1–23.

27. *Pierre v. Gabriel Chouteau* (November term, 1842) and *Mary Charlotte v. Gabriel Chouteau* (May 24, 1845), SLCC, record of slave cases compiled by Moore and Conley; *The Vermont Phoenix,* July 19, 1887, article reprinted from the *St. Louis Globe-Democrat;* Gabriel Chouteau was the son of Auguste Chouteau, who accompanied Laclede when he left New Orleans in 1763 for Fort de Chartres in Illinois territory and the subsequent founding of St. Louis. Cunningham and Blythe, *Founding Family,* 5.

28. Howard L. Conard, *Encyclopedia of the History of Missouri,* vol. 1, 590; William E. Foley and Charles David Rice, "Pierre Chouteau, Entrepreneur as Indian Agent," 387.

The Missouri Supreme Court did not announce a decision in the Dred Scott case until the court's March term in 1852. By then proslavery threats, which had in earlier years echoed in the rotunda of the St. Louis Courthouse from the crowds attending rallies of the Committee of One Hundred, had found a welcome home in the Missouri statehouse in Jefferson City and in the more sedate judicial chambers of Missouri's highest court.

By 1852, Missouri proslavery forces, in defense of their $100 million investment in black slaves, had succeeded for the most part in seizing political control of Missouri and its government. They had ceased listening to the state's venerated elder statesman, Senator Thomas Hart Benton, taking their cues instead from followers of Southerners like Senator John C. Calhoun of South Carolina, who pledged that he would sacrifice the nation itself to preserve the sovereignty of the slave states.[29] As a result, Senator Benton, who had dominated Missouri politics for more than thirty years and had been a U.S. Senator since the days when the state was a territory, became one of the first political casualties as proslavery forces in Missouri moved to align the state more closely with its sister slave states in the South.

Senator Benton was a Southerner by birth and a slave-owner, but he believed first and foremost in preserving the Union, even if it meant compromises on slavery issues. This position made him a political foe of Southerners like Calhoun, but it won him some acclaim—which he certainly did not want or need—from Northerners like Roswell Field's old friend Zebina Eastman, who was editing an abolitionist newspaper in Illinois.[30] Missouri proslavery forces were also critical of Benton's rather lukewarm and compromising positions on Texas, the Oregon territory, and the Wilmot Proviso.

This hostility to Benton split the Democrats in Missouri into pro-Benton and anti-Benton factions, and in 1848 the anti-Benton forces within Missouri's General Assembly succeeded in adopting a set of directives known as the "Jackson Resolutions." Among other things, these resolutions denied federal control over slavery in any territory and pledged Missouri's "hearty cooperation with the slave-holding states, in such measures as may be deemed necessary for our mutual protection against the encroachments of northern fanaticism." They further directed Senator

29. In 1861, Missouri Governor Claiborne Jackson estimated the state had 114,931 slaves with a total value of $100 million. Trexler, *Missouri Slavery*, 44; "After the election of 1848, the anti-Benton group in Missouri began actively working towards Old Bullion's defeat in 1850 and for Missouri's alignment with the South. Through the appointment of many anti-Benton men to state offices, and through the skillful election of anti-Benton officials to the Bank of Missouri and its branches, Benton's opponents built up a strong state political machine." Marshall D. Hier, "The Jackson Resolutions of 1849, Extracts from the Diary of the Author," 50.

30. Eastman in his newspaper said of Benton, "While trucking and tricksters abound there is one man, a Southerner and slave holder, who dares speak out and upon slave soil. We refer to old Bullion [Benton]." *The Western Citizen* (Chicago), June 8, 1852.

Benton and the other Missouri congressional delegates in Washington "to act in conformity" with them in casting Missouri's votes in Congress.[31]

Senator Benton denounced the resolutions. He accused those who drafted them of "disrupting the national Union and of misleading the people of Missouri into cooperation with the slave-holding states for that purpose." Benton took his cause to the people, traveling from one Missouri town to another in a campaign many consider the most hard-fought political battle ever waged in the state. Benton told his audiences, "I do not admit a dissolution of the Union to be a remedy to be prescribed by statesmen for the diseases of the body politic, than I admit death, or suicide, to be a remedy to be practiced by physicians for diseases of the natural body."[32]

But the charges by the state's proslavery forces mortally wounded the old warrior. After forty ballots in the Missouri General Assembly early in 1851, Henry S. Geyer, St. Louis lawyer and Whig, was elected the new senator from Missouri.[33] The victory gave Geyer a national presence, and also a Washington address. From the nation's capital, Geyer, in a few years, had a convenient location from which to represent John F. A. Sanford before the United States Supreme Court.

Had the controversy between the anti-Benton and pro-Benton forces been confined solely to the Missouri legislature, the outcome in the case of *Dred Scott v. Emerson* might have been different. Unfortunately for the Scotts, politics played as prominent a role in the judicial chambers of the Missouri Supreme Court as it did in the Missouri General Assembly. In fact, the controversial Jackson Resolutions were drafted within the chambers of the Missouri Supreme Court.[34] The author was William B. Napton, one of the three justices of the court. Both he and Justice James B. Birch, a newspaper editor from western Missouri, were not only anti-Benton but also strongly proslavery; both were also capable—and ready—to discard legal precedent to achieve political ends.[35] John F. Ryland, the third justice on the court, was less militant in his views on slavery but also, as it turned out, less consistent.

31. P. Orman Bay, *The Repeal of the Missouri Compromise, Its Origins and Authorship*, 39.

32. Ibid., 50; March, *History of Missouri*, vol. 1, 830.

33. Bay in his biographical sketch of Geyer says, "Captain Geyer had often expressed a desire to obtain a seat in the United States Senate and when he finally succeeded in 1851, his friends entertained strong hope that he would make a fine reputation as a statesman; but in this they were greatly disappointed, for he fell far below public expectation. The fact is, he was a mere lawyer, and as much out of his place in the Senate as he would have been at the helm of a ship." Bay, *Reminiscences*, 152.

34. In his diary, Justice Napton says, "These resolutions were written by me, at the request of C. F. Jackson, on Saturday night and read the following morning in my office at the Capitol (Jefferson City) to Jackson, Judge [William] Scott, C[arty] Wells, and G. W. Hough, who each approved of them, and were subsequently introduced and passed the Legislature." Hier, "Jackson Resolutions," 35.

35. Birch filed a suit for slander against Benton in 1849, alleging that Benton in a public speech described Birch as a "sheep-killing cur dog" who had whipped his wife and knocked

Briefs were filed by the attorneys with the court on March 8, 1850, and were primarily restatements of positions that had been taken earlier in Judge Hamilton's court. The briefs meant little, however, for the justices were very aware of the Dred Scott case as well as its political implications and, as later revealed, they had already decided to overturn the jury's verdict in the lower court that granted freedom to the slaves. Years later, Judge Napton allowed that he was determined "to overrule the old decisions of our court" when the Dred Scott case "came up to the supreme court of this state while I was on the bench." He added, "I made up my mind on it and communicated my views to Judge Ryland and Judge Birch then my colleagues."[36]

Whether John Sanford had advance knowledge of Napton's views, and whether this influenced his decision to appeal, is unknown. But the justices apparently felt little hesitation in discussing the Dred Scott case outside the court's chambers. Edward Bates, law partner of Hamilton Gamble and friend of Roswell Field, wrote in his diary, "Judge Ryland last afternoon told me that the majority of the Court—Judges Napton & Birch—were about soon to give an opinion over-ruling all former decisions of the Supreme Court declaring negro slaves emancipated by a residence northwest of the Ohio, in virtue of the Ordinance of 1787. They assume, he says, that Congress has no power to legislate upon the subject of slavery in the territories, and consequently, all the enactments on that subject are merely void. Judge Ryland expects to write a counter opinion."[37]

Edward Bates's intelligence from Judge Ryland proved correct in one respect, and incorrect in others. When the decision of the Missouri Supreme Court was finally rendered in 1852, it was, as predicted, adverse to Dred Scott, but the majority opinion was not written by Judge Napton or Judge Birch. Judge Napton had planned to write it, but delayed doing so while awaiting the arrival of some law books not available in Jefferson City. The delay denied him his moment in history, for by 1851, when he was ready to write the decision, he had been voted out of office. He and Judge Birch were both the victims of irate pro-Benton voters, largely in St. Louis, seeking to right the wrong that had been done to Senator Benton.[38]

Politically, St. Louis was never very typical of Missouri. When the General Assembly failed to return Thomas Hart Benton to the U.S. Senate, St. Louis voters in 1852 "triumphantly elected" the veteran politician, then seventy years old, to a seat in the U.S. House of Representatives as consolation. Unlike parts of rural Missouri that retained a strong Southern slave heritage, St. Louis, by contrast,

---

out three of her teeth, because she had remonstrated against Birch's illicit association with "a negro wench" belonging to Birch. Stewart, *Bench and Bar*, 377.

36. Journal, William B. Napton Papers, 1857, 223, MHS.

37. Diary of Edward Bates, October 26, 1850, Bates Family Papers, MHS.

38. Journal, William B. Napton Papers, 1857, 223, MHS.

was increasingly sharing new interests with the large commercial and industrial centers of the East. Almost from its inception, the city had strong antislavery elements. Joseph Charless, father of Charlotte Blow's husband, had been a leading opponent of slavery when he edited Missouri's first newspaper in territorial days. St. Louis merchants, bankers, and industrialists were also well aware that where free labor existed, cities flourished and grew. And like other eastern cities, St. Louis was attracting large numbers of immigrants, many of them Germans, who— almost to a man—opposed slavery and identified with Senator Benton and the Democratic Party. Furthermore, as early as 1848, St. Louis harbored a strong Free Soil movement—headed primarily by Francis P. Blair Jr. and his brother, Montgomery—along with newspapers like the *Missouri Barnburner* and churches like those of the Unitarians and Presbyterians, all of whom often openly criticized slavery and were suspected by Southerners of advocating the "black vomit" of abolitionism.[39]

It was therefore no surprise that when voters of Missouri were given their first opportunity to vote, in the summer of 1851, for the justices of the Missouri Supreme Court, the election would become a referendum on the politics of Thomas Hart Benton, pitting the heavy concentration of pro-Benton Democrats of St. Louis against the anti-Benton Democrats of rural Missouri.[40] Members of the St. Louis bar, realizing the judicial dangers of a factious high tribunal, selected as their candidate Hamilton R. Gamble, a highly respected attorney and a Whig who appealed to both Democratic factions. In a petition signed by 151 members of the St. Louis bar, Gamble was asked for permission to have his name placed on the ballot. The St. Louis bar cited the "public good" and the need to calm the concerns of the people on the "administration of the laws." Among the signers was R. M. Field, whose prominent signature with a sweeping flourish left little doubt as to his loyalty to his good friend. The petition was transmitted to Gamble by Charles Drake, member of the Blow family and Dred Scott's former attorney.[41] Several notable names were missing among the signers. Henry Geyer did not sign, though

39. Scharf, *History of St. Louis City and County,* vol. 1, 593; William Nisbet Chambers, *Old Bullion Benton, Senator from the New West,* 387; Benjamin Merkel, *The Anti-Slavery Controversy in Missouri, 1819–1865,* 5; James Neal Primm, "Missouri, St. Louis, and the Secession Crises," in *Germans For A Free Missouri: Translations from the Radical Press,* translated by Steven Rowan, 6; Merkel, *Anti-Slavery Controversy,* 14; Mrs. Emerson's attorney, Lyman Norris, used the expression "black vomit" to describe the words of those with antislavery sympathies in his closing arguments in Judge Hamilton's court on January 12, 1850.

40. When the Missouri Constitution was drafted in 1820, elected court officials were rare, but as the years progressed more and more states subjected the judiciary to the democratic election process, and Missouri joined their ranks in 1850 when justices of the state supreme court became elected officers with six-year terms. Dunne, *Missouri Supreme Court,* 45.

41. Petition to Hamilton Gamble from the St. Louis bar, March 22, 1851; Letter to Hamilton R. Gamble from Charles D. Drake, April 11, 1851, Hamilton R. Gamble Papers, MHS.

he may have been in Washington, nor did the petition include the signatures of Irene Emerson's two attorneys: Hugh Garland and Lyman Norris.[42]

The election was held in August and Hamilton Gamble received the largest number of votes, and he was named to the presidency of the court. The other two justices elected were the incumbent John Ryland, who ran under the pro-Benton label, and William Scott, an ardent proslavery and anti–Benton Democrat.[43] The presence of Gamble and Ryland on the court, in place of Napton and Birch, gave the appearance that perhaps the new court might be less proslavery than the old one, and this probably gave Dred Scott's supporters some encouragement. But in Missouri politics, appearances could be—and often were—deceiving.

On October 20, 1851, two months after the election, the Missouri Supreme Court met at St. Louis, and at first it seemed that a heavy court docket might delay a decision on the Dred Scott case. Roswell Field himself had seven cases before the Missouri Supreme Court during that term. However, on November 29, 1851, the case was taken under consideration, new written briefs were filed, and Justice Scott was designated to prepare the court's opinion. The designation of Scott as the author removed what little hope might still have remained among Scott's supporters that an opinion from the new court might be favorable to the slave. The confirmation came on March 22, 1852, when the court met in St. Louis for its March term.[44]

Over the years, historians have devoted considerable study to the decision of the Missouri Supreme Court in *Dred Scott v. Emerson,* and much attention has been focused on the briefs submitted by Lyman Norris, Mrs. Emerson's attorney, and by Alexander Field, Scott's attorney.[45] To what extent did the decision serve

42. Lyman Decatur Norris was perhaps the most mysterious individual involved in the Dred Scott case. He was proslavery and a bitter racist, as evidenced by his brief filed in the second Missouri Supreme Court hearing. Justice Scott's majority opinion was largely taken from Norris's brief. Except for his name in four city directories from 1851 to 1854, he is not mentioned in other reference works. He never established a residence in St. Louis, taking his board in a hotel. His background, his education, where he came from, and where he went after 1854 are unknown. He was obviously well versed in the arguments of proslavery forces, which raises the question of whether he was perhaps brought to St. Louis from a Southern state by proslavery forces for the singular purpose of working on the Dred Scott case. His law partner, Hugh Garland, on the other hand, is given biographical mention in local histories. Garland was old and in bad health, which may explain Norris's prominent role. When Field and Garland met to draft the agreement on facts in 1853, Norris apparently had no part in it, and may already have left the city.

43. Fehrenbacher, *Dred Scott,* 263; "There was then no office of Chief Justice," and Gamble was voted by his associates to the presidency of the court. Philips, "Hamilton Gamble," 3.

44. Field's seven cases are listed in 15 and 16 *Missouri Reports* for the March Term, 1852, when the state supreme court met in St. Louis. A case in which Field was the attorney, *Walker, appellant v. City of St. Louis, respondent,* is listed on page 563, immediately preceding the Dred Scott case on page 576; Ehrlich, *They Have No Rights,* 61, 64; "As the case moved into the Supreme Court, personal politics and the politics of slavery entered into it." McCandless, *History of Missouri,* 260.

45. Actually, the case before the Missouri Supreme Court was titled *Scott, a man of color, defendant in error, v. Emerson, plaintiff in error.* 15 *Missouri Reports,* 366.

as a prelude to the later *Dred Scott v. Sandford* in the federal courts? Historians also wonder if the 1850 pronouncements of U.S. Justice Roger Taney in *Strader v. Graham,* implying that the laws of one state did not necessarily need to be influenced by the laws of another, gave encouragement to the Missouri high court to abandon comity.[46]

Regardless of the judicial analysis and study undertaken by historians, the Missouri Supreme Court decision in *Dred Scott v. Emerson* remains finally a political rather than a judicial decision; from a twentieth-century American perspective it was also a tragic commentary on the times. The court subordinated judicial considerations to the emotions of the moment, creating little more than a formalized expression of anger and outrage.

In the majority opinion, concurred in by Judge Ryland, Judge Scott never once mentioned Missouri's precedent-setting case of *Winny v. Whitesides,* in which the Missouri Supreme Court first ruled that residence by a slave in free territory entitled that slave to freedom upon return to Missouri.[47] Instead, he simply dismissed as meaningless all legal and statutory precedents in Missouri concerning comity by declaring:

> Every State has the right of determining how far, in a spirit of comity, it will respect the laws of other States. Those laws have no intrinsic right to be enforced beyond the limits of the State for which they were enacted.[48]

He then added, "It is a humiliating spectacle, to see the courts of a state confiscating the property of her own citizens by the command of a foreign law." As to why the Missouri Supreme Court would, after three decades, decide that it no longer would enforce the legal precedents it had earlier established, Scott said:

> Times are not now as they were when the former decisions on this subject were made. Since then not only individuals but States have been possessed with a dark and fell spirit in relation to slavery, whose gratification is sought in the pursuit of measures, whose inevitable consequences must be the overthrow and destruction of our government. Under such circumstances it does not behoove the State of Missouri to show the least countenance to any measure that might gratify this spirit . . . Although we may, for our own sakes, regret that the avarice and hard-heartedness of the progenitors of those who are not so sensitive on the subject, ever
> · introduced the institution among us, yet we will not go to them to learn law, morality, or religion on the subject.[49]

Nowhere does Justice Scott come closer to revealing the true political nature of the Supreme Court's decision in the Dred Scott case than in his closing remarks.

46. Fehrenbacher, *Dred Scott,* 261.
47. 1 *Missouri Reports,* 473.
48. 15 *Missouri Reports,* 368.
49. 15 *Missouri Reports,* 372.

Had they not been delivered within the chambers of the state's highest court, they might well, for all their righteousness, have been uttered in the rotunda of the St. Louis Courthouse at a meeting of the Anti-Abolitionist Society. Scott said:

> As to the consequences of slavery, they are much more hurtful to the master than the slave. There is no comparison between the slave of the United States and the cruel, uncivilized negro in Africa. When the condition of our slaves is contrasted with the state of their miserable race in Africa; when their civilization, intelligence and instruction in religious truths are considered, and the means now employed to restore them to the country from which they have been torn, bearing with them the blessings of civilized life, we are almost persuaded that the introduction of slavery amongst us was, in the providences of God, who makes the evil passions of men subservient to his own glory, a means of placing that unhappy race within the pale of civilized nations.[50]

It remained for Justice Hamilton R. Gamble, in his dissenting opinion, to advise his two colleagues that the purpose of the Missouri Supreme Court was to make judicial decisions, not to determine public policy. Justice Gamble reminded Justices Scott and Ryland of *Winny v. Whitesides.* Citing seven other similar Missouri cases, he said, "In this state it has been recognized, from the beginning of the government, as a correct position in law, that a master who takes his slave to reside in a State or Territory where slavery is prohibited, thereby emancipates his slave."[51] Gamble added:

> I regard the question as conclusively settled, by repeated adjudications of this court, and if I doubted or denied the propriety of those decisions, I would not feel myself any more at liberty to overthrow them than I would any other series of decisions, by which the law upon any other question was settled. There is with me, nothing in the law relating to slavery, which distinguishes it from the law on any other subject, or allows any more accommodation to the temporary public excitements which are gathered around it.[52]

Then, obviously referring to Justice Scott's statement that times "now are not as they were when the former decisions on this subject were made," Gamble replied, again referring to the many earlier cases granting freedom to slaves:

> The cases here referred to are cases decided when the public mind was tranquil, and when the tribunals maintained in their decisions the principles which had always received the approbation of an enlightened public opinion. Times may have changed, public feeling may have changed, but principles have not and do not change; and, in my judgment, there can be no safe basis for judicial decisions but in those principles which are immutable.[53]

50. Ibid.
51. Ibid., 376.
52. Ibid.
53. Ibid., 378.

The Missouri Supreme Court had announced its decision on March 22, and the following day, Irene Emerson Chaffee, through her attorneys, filed in the Circuit Court of Judge Hamilton an order to the court asking it to produce the bonds the Blow family had signed covering Dred and Harriet's court costs, the slaves themselves, and the wages the slaves had earned "by virtue of said hiring with the six per cent interest, allowed by law."[54] As far as Mrs. Chaffee was concerned, the matter had been settled by the Missouri Supreme Court's decision and she was ready to reclaim her slaves, along with the wages they had earned while under custody of the court.

What exactly was to happen to Dred and Harriet Scott and their two children at this point is unknown. Irene Chaffee was now in Massachusetts and she obviously had no intention of moving the slaves there. Her father was dead and his plantation had been sold. Her brother, John Sanford, lived in New York, and while he came to St. Louis often, he probably had no need for the slaves, since he had sold those he had inherited from his father four years earlier.

Among the other possible alternatives, of course, was the obvious one that Southerners often turned to when they no longer needed their slaves. They simply auctioned them off or sold them to slave trader Bernard Lynch, who herded them into his slave pen. When he had sufficient number, he sold them by lot downriver to work on the large cotton and rice plantations.

Fortunately, Dred, Harriet, Eliza, and Lizzie were spared that terrifying alternative. Judge Alexander Hamilton, who on previous occasions in his court had evidenced compassion for the slaves, did a very unusual and unexpected thing. He denied Irene Emerson Chaffee's motion to reclaim her slaves.

The court's record book simply states, "Said motion be overruled."[55] No reason was given.

---

54. Notice to the circuit court of St. Louis, dated March 23, 1852, for Irene Chaffee by her attorneys, *Dred Scott v. Emerson* and *Harriet v. Emerson,* typescript copies of court records, Dred Scott Collection, MHS.

55. Record book 22, 111, SLCC.

14

A New Beginning

During the spring of 1852, when the Dred Scott case seemed hopelessly lost and every chance for Dred and Harriet to escape slavery condemned by Missouri law to almost certain failure, Roswell M. Field became Dred Scott's attorney.

Six years of bitterly fought litigation had taken place since Dred and Harriet filed their petitions for freedom; two trials in the St. Louis Circuit Court and two hearings before the Missouri Supreme Court had achieved absolutely nothing. Now pending in Judge Alexander Hamilton's court was the request from the triumphant Irene Chaffee that her slaves be returned, along with their four years of wages and the forfeiture of the bonds put up by the Blow family to cover the slaves' court costs. Also, Harriet and Dred Scott were once again without legal counsel. David N. Hall died in the spring of 1851, and Alexander P. Field, who had wandered into St. Louis from Illinois and Wisconsin in the 1840s, was now, in the early 1850s, wandering off to a new law career in Louisiana.[1]

To make matters worse, Dred and Harriet's strongest supporters, the Blow family, after paying the legal fees due to the firm of Field and Hall, had apparently decided by the spring of 1852 that they had reached the limits of their financial support and they could no longer pay the Scotts' legal costs when further litigation seemed so hopeless. This decision must have been a difficult and emotional one for the Blow family, since the withdrawal of their financial support would likely doom Harriet, Dred, and their two children to the slave auction block. Now that attorney Charles Drake, their brother-in-law, had moved temporarily to Cincinnati, it was probably in desperation that Charlotte Blow Charless and the other members of the

1. Lawson, *State Trials,* 227.

Blow family turned to the only remaining lawyer in the family, Charles Edmund LaBeaume.[2] The question the Blows probably asked LaBeaume was: what legally can be done to save the Scotts?

LaBeaume was no newcomer to the Dred Scott case. As a member of the Blow family he had been involved in it from the beginning, and in 1851 he had hired Dred and Harriet from the sheriff to spare the Scotts possible abuse from indifferent employers. A descendant of one of the city's early French families, he was a brother of Eugenie LaBeaume, who had married Peter E. Blow. In practicing law, LaBeaume shared office space first with Samuel M. Bay, and then with Field and Hall—all of whom had served as attorneys for the Scotts.[3] Some historians have found LaBeaume's involvement in the Dred Scott case puzzling, and have wondered about his motives, but it seems quite probable that LaBeaume, as a relative, was simply providing legal assistance and guidance to the Blows.

According to Roswell Field, it was LaBeaume who got Field involved in the case, coming to see him shortly after the Missouri Supreme Court decision. "I was applied to by C. E. LaBeaume, Esq. for advice," is the way Field phrased it.[4] What LaBeaume asked Field was probably the same question the Blows had asked LaBeaume: what legal action might yet be undertaken to free Harriet and Dred Scott?

In typical legal style, Field's explanation of how he became involved in the Dred Scott case is factual, concise, to the point, and very likely truthful. What Field does not reveal is why, out of all the lawyers in St. Louis, LaBeaume came to him for help, and why Field, a prominent and successful lawyer, not only gave LaBeaume advice but also agreed to take on an almost hopeless slave suit for freedom without compensation.

Unfortunately, there seems to be no evidence to provide definite answers to these questions, and Field has left few clues behind for historians to discover. However, it seems likely that before LaBeaume ever called at Field's law office on Chestnut Street, he knew that Field, though primarily a real estate lawyer, was interested in the Dred Scott case, and might be receptive to serving as legal counsel for the two slaves without fee. Just how LaBeaume became aware of Field's interest is not clear, but given Field's reticence it is unlikely that he went about the city proclaiming his views on the case. More likely, LaBeaume was pointed in the direction of Roswell Field by one or both of Field's two good friends, Judge Hamilton or Justice Gamble, both of whom were involved in the Dred Scott case. As friends and fellow lawyers, they had discussed the case with Field and would likely have been aware of his personal opinions on the suits and on the Missouri

2. Hyde and Conard, *Encyclopedia of the History of St. Louis,* vol. 1, 598.

3. The LaBeaumes were one of the few Protestant families in early French St. Louis. Bryan, "Blow Family," pt. 1, 229; Ehrlich, *They Have No Rights,* 74.

4. Typescript copy of letter from Roswell Field to Montgomery Blair dated January 7, 1855, Dred Scott Collection, MHS.

high court's decision. In any case, sometime between March 23, 1852, when Irene Chaffee asked for the return of her slaves, and June 29, 1852, when Judge Hamilton officially denied that request, Hamilton learned that Roswell Field had become the new attorney for Dred and Harriet Scott and that litigation to seek the slaves' freedom was far from over.[5]

Roswell Field's reasons for taking on the Scotts' case are equally vague. But given Field's background in the law, his reasons seem clear enough, though they have often been obscured by those seeking to find political motivations for the Dred Scott case. Some historians view Field as part of an abolitionist conspiracy, others as a dupe for proslavery forces, yet others see Field as part of a collusion of interested parties seeking to use the Dred Scott case as a means of bringing major slavery issues before the United States Supreme Court.

Generally, most historians have attributed Roswell Field's interest in the case to his antislavery sentiments. One historian has described him as "an outspoken abolitionist" and another as "a native of Vermont with strong antislavery sentiments."[6] The latter view is probably closer to the truth, for Field was certainly no abolitionist, as evidenced by his heated arguments with his friend Zebina Eastman back in Vermont before he ever came to St. Louis. Perhaps Field can most aptly be described, not as an antislavery lawyer, but as a lawyer who was antislavery, and one who was probably more interested in the legal aspects of slavery than in its moral and ethical issues.

It is from a judicial viewpoint that Roswell Field's involvement in the Dred Scott case can best be understood. As Field himself later said, it was the "much vexed" question of the law regarding the freedom of a slave taken into free territory that required judicial attention. The issue of slavery itself—or, as Field phrased it, the "cause of humanity"—was secondary.[7] It was not the issue of Dred and Harriet's condition as slaves that Field, as the Scotts' attorney, sought first and foremost to correct, but the misapplication of Missouri slave law. Field shared Judge Hamilton's opinion that Dred and Harriet Scott were entitled to freedom according to Missouri law, as well as Justice Gamble's opinion that Missouri's highest court had completely disregarded all legal precedent in denying freedom to the Scotts.

That Field's reasons for serving as counsel for the Scotts were legal in nature are confirmed by Melvin L. Gray, Field's closest friend in St. Louis. Like Field, Gray was a native of Vermont and a lawyer who had come to St. Louis three years after his friend. Gray would later serve as executor of Field's estate, and, after Field's

5. Record book 22, 52; record book 22, 111, SLCC.

6. Ehrlich, *They Have No Rights*, 78; Kenneth M. Stampp, *America in 1857, a Nation on the Brink*, 85.

7. Typescript copy of letter of Roswell Field to Montgomery Blair, December 24, 1854, Dred Scott Collection, MHS.

death, would look after his surviving sons.[8] In 1893, Melvin Gray was asked by the youngest son, Roswell, about his father's involvement in the Dred Scott case. Replied Gray:

> It may have been his purpose and intention that the case should go to the U.S. Supreme Court, that the opinion of that court might be obtained, but certainly your father was not acting under the influence of southern men, but he may have scented the battle from afar and desired a decision by the highest tribunal in the land.[9]

In many respects, Roswell Field's actions in the Dred Scott case reflect the same intensity he displayed two decades earlier in Vermont when, confident that the decision would be in his favor, he sought a judicial resolution to the vexing question of his marriage to Mary Almira Phelps. Now in 1852 in Missouri, with Dred and Harriet Scott as clients, Field was seeking a judicial resolution to questions concerning the freedom of slaves taken onto free soil, again confident that the ultimate decision would be a favorable one. And just as Field, two decades earlier, had taken his marriage case all the way to Vermont's highest court for resolution, Field was now ready and willing to take the Dred Scott case all the way to the United States Supreme Court if necessary to gain freedom for the Scotts. Furthermore, as Susanna Torrey had once done, the Missouri Supreme Court in its decision had displayed a total disrespect for the law that, by Field's way of thinking, should not be allowed to go unchallenged. Justices Scott and Ryland had placed their personal fidelity to slavery above their fidelity to the law. As Field saw it, it was not only a debasement of the law but also a wrong that needed to be righted.

As commendable as such motives might have been, they did not look beyond the legal resolution to the ultimate consequences. Just as Field had not foreseen the consequences of his legal actions against Susanna Torrey, now he seemed once again to be overlooking the possible long-term consequences of his actions on behalf of Harriet and Dred Scott. Observes historian Don Fehrenbacher:

> In view of the odds against success, one may question the wisdom of undertaking the suit, but not the honesty of its purpose. Field appears to have been determined that Dred Scott should obtain a hearing before the nation's highest tribunal. The worst that can be said is that he and his associates failed to look beyond the goal to the possible consequences of submitting such an issue to a hostile Supreme Court.[10]

---

8. Stewart, *Bench and Bar,* 191; The friendship between Melvin Gray and Roswell Field's sons was, as one biographer put it, "strong and lifelong." "Memorial Sketch of Mr. Melvin L. Gray," 48; When Roswell Field's sons wrote *Echoes from the Sabine Farm* they dedicated the book to Melvin Gray with this verse by Eugene Field: "And lo, sweet friend! behold this cup, / Round which the garlands intertwine; / With Massic it is foaming up, / And we would drink to thee and thine / And of the draught thou shall partake, / Who lov'st us for our father's sake." Eugene and Roswell Martin Field, *Echoes From a Sabine Farm.*

9. Letter from Melvin L. Gray to R. M. Field, June 30, 1893, Field Collection, JL.

10. Fehrenbacher, *Dred Scott,* 275.

In discussing legal strategy with LaBeaume, Field probably first suggested that the case of *Dred Scott v. Irene Emerson* be appealed from Missouri's highest court to the United States Supreme Court. This would have been the most direct way. But such an appeal, Field probably added, would in all likelihood be dismissed by the court for lack of jurisdiction.[11] However, during their conversation, LaBeaume mentioned to Field that John Sanford, and not his sister, was now the owner of the Scotts; based on this new bit of information Field told LaBeaume that, rather than a direct appeal from Missouri, he recommended that the Scotts file a new case in the federal courts under the U.S. Constitution's diversity of citizenship clause. Because the Scotts were residents of Missouri and Sanford was a citizen of New York, the United States courts had jurisdiction since the issue involved was one between citizens of different states.[12]

Sanford's claim that he owned the Scotts has been most troubling to historians, for, in the absence of any documents showing transfers of slaves within the Sanford family, his ownership appears dubious and his involvement in the case contrived. Why would he claim ownership when the slaves were really not his? What were his motives? Questions like these are unlikely ever to be answered with any assurance. All that can be said with certainty is that John Sanford, for whatever reasons, was quite willing to assume the role of owner even without a certificate of ownership and to be sued in court by the slaves.

Yet given what is known about the Sanford family, John Sanford's position is not difficult to understand. The Scotts had always been treated as more or less communal property by members of the Sanford family. For several years after Dr. Emerson's death, Irene's brother-in-law, Captain Henry Bainbridge, had had control of the slaves, even taking Dred to Texas. Later, Irene's father, Colonel Sanford, used the slaves on his plantation and then hired them out, collecting their wages for his daughter. And when Irene Emerson left St. Louis to become Mrs. Irene Chaffee of Massachusetts, it was John Sanford who, in his sister's absence, made the legal decisions concerning the slaves' suits for freedom.

A newspaper account reports that Sanford consented to participate in the case "after enduring an amount of importunity, badgering, and worrying, from persons having no other than a political interest in the case."[13] The names of those doing the badgering are not mentioned, but if the report contains any element of truth these interested parties may well have been the proslavery members of the Chouteau

11. Field probably based this observation on the United States Supreme Court's refusal to accept jurisdiction in the slave freedom case of *Strader v. Graham,* which had come up from the Court of Appeals of Kentucky, that state's highest court. In this case, the court avoided the highly charged slavery issues by denying jurisdiction. Chief Justice Taney ruled that nothing in the United States Constitution "can in any degree control the law of Kentucky upon this subject."

12. Typescript copy of letter from Roswell Field to Montgomery Blair, January 6, 1855, Dred Scott Collection, MHS.

13. Fehrenbacher, *Dred Scott,* 275.

family and Sanford's father's old friends from the Anti-Abolitionist Society and the Committee of One Hundred.

On November 2, 1853, Roswell Field instituted the now-famous case of *Dred Scott v. John F. A. Sanford* by filing suit for the Scotts' freedom in the Circuit Court of the United States in the District of Missouri. On the same day, C. Edmund LaBeaume and Taylor Blow bonded themselves to Sanford for two hundred dollars to cover court costs that might accrue to Dred Scott as a result of the suit.[14]

The declaration filed by Field for Dred Scott in federal court was similar to the initial plea of trespass filed by Dred Scott in Judge Krum's court in 1846, but there were some notable differences. For one thing, the suit was filed under common law rather than statutory law, and therefore required no petition to the court for permission to sue. In the federal suit, the action was brought directly by Dred Scott against John Sanford without first asking the court's permission.

Another difference was that Harriet Scott, along with the children Eliza and Lizzy, were now made an official part of the initial declaration, joining with Dred Scott in his suit against Sanford. Harriet was no longer simply *Harriet, a woman of color,* as she was described in her suit in Missouri against Irene Emerson, but was instead "Harriet Scott, then and still the wife of the plaintiff." Also given last names in the federal action were the two children, now named as "Eliza Scott" and "Lizzy Scott," daughters of Dred and Harriet Scott.[15] If Roswell Field, as attorney for the Scotts, did nothing else for Dred and Harriet Scott, he restored to them at least in the court records the dignity of a family name, recognizing their lawful marriage and the two children born of that marriage.

There was also one final difference: the financial stakes in the litigation had increased significantly. In the initial suits filed in the Missouri courts, Dred and Harriet had each asked ten dollars in damages. In the federal filing, the damages

14. Typescript copies of declaration and bond, both dated November 2, 1853, Dred Scott Collection, MHS; In the United States Circuit Court of Missouri documents the name is spelled Sanford, but when the case reached the Supreme Court in Washington, the name became Sandford. Printed transcript of lower court proceedings, Supreme Court of the United States, no. 137, Archives, United States Supreme Court, Washington, D.C. (USSC).

15. Copy of declaration, November 2, 1853, Dred Scott file, USDC; Most original Dred Scott court documents are locked away in safes. A scholar in the late 1800s described the declaration written by Field. "The papers still on file in the United States Circuit Court have a quaint, old-fashioned look . . . The complaint is written on a sheet of rapidly yellowing foolscap . . . It has no water marks, and the faint line-ruling, although done on a primitive ruling rack, is remarkably even. In place of the marginal line Roswell Field . . . had creased the paper about an inch to the right of the fold of the sheet. The maker's stamp, embossed in the upper left hand corner [reads] Owens & Hurlburt, So. Lee, Mass. Every piece in the case has their imprint upon it . . . On the blue paper the quill-pen placed ink stares just as blackly as on the day it was lain, and in places black crystals clinging to the heavier lines show the sand-box was shaken over the document to dry the ink." Undated manuscript entitled "Dred Scott, Life of the Famous Fugitive and Missouri Litigant," T. W. Chamberlain Collection, MHS.

claimed for Dred and Harriet were nine thousand dollars, not an insignificant amount in 1853.[16]

In all other respects, however, this was a suit for damages in the traditional form of an action of trespass. The declaration was written in the handwriting of Roswell Field, and it was in his precise and vivid words that he described the complaint.

> Dred Scott, of St. Louis, in the State of Missouri, and a citizen of the United States, complains of John F. A. Sanford, of the city of New York, and a citizen of New York, in a plea of trespass, for that the defendant heretofore, to wit: on the 1st day of January, A.D. 1853, at St. Louis, in the county of St. Louis, and State of Missouri, with force and arms assaulted the plaintiff, and without law or right held him as a slave, and imprisoned him for the space of six hours and more, and then and there did threaten to beat the plaintiff, and to hold him imprisoned and restrained of his liberty.[17]

Sanford was in St. Louis when Field filed Scott's new case in federal court, and Thomas S. Bryant, marshall for the court, served a summons on Sanford that same day. Sanford declined to have the summons read to him and asked that a copy be mailed instead. On April 7, 1854, some five months later, he made his reply. Through his attorney Hugh Garland, Sanford filed a plea of abatement challenging the court's jurisdiction and urging the court not to take "further cognizance of the action" because, as Sanford claimed:

> Dred Scott, is not a citizen of the State of Missouri, as alleged in his declaration, because he is a negro of African descent; his ancestors were of pure African blood, and were brought into this country and sold as negro slaves.[18]

In reply, Field filed a demurrer challenging Sanford's plea and pointing out that Sanford did not show sufficient cause to preclude the court's jurisdiction in the case and that, while Scott was of African descent, that fact in itself did not bar him from citizenship or the right to sue.

The issue would be decided by Judge Robert W. Wells, who arrived in the city on April 1 for the commencement of the spring term of the United States court. Wells, a native Virginian, was some ten years older than Field, and prior to being named judge of the federal court in St. Louis he had been attorney general for the state of Missouri. Though a slaveholder most of his life, Wells favored a gradual system of emancipation and felt slavery hampered Missouri's economic development.[19]

16. Typescript copies of pleas of trespass for Dred and Harriet Scott, Dred Scott Collection, MHS; Copy of declaration of Dred Scott dated November 2, 1853, Dred Scott file, USDC.

17. Ibid.

18. Typescript copy of John Sanford plea of abatement, April 7, 1854, Dred Scott Collection, MHS.

19. *Missouri Republican,* April 3, 1854; Bay, *Reminiscences,* 539.

When Wells arrived in St. Louis, there were no permanent quarters for a courtroom and space had to be leased. For the spring term in 1854, the site selected for a courtroom was No. 38 Main Street, where the accommodations were so inadequate that the *Missouri Republican* felt they were a "mortifying reflection on the justice of the government." The paper wrote, "At the present term, the Court is compelled to occupy the second story of a building on Main Street in the midst of the noise and confusion of the trade on the street, and is worse off in accommodations than many of the clothing stores or drinking houses in the city."[20]

On April 24, above the noise and din from the street below, Roswell Field and Hugh Garland argued the issue of Dred Scott's citizenship before Judge Wells.[21] Garland cited a number of decisions in other jurisdictions in which blacks were not determined to be citizens within the meaning of the Constitution. Field replied that there was no consistent pattern among the states, that in some states blacks were entitled to vote and in others they were not, and that simply being black and a descendant of African slaves did not of itself bar citizenship.

Judge Wells gave his decision the following day, upholding Field's demurrer and denying Sanford's plea that the court lacked jurisdiction. While recognizing that slave states denied free blacks the right to sue, Wells pointed out that this gave blacks a special privilege and immunity denied whites, for if blacks could not sue in court, neither could they be sued. Further, he asked, if blacks who were foreign aliens could sue in the courts, why not native-born blacks?[22]

The decision by Judge Wells in favor of Scott walked a fine line between the rights of free blacks and slave blacks, and did not at all resolve the basic issues that surfaced again before the United States Supreme Court. Not mentioned by Wells or the opposing counsel was the question of Dred Scott's own status as a black man. Was he free or slave?

Thus, with Judge Wells's ruling, and with the question of jurisdiction out of the way, Sanford entered a plea of not guilty to the charges made in Scott's declaration, and the case was readied for trial. To the other charge of assault and battery, Sanford claimed he had only "gently laid his hands" on the slaves as he "had a right to do."[23]

Sometime before May, Roswell Field and Hugh Garland sat down together and wrote an "Agreed-Upon Statement of Facts," which was entered into the court record when the trial was held. These agreed-upon facts covered the life of Dred Scott for two decades, starting in 1834 when he was a slave of Dr. Emerson and

20. *Missouri Republican,* April 20, 1854.

21. Lawson, *State Trials,* 248.

22. Ehrlich, *They Have No Rights,* 84; Judge Wells later said, "In regard to the right of a free negro to sue in the Courts of the U.S., it may be viewed as a privilege extended or attempted to be extended to negroes against the feelings or policy of the people of Slave States. It was so viewed and treated in the Circuit Court." Typescript copy of letter from Robert Wells to Montgomery Blair, February 12, 1856, Dred Scott Collection, MHS.

23. Typescript copy of plea of John Sanford dated May 4, 1854, Dred Scott Collection, MHS.

ending when his suit against Irene Chaffee was returned by the Missouri Supreme Court to the St. Louis Circuit Court "where it has been continued to await the decision of this court."[24] The statement, written in Field's handwriting but signed also by Garland, has special significance. It probably signaled the point at which Dred Scott's freedom no longer depended upon proving residence on free soil, but rather on proving that freedom, once gained on free soil, could be retained upon return to slave territory.

Unlike the earlier trials in Missouri's lower courts, the statement of facts eliminated the need for Field to call upon witnesses to attest to Dred Scott's sojourn in Illinois and Fort Snelling, or his bondage upon his return to Missouri. These issues were covered in the statement, and were settled and agreed upon by the two attorneys. Also mentioned as a fact in the statement was the obviously incorrect claim that Sanford owned the slaves and that "Dr. Emerson sold and conveyed the plaintiff, said Harriet, Eliza and Lizzie, to, the defendant, as slaves, and the defendant have ever since claimed to hold them and each of them as slaves." Agreement on this fact conveniently eliminated any need to prove in court that John Sanford was indeed the owner of the slaves.[25]

The case came to trial on May 15, 1854, a rather chilly day in St. Louis with rain and cold, and westerly winds, which, according to the newspaper, required many to don heavy coats and relight their stoves. The federal court had been in session for some six weeks and was nearing the end of its spring term, with most of the major cases before it having been heard. *Dred Scott v. John F. A. Sanford* came to trial on the second to last day of the court's session, and Judge Wells was eager to move things along for it had been a very crowded spring court docket. Further delay would set the Dred Scott case back an entire year, to the court's next term in April 1855.[26]

After Judge Wells had announced fines of ten dollars for several jurors who had failed to appear at court, a panel of twelve jurors was selected and sworn in, and Roswell Field read to the court the "Agreed Upon Statement of Facts." There were no witnesses or other testimony presented by Garland or Field.[27]

At that point, Field asked the court to give the following instructions to the jury: "That upon the facts agreed to by the parties, they ought to find for the plaintiff."[28]

24. Printed copy of transcript of proceedings in the U.S. Circuit Court for the District of Missouri in *Scott v. Sandford,* archives, USSC; Copy of "Agreed Upon Statement of Facts," Dred Scott file, USDC.

25. "Agreed upon Statement of Facts"; It was the failure of Dred Scott's attorneys to prove that Irene Emerson actually owned the slaves in the first state trial in 1847 that brought about the second state trial.

26. *St. Louis Daily Evening News,* May 15, 1854; "The U.S. Court adjourned yesterday and all cases not heard this term will go over until the April term 1855." *St. Louis Daily Evening News,* May 18, 1854.

27. *St. Louis Daily Evening News,* May 15, 1854; Lawson, *State Trials,* 251.

28. Lawson, *State Trials,* 251.

Judge Wells refused to give such instructions, and instead instructed the jury that based "upon the facts in this case, the law is with the defendant" and not with Scott, the plaintiff. In giving this instruction, Judge Wells was simply echoing the earlier decision of the Missouri Supreme Court that slaves sojourning in free territory once again become slaves upon their return to Missouri.[29]

Based on this instruction from Judge Wells, the jury found for Sanford, and James Hardy, jury foreman, reported that it was the decision of the jury that "Dred Scott was a negro slave and the lawful property" of John Sanford, as were Harriet, his wife, and Eliza and Lizzy, his two daughters.[30]

Field's immediate response was a motion to set aside the verdict, requesting at the same time that a new trial be granted on the grounds that "the court had misdirected the jury in the matter of the law." Wells overruled the motion. Field then presented a bill of exceptions, which Judge Wells approved. The result was the appeal of the case of *Dred Scott v. John F. A. Sanford* to the United States Supreme Court.

Probably unknown to Judge Wells or the twelve men on the jury, Roswell Field's good friend, Judge Alexander Hamilton, had five months earlier anticipated the verdict in the federal court and had already noted the outcome in the record books of the St. Louis Circuit Court. On January 25, 1854, in the pending case of *Dred Scott v. Irene Emerson,* Judge Hamilton wrote, "Continued by consent, waiting decision of U.S. Supreme Court."[31] Judge Hamilton's notation evidences not so much his unusual psychic power as it does his likely awareness that *Dred Scott v. John F. A. Sanford* was headed to the United States Supreme Court no matter what verdict was reached by the jury in Judge Wells' court.

As for Judge Wells, he later admitted that his sympathies were for the Scotts, even though his instructions to the jury led to a verdict against them. Two years after the trial he told Montgomery Blair, "I may say to you, however, that my feelings were deeply interested in favor of the poor fellow, and I wish the law was in favor of his freedom."[32]

As for St. Louis, the city still displayed no interest in the Dred Scott case, and the local newspapers, for the most part, ignored it. Thomas C. Reynolds, later to become lieutenant governor of Missouri, recalled that the case was so unimportant that it did not even "create a local stir."[33]

29. Ibid., 252; Judge Wells later commented, "The U.S. Courts follow the State courts in regard to the interpretation of their own laws. I was bound to take the interpretation of the laws of Mo., in this case, from the Supreme Court of the State." Typescript copy of a letter from Robert Wells to Montgomery Blair, February 12, 1856, Dred Scott Collection, MHS.

30. Typescript copy of jury's verdict, Dred Scott Collection, MHS.

31. Record book 24, November Term 1853, SLCC.

32. Typescript copy of a letter from Robert Wells to Montgomery Blair, February 12, 1856, Dred Scott Collection, MHS.

33. Undated letter of Thomas C. Reynolds, T. W. Chamberlain Collection, MHS.

During Dred Scott's trial in May 1854, the St. Louis newspapers were reporting the debates in Washington on the Kansas-Nebraska Bill over the issue of slavery in the territories. Within two weeks President Franklin Pierce signed the bill into law, repealing the slavery prohibition of the Missouri Compromise and replacing it with a vague principle of popular sovereignty whereby voters in newly created territories, and not Congress, decided whether their state was to be slave or free. The act in effect opened the western territories to slavery. The *St. Louis Daily Evening News* termed the matter a "great excitement" and the *St. Louis Intelligencer* warned citizens of St. Louis that they were "in the midst of a revolution."[34] That the political issues in the Kansas-Nebraska Act might in some way be connected to a current St. Louis slave case now on its way to the United States Supreme Court had not yet dawned on the people of Missouri, perhaps not even on Roswell Field.

Likely of more concern to Dred and Harriet Scott were the advertisements appearing in the St. Louis newspapers during May 1854 for the Bolton Dickins Company. The ads read:

ONE THOUSAND NEGROES WANTED
Our Mr. Dickins having located himself in St. Louis, Mo. for the purpose of purchasing for the Southern Market will pay the HIGHEST PRICES for all good negroes offered. No. 52 Second Street between Olive and Pine Streets under the sign "Negroes Bought Here."[35]

34. *St. Louis Daily Evening News,* May 15, 1854; *St. Louis Intelligencer,* May 16, 1854.
35. *Daily St. Louis Intelligencer,* May 18, 1854.

Appeal to the Nation

It is difficult to imagine how Roswell Field felt following the verdict against Dred Scott and his family in the United States Circuit Court. On one hand, it represented yet another defeat for the Scotts in their efforts to obtain freedom. This verdict in the federal court, following in the wake of the adverse decision by the Missouri Supreme Court two years earlier, seemed only to confirm what Missouri Justice Scott told Dred and Harriet, namely, that "times are not now as they were when the former decisions on this subject were made."[1]

On the other hand, the verdict opened the way for an appeal to the highest tribunal in the land, the Supreme Court, and this may well have been Field's goal from the start. Thus, instead of viewing the verdict as a defeat, Field may actually have felt assured that the legal strategy he and LaBeaume had worked out in 1852 was on course, and that his ultimate goal of obtaining resolution of the issues by the United States Supreme Court was now within sight.

If Field was disappointed by the decision in Judge Wells's court, he gave little sign of it. Within ten days afterward, he was already actively at work setting up the legal machinery for the appeal to the Supreme Court. The steps he took in the early days following the verdict not only prepared the case for trial in the Supreme Court, but even more significantly moved *Dred Scott v. John F. A. Sanford* further into the maelstrom of Missouri politics, and onto the national stage, where it became a cause célèbre.

In the first of these actions, on May 25, 1854, ten days after the trial, Field sent a letter to attorney Montgomery Blair in Washington, asking Blair to join as fellow

---

1. 15 *Missouri Reports,* 372, MSC.

counsel in the case by representing the Scotts before the high court. Although Field did not know it, Blair was away from Washington in California, where he had gone to settle the estate of his deceased brother, James Blair.[2]

In inviting Montgomery Blair to assist him in the case, Field could not have taken a step better calculated to attract the attention of Dred Scott's enemies in Missouri. The Blairs were one of the most politically influential families in St. Louis and Washington—and also one of the most contentious. Wherever controversy existed in the body politic, the Blairs were probably somewhere nearby.

Field had known Montgomery Blair for about fifteen years, and like Field, Blair arrived in St. Louis in 1839 as a young attorney. Unlike Field, Montgomery Blair had a well-known last name and good connections, and upon arriving in the city entered the law office of Senator Thomas Hart Benton. Montgomery's father, Francis Preston Blair, a confidant and adviser to President Andrew Jackson, was publisher of the *Congressional Globe,* and had amassed a fortune that enabled him, along with his wife, family, slaves, and horses, to live a luxurious life in the nation's capital. A mansion on Pennsylvania Avenue across from the White House, and a Maryland estate named Silver Springs, permitted the Blairs to entertain presidents, ambassadors, and congressmen in "oriental magnificence"—a sharp contrast to the leveling tenets of Jackson's party of the Democracy, which the Blairs all strongly supported.[3] While the family was part of Washington's Southern aristocracy in its heyday, the Blairs were opposed to the expansion of slavery, and strongly believed in the federal Union.

Francis Blair encouraged Montgomery, after graduation from West Point and Transylvania University in Kentucky, to settle in St. Louis, as he would likewise encourage his youngest son, Francis P. (Frank) Blair. St. Louis was home to the family's good friend, Senator Benton, with whom the Blairs shared a common political ideology and a vision of St. Louis as a future great city of the world. The Blairs backed up this enthusiasm for St. Louis by making sizable investments in real estate; to enhance the value of these investments, they also joined with Benton in his efforts to make St. Louis the eastern terminus of the transcontinental railroad to the Pacific.[4]

2. Smith, *Blair Family,* vol. 1, 385.
3. Ibid., 158.
4. "The families of Benton and Blair were on the friendliest terms. The two fathers loved each other, and, as far as I am able to learn, never quarreled. Both of them were keen observers and sought knowledge in every direction. Benton was not so great a reader as Blair. They each had large libraries for their day. How they discovered the most minute details of the countless political movements, or of any problem of interest to the country, is almost a mystery. Benton sat like a watchdog in the Senate; Blair listened to the news gatherers and read letters and newspapers, whether he was the powerful editor of the *Globe* or the retired citizen of Silver Springs. Their many conversations naturally led them to a common body of knowledge and understanding." Ibid., 266, 203.

Like Field, Montgomery Blair centered his legal practice on real estate law, in which he was quite successful. While a product of the South, Blair was almost puritanical in his tastes and habits, and shared with Field a certain streak of self-righteousness. Further, like Field, Blair could be an "implacable and intolerant enemy when his favorite beliefs and principles were at stake," and was, it was also noted, "fearless, tactless, independent of thought, and absolutely outspoken."[5]

Blair wasted no time in establishing himself in St. Louis. While Field was struggling to pay his room and board, Blair was serving as United States district attorney, and in 1843 as judge of the court of common pleas. Joining Montgomery in St. Louis in the early 1840s was his younger brother Frank, who quickly became immersed in Missouri politics. Frank Blair was strongly antislavery; he became one of the founders of the "free soil" movement in Missouri and later a leader of the Free Soil party. In 1848 he established the *Missouri Barnburner,* the first free-soil newspaper in the West, and after this paper's demise, he took control of the *Missouri Democrat,* editing it to serve as Senator Benton's voice in Missouri. In 1852 he was elected to the Missouri legislature, where he was allied with Senator Benton's supporters.[6]

In 1853, Montgomery was summoned back to Washington by his father. Francis Blair wanted his son to practice before the Supreme Court, and he also sought a position for him in President Franklin Pierce's cabinet. The office targeted was that of attorney general. Pierce, however, did not select Blair for the post, but instead appointed him United States solicitor in the Court of Claims. While the Dred Scott case was before Judge Wells's court in 1853, Blair was establishing his law office in Washington and moving his family into his father's mansion on Pennsylvania Avenue. The elder Blair had moved to Silver Springs, and returned to Washington only for the winter social season. Montgomery immediately added a third story to the mansion so the Blair hospitality could be "enjoyed by a large circle of friends."[7]

In late December 1853, when Montgomery returned from California, Roswell Field's second letter, written in St. Louis on Christmas Eve, reached Blair. Field asked Blair whether he "or any other professional gentleman at W[ashington] should feel interest enough in the case to give it such attention as to bring it to a hearing & decision by the court." By such action, Field said, "the cause of humanity may perhaps be subserved! at all events a much disputed question would be settled by the highest court in the nation." Blair consulted with his father at

5. Elbert B. Smith, *Francis Preston Blair,* 92.

6. Hyde and Conard, *Encyclopedia of the History of St. Louis,* vol. 1, 174, 286.

7. Smith, *Blair Family,* vol. 1, 286; Letters of support for Montgomery Blair. John T. Ryland to the President, January 19, 1853, and Judge R. W. Wells to General Pierce, January 19, 1853, Blair Family Collection, Library of Congress, Washington, D.C.; Hyde and Conard, *Encyclopedia of the History of St. Louis,* vol. 1, 174; Smith, *Blair Family,* vol. 1, 291.

Silver Springs, and also with Gamaliel Bailey, editor of the antislavery *National Era,* and accepted. Bailey agreed to underwrite some of Dred Scott's court costs.[8]

In response to accusations that the Dred Scott case was politically conceived, Blair would later say that he agreed to serve as Washington counsel at the request of Roswell Field, a fellow Missouri lawyer whom he had known for fifteen years and who had no interest in politics. Said Blair:

> In Missouri, and generally, I believe, in the Southern States, almost every lawyer feels bound to give his services when asked in such a case arising in the community in which he belongs. Having risen at that bar, considering myself still a citizen of Missouri, although for the present pursuing my profession at the seat of government, I did not hesitate to become the counsel for the plaintiff here, as I should have done there.[9]

Other than Thomas Hart Benton himself, Field could not have selected anyone more closely identified with the antislavery and pro-Benton faction in Missouri. From the time of their first arrival in the state, both Montgomery and his brother Frank had been viewed as the senator's "political lieutenants," and during Benton's hard-fought battle several years earlier to retain his Senate seat, the two young men had earned their Benton labels by traveling the state making speeches and conducting rallies on the senator's behalf.[10] In 1849, Frank Blair wrote in the *Missouri Republican*:

> For those therefore who maintain the Jeffersonian doctrine of the power and duty of Congress to prohibit slavery in the territories now free—to those who maintain Benton in his position in the Senate; and to those who desire to put down the conspiracy now on foot for the severance of the Union, and the formation of a Southern Confederacy, I appeal for support for Col. Benton.[11]

By 1854, the political factions in Missouri were more polarized than ever as Benton, after his defeat by Henry Geyer in 1850, sought to regain his control and power in the state.[12] The Whig party in Missouri was in its death throes and the party of the Democracy hopelessly divided. On one side there was the proslavery, anti-Benton wing headed by Missouri Senator David R. Atchison and Claiborne Jackson; on the other there was the pro-Benton, antislavery wing represented by Benton and the Blairs.[13] By 1854, when the Dred Scott case reached the United

---

8. Typescript letter from R. M. Field to Montgomery Blair, December 24, 1854, Dred Scott Collection, MHS; Smith, *Blair Family,* vol. 1, 386; Ehrlich, *They Have No Rights,* 91.

9. Typescript copy of article in the *National Intelligencer,* December 24, 1856, Blair Family Collection, Library of Congress, Washington, D.C.

10. Smith, *Blair Family,* 303.

11. Letter signed "a radical." *Missouri Republican,* January 18, 1849.

12. P. Orman Bay, *Missouri Compromise,* 27.

13. Smith, *Blair Family,* vol. 1, 299.

States Supreme Court, the hostility between these two factions had reached a fever pitch. Not only was it Senator Atchison's seat that Benton was seeking in his bid to return to power in Missouri, but more importantly the two groups were bitterly divided on the volatile issues raised by the Kansas-Nebraska Act. This act, which abolished the Missouri Compromise and opened the northern territories to possible slavery, had long been a goal of proslavery Southerners in Missouri and elsewhere. Among Missouri's congressional delegation only Benton had opposed the bill's passage in Congress, and his opposition was strongly supported by the Blairs. The Blairs, who could tolerate slavery where it already existed, were against expanding slavery into new states entering the Union. The Blairs said:

> We cannot understand how those who recognize the evils of slavery, who see it as we see it in the valley of the Mississippi, cannot avoid seeing how it retards the growth and prosperity of communities, impairs enterprise and paralyses the industry of people and impedes the diffusion of knowledge amongst them, to say nothing of the aristocratic tendencies and degradation which it attaches to labor.[14]

Dred Scott's suit for freedom had always been tainted by the politics of slavery, but now in 1854 the case became a focus of attention in the bitter conflict between the pro-Benton and anti-Benton factions in Missouri. Even worse for Dred and Harriet, their suit for freedom had by 1854 also become enmeshed in a state conflict over the admission of Kansas to the Union.

What made the issue of Kansas so acute for Missourians was Missouri's rather peculiar geographical location as a part of the South. With its eastern and northern boundaries exposed to the free soil of Illinois and Iowa, and only its southern boundary with Arkansas bordering on a slave state, the question of the western boundary—Kansas—took on special significance. Missourians seemed to sense, perhaps correctly, that if the state were bounded on three of its four sides by free soil, it would only be a matter of time before slavery would be forced to beat a retreat from the state. Therefore, the "spectre of a 'horde of negro-stealing Abolitionists' permanently settled in Kansas with the avowed purpose of strangling the 'peculiar institution' was both irritating and economically appalling to the hardheaded, self-made frontiersman, who resented any interference with his God-given institution."[15]

Proclaimed one Missourian in 1855, "What shall Missourians do? If Kansas be settled by Abolitionists, can Missouri remain a Slave State? If Missouri goes by the board what will become of Kentucky? Maryland? Virginia?" Senator Atchison warned Missouri slave-owners, "Will you sit here at home and permit the nigger thieves, the cattle, the vermin of the North to . . . run off with your negroes and

---

14. Ibid., 263.
15. Trexler, *Missouri Slavery,* 187.

depreciate the value of your slaves?"[16] The issues were emotional ones, not only along the border between Kansas and Missouri where they often erupted into violence, but in the rest of the state and throughout the nation as well.

Thus, with yet another aspect of Missouri politics injected into the Dred Scott case, Roswell Field took still another action aimed at focusing more attention on Dred and Harriet's freedom suit. In the spring of 1854, within weeks after the unfavorable verdict in the United States Circuit Court, Field made—or at least consented to—a public appeal directly to the nation on behalf of his client, Dred Scott. This effort, like Montgomery Blair's selection as legal counsel, would hardly go unnoticed by John Sanford and the proslavery forces now lining up in his support.

On July 4, 1854, no doubt a symbolic date selected by Scott's supporters, a twelve-page printed pamphlet made its public appearance. Claiming to be the voice of Dred Scott, the pamphlet was a cry for help from "a poor black man and his family" for assistance from his fellow men.[17]

Who the author, or authors, of this pamphlet were is unknown. Montgomery's son, Gist, later said his father wrote the pamphlet, though this is very unlikely since Blair was in California at that time. Field said the author was C. Edmund LaBeaume. Other possibilities include Field himself, or perhaps one of Frank Blair's friends in the print shop of the *Missouri Democrat,* or perhaps even Dred Scott, for while Scott could not read or write, many of the thoughts expressed may have come from him.[18]

The true author is likely never to be known, but Field, as legal counsel for the slave, was probably aware of the pamphlet before it was printed and likely approved of its issuance. If LaBeaume was indeed the author, as Field claimed, it would have been unthinkable for him to have undertaken to write the tract without agreement from Field as Scott's attorney.

Such an effort to focus public attention on the Dred Scott case would not have been an untried step for Field to take in a legal suit, for he had taken similar action back in Vermont when he published his charges against Susanna Torrey in the *Bellows Falls Intelligencer.* In that case, Field believed that the need "to bring the facts before the publick" was just as important as bringing the facts before the court.[19] Without question, Field saw publicity as a strategy in court litigation, and

16. Ibid.

17. The twelve-page Dred Scott pamphlet is apparently no longer extant. Once in the Law School Library at the University of Missouri at Columbia, it turned up missing in 1988. John Lawson, in his 1921 work *American State Trials,* vol. 13, 243, quotes at length from the pamphlet.

18. Letter of Gist Blair to W. F. Smith, December 31, 1928, Blair Family Collection, Library of Congress, Washington, D.C.; Typescript copy of letter from R. M. Field to Montgomery Blair, January 7, 1855, Dred Scott Collection, MHS; The pamphlet says Dred "had several children" other than Eliza and Lizzie "all of whom are dead," a fact that would have been known only to Scott himself.

19. Roswell Field pleading, *Clark v. Field,* Windsor County Superior Court, 1838, Vermont State Archives, Middlesex, Vt.

just as he fed information about his Vermont suits to his friend Zebina Eastman for publication in the *Vermont Free Press* twenty years earlier, he may have encouraged publicity in 1854 in the Dred Scott case. Such actions by Field might explain the appearance of a decidedly pro-Scott article in the *Daily Morning Herald* on May 18 following the federal court decision—the only public notice taken by any St. Louis newspaper. The article reported briefly on the nature of Dred Scott's case and then concluded:

> The case will be taken by writ of error to the Supreme Court of the United States. Dred is of course poor and without powerful friends. But no doubt he will find at the bar of the Supreme Court some able and generous advocate, who will do all he can to establish his right to go free.[20]

The stated purpose of the Dred Scott pamphlet was to solicit money, and perhaps legal support, from Northerners opposed to slavery and from those in Missouri who might be sympathetic to the plight of a slave. In this effort, we have Field's own words that the pamphlet was not successful, apparently gaining little if any support or recognition.[21] However, while unsuccessful in its primary mission, the pamphlet was almost certain to have rankled Southerners who read it, not only in Missouri but elsewhere.

In the pamphlet Dred said he brought suit "to get the freedom of myself, my wife and children." He claimed to be of "pure African blood" with "not a drop of white man's blood in my veins"; his ancestors were "free people of Africa." He described his early life with Peter Blow and later with Dr. Emerson.[22] After referring to the Ordinance of 1787 and the Missouri Compromise of 1820, Dred said:

> The judge said that according to these laws while I was in Illinois and Wisconsin I was a free man—just as good as my master—and that I had as much right to make a slave of a white man as a white man to make a slave of me. I was sorry nobody ever told me that while I was there. Yet I was glad to have the judge talk so for I thought he would set me free. But after a little while the judge said that as soon as my master got me back this side of the line of Missouri my right to be free was gone; and that I and my wife and my children became nothing but so many pieces of property. I thought it hard that white men should draw a line of their own on the face of the earth and on one side of which a black man was to become no man at all, and never say a word to the black man about it until they got him on that side of the line.[23]

Scott then stated that his case was now before the Supreme Court in Washington and that he had no money "to pay anybody at Washington to speak for me." Scott pleaded:

20. *Daily Morning Herald,* May 18, 1854.

21. "The record on Dred's case was printed here and sent I believe to many in eastern states. It does not seem to have attracted any attention." Field to Blair, January 7, 1855, Dred Scott Collection, MHS.

22. Dred Scott pamphlet, Lawson, *State Trials,* 244.

23. Ibid.

My fellow country-men, can any of you help me in my day of trial? Will nobody speak for me at Washington, even without hope of other reward than the blessings of a poor black man and his family? I do not know. I can only pray that some good heart will be moved by pity to do that for me which I cannot do for myself; and that if the right is on my side it may be so declared by the high court to which I have appealed.[24]

The pamphlet ends with Dred Scott's "X" mark, followed by a complete copy of the St. Louis federal court record and pleadings.

Since neither attorneys nor cash were forthcoming from the East in response to Dred's plea, all the pamphlet probably did was enrage those Southerners who read it, and further to alert John Sanford and his supporters to the determination of Scott's friends to win the case using every means available, even if it meant soliciting money and help from Northern abolitionists.

From a Southern perspective the pamphlet contained some inflammatory words and statements. The very date selected for the pamphlet—July 4—in itself would have raised the ire of those Southerners who believed that blacks, slave or free, were not citizens of the United States, and thereby not entitled to the freedoms set forth in the Declaration of Independence. Judge Krum had ruled eight years earlier in *The State v. Charles Lyons* that blacks, though free, were of a race permanently set apart by reason of their African slave heritage and excluded from the fruits of the American Revolution. Other statements in the pamphlet that Dred Scott as a free man was "just as good" as his master, and that Scott's blood was pure African and not tainted "by a drop of white man's blood," were also likely to have angered any Southerner who read them.[25]

As a result of these efforts to focus attention on the Dred Scott case and to solicit support from the Blair family, and from Northern abolitionists, it should have come as no surprise to Roswell Field and Scott's friends that John Sanford, in responding to these developments, sought to marshall an equally impressive display of support and power for his cause. This took the form of two new defense attorneys; one the foremost attorney at the Missouri bar, Henry S. Geyer; and the other a nationally acclaimed constitutional lawyer, Reverdy Johnson.[26] As Roswell Field and Montgomery Blair viewed this new defense lineup, they probably realized, if they had not before, that gaining freedom for Dred and Harriet Scott before the United States Supreme Court was not going to be easy.

Geyer and Johnson replaced Sanford's previous attorneys. Hugh Garland had been in poor health for some time, and a St. Louis woman who saw him in Washington early in 1854 wrote home to a friend that Garland was "so broken down with trouble of one kind or another that one has to be very civil to him

24. Ibid.
25. *St. Louis Daily Union,* December 16, 1846; Scott pamphlet, Lawson, *State Trials,* 244.
26. Fehrenbacher, *Dred Scott,* 282.

to draw him out at all." In October 1854, four months after the Scott trial in the federal court, Garland died.[27] His partner, Lyman Norris, who had assisted him, and whose arguments had greatly influenced the Missouri Supreme Court two years previously, had apparently left the state.

Even if Garland had been in good health and Norris had remained in Missouri, it is doubtful that Sanford and his supporters, aware of the mounting importance of the Dred Scott case, would have allowed them to represent Sanford before the United States Supreme Court. Since Garland's entry into the Dred Scott litigation in 1850, the Dred Scott case had taken on issues far more important to the South than the mere freedom of some Missouri slaves. Sanford was still the named defendant in the suit, but the real defendant in 1854 had become slavery itself.[28]

The selection of Geyer and Johnson for the defense was clearly an effort to outclass the Scott supporters with a dazzling display of legal talent before the Supreme Court. It would not have been easy to find a new defense attorney from Missouri whose legal stature exceeded that of Roswell Field, nor would it have been easy to find a Washington attorney with credentials more impressive than those of Montgomery Blair. Yet, it appears, John Sanford succeeded in doing just that.

Among St. Louis lawyers, there were perhaps only two whose reputations as attorneys outshone Roswell Field. One was Hamilton R. Gamble, and the other was Henry S. Geyer. Of Geyer, W. V. N. Bay had this to say in his 1878 book on the Missouri bench and bar:

> If called upon to decide who, in our judgment, was the greatest lawyer at the Missouri bar, we should unhesitatingly say Henry S. Geyer; not that he was the superior of Gamble, Leonard or Field, in his knowledge of the law relating to real estate; nor that he was the equal of Josiah Spaulding as a commercial lawyer; nor equal to Edward Bates in impassioned eloquence; yet, taking everything into consideration, he was the superior of all.[29]

Geyer was not known as a lawyer who focused on slave cases, although he seems to have represented proslavery clients in many of the major slave cases that came before the courts in those days. When the Anti-Abolitionist Society in St. Louis sought to rid the streets of free blacks, it was Geyer who represented the state

27. Letter from Anne Lane to Sarah Glasgow dated February 20, 1854, William Carr Lane Papers, MHS; *Missouri Republican,* October 15, 1854.

28. John Sanford was officially notified on June 17 that he was to "appear at a Supreme Court of the United States, to be holden at Washington on the first Monday of December next." Printed copy of the proceedings in the United States Circuit Court of Missouri, archives, USSC.

29. Bay, *Reminiscences,* 148; An example of Geyer's skill as a lawyer is described in a two-part article by Marshall D. Hier, "Henry S. Geyer's 'Sale of Indulgences,' The 1840 Darmes Case," 40–42.

against Charles Lyons when he appeared in Judge Krum's court on charges of being in the city without a license. When the slave descendants of Marie Jean Scypion sought to escape bondage, it was Geyer who fought their freedom on behalf of his client Pierre Chouteau. When the anti–Benton, proslavery forces defeated Benton in 1850, it was Geyer, a Whig, who was chosen by a proslavery Democratic and Whig coalition to fill Benton's Senate seat.

Geyer's experience in law and government was impressive. A veteran of the War of 1812, he came to Missouri from Maryland and in 1818 became a member of the Missouri Territorial Legislature, as well as state representative and speaker of the house during Missouri's first three general assemblies. Geyer helped establish public schools and a state university for Missouri, and coauthored the first revision of Missouri's laws in 1825. For more than thirty years there was hardly an important legal case in St. Louis in which he was not involved as an attorney.

Reverdy Johnson's reputation, on the other hand, was national. Like Geyer, he was born in Maryland, and was said to enjoy a warm friendship with another Maryland native, Chief Justice Roger Taney. Johnson, a former senator and attorney general, was considered the foremost constitutional lawyer in the nation. He later said he had been introduced to the Dred Scott case by "a southern gentleman," believed by some to have been Garland, but it could also have been John Sanford.[30]

Both Geyer and Johnson, like Field and Blair, agreed to serve their clients and argue the case without compensation—convincing proof that the Dred Scott case, instituted eight years earlier to obtain the freedom of a Missouri slave family, had during the succeeding years transcended that objective, and was now encompassing issues of greater significance; in 1854, however, the scope of these issues still had not been fully comprehended by Missourians or the nation. On December 30, 1854, attorney Nathaniel Holmes, representing Roswell Field, formally filed the case with the United States Supreme Court in Washington. It would be known to the court, and to history, as *Dred Scott, Plaintiff in Error vs. John F. A. Sandford, Defendant in Error.*[31]

More than a year elapsed before the justices on the Supreme Court took official cognizance of the case. The docket was already full, and the court was forced to continue the case until the next court term.[32] That left a year for Roswell Field and Montgomery Blair to develop their arguments and write a brief.

In appealing the Dred Scott case to the United States Supreme Court, Field indicated he had two questions he would like to have decided by the court. The first was the "much vexed" question of "whether the removal by the master of

---

30. Fehrenbacher, *Dred Scott,* 282, 89.
31. "Plaintiff prays judgment of reversal" of proceedings of the lower court, *Dred Scott, plaintiff in error, v. John F. A. Sandford, defendant in error,* case 3230, docket G, 3388, archives, USSC.
32. Fehrenbacher, *Dred Scott,* 283.

his slave to Illinois or Wisconsin works an absolute emancipation of the slave." The second question upon which Field felt "it was very desirable" to "obtain the opinion of the court" was that of black citizenship and whether "every person *born in the United States & capable of holding property"* is "a *citizen* having the right to sue in the United States courts."[33]

Both of these questions directly involved Dred Scott and his freedom. Therefore, at least at this point in the litigation, Field was still placing the needs and wishes of his client foremost. If Field had other issues he hoped would come before the court, he never mentioned them. Neither were any other issues covered in the brief that Montgomery Blair filed with the court a year later on Scott's behalf. During the whole of the litigation before the Supreme Court, there is no indication that Field and Blair ever sought anything from the court other than the freedom of Dred Scott and his family. Field and Blair simply wanted the court to uphold and sanction Missouri's time-honored laws on slave freedom and citizenship. Political issues, when they were introduced, came in the arguments of Sanford's attorneys, whose overall objective seemed directed not at protecting slavery where it already existed, but in expanding it into areas where it did not exist.

Field's exclusive focus on slave freedom and citizenship, and his failure to anticipate the introduction of related issues such as the Missouri Compromise, has prompted some historians to be critical of Field's strategy in handling the case. This criticism may have some merit. During most of the time that the case was before the Supreme Court, Field and Blair continued to concentrate on the issues of Dred Scott's freedom and citizenship, and not until the final arguments, just prior to the decision, did they argue the political territorial question.

During 1855 and the early months of 1856, before the court took up the Dred Scott case, Field and Blair corresponded back and forth between Washington and St. Louis, and probably also had several face-to-face discussions about the case when Blair visited St. Louis, which he did on occasion.[34]

What appears to have concerned Field the most during this period was his fear that the Supreme Court, reflecting a prudent sensitivity to the slavery issues involved in the case, might simply dispose of the case by upholding the lower court's verdict, and not rule on Field's two questions. Even as late as March 1856, Roswell Field wrote Blair that he "observed that many newspaper correspondents are speculating on the possibilities of the court's evading the main question by turning the case off on some minor point." Field was also concerned about the

33. For the first question, see typescript copy of letter from Roswell Field to Montgomery Blair, December 24, 1854, Dred Scott Collection, MHS; On the second question, emphasis indicated by italics reflects Field's underlining. Typescript copy of letter from Roswell Field to Montgomery Blair, January 7, 1855, Dred Scott Collection, MHS.

34. Blair was a pallbearer at the funeral of Senator Benton's wife in March 1855, and requested that the funeral oration on March 26, 1855, at the Second Presbyterian Church in St. Louis be published. Pamphlet, Collections, MHS.

court's reaction to Judge Wells's ruling permitting Dred Scott to sue in the federal courts as a citizen. If this ruling were allowed to stand, Field told Blair, it would give blacks the constitutional right to sue in federal courts and to have a trial by jury, and thus "the Fugitive Slave act would undoubtedly become of little value." Field felt that the Supreme Court, for this reason, might find it a "strong argument against allowing black men to sue as citizens."[35]

As to Scott's claim to freedom because of his residence on free soil, Field told Blair he felt this was the "principal question." On this subject, Field called Blair's attention to Judge Gamble's dissenting opinion in the Dred Scott case. Said Field, "The American cases are nearly uniform in holding that a removal of a slave by his master into a free state makes him free forever." Field further added that "there has never been any judgment of the State court declaring Dred a slave."[36]

Field's concerns that the court might seek a way to avoid ruling on the issues of Dred Scott's freedom and citizenship because of their controversial nature were not without some foundation. Ever since Chief Justice John Marshall, the Supreme Court had tended to use its "power sparingly where the constitutionality of state legislation was at stake." Chief Justice Taney had been quoted as saying that powers given the federal courts by the Constitution "are judicial powers and extend to those subjects only which are judicial in their character; and not those which are political."[37]

As Roswell Field and Montgomery Blair were to learn later, there could be exceptions.

Montgomery Blair filed his brief for Dred Scott with the court on February 7, 1856, more than a year after the case was docketed and nearly ten years after Francis Murdoch had filed petitions in the St. Louis Circuit Court for the freedom of Dred and Harriet Scott. On the following day, a brief was filed by Henry Geyer for John Sanford.[38]

In his history of the Missouri bar, historian Bay says that the arguments presented in Scott's brief were "no doubt prepared to some extent" by Roswell Field.[39] This is true, for the two questions Field wanted the court to resolve are the only two issues argued in the brief. Of the brief's ten printed pages, the first four pages offer arguments on the question of slave residence on free soil, and the remaining six

35. Quotes are from typescript copy of letter from Roswell Field to Montgomery Blair, March 12, 1856, Dred Scott Collection, MHS; and typescript copy of letter from Roswell Field to Montgomery Blair, January 7, 1855, Dred Scott Collection, MHS.

36. Ibid.

37. Fehrenbacher, *Dred Scott,* 230; quote from an 1838 court decision, ibid.

38. Printed copy of Montgomery Blair's brief bearing the handwritten initials "MB," and containing editing marks and revisions. Printed by Gibson Printer, 511 Ninth Street, Washington, D.C., Blair Family Collection, Library of Congress, Washington, D.C.; Henry Geyer's brief filed during the first round of arguments before the court has never been found by historians.

39. Bay, *Reminiscences,* 241.

pages present arguments on the question of black citizenship. However, while the subject matter covered in the brief is Field's, as are many of the legal citations, Field probably did not participate in actually writing the brief. This was very likely done by Montgomery Blair. The wording bears very little, if any, resemblance to that usually found in Field's writings. The words lack Field's customary precision and clarity; the sentences are long and rambling, and in some instances are not very clear—rare occurrences in most of Field's prose.

The arguments presented in the brief for Dred Scott's freedom based on residency on free soil follow closely Justice Gamble's dissenting opinion in the Missouri Supreme Court decision, and a key paragraph in Gamble's dissent is quoted. Also, the Missouri legal precedents for slave freedom cited by Gamble are repeated in the brief. In his arguments, Blair says that earlier decisions by the Missouri Supreme Court "seem to have so fully settled the question, that since that time there has been no case bringing it before the court for any consideration until the present." Blair does not avoid mentioning the Missouri Supreme Court's majority opinion given by Justice Scott, and quotes some sentences from it, but he tosses it off as simply reflecting the "vexed topics of the politics of the day."[40]

On the subject of black citizenship, Blair cites the definition of a citizen given in a dictionary of the era when the Constitution was written, in which a citizen was defined as "a freeman of a city, not a foreigner, not a slave." Blair admitted that Americans have held blacks to be inferior politically and socially, but said that the right to sue in court was a civil right, not a political or social right. He also admitted that the practices of states varied in granting civil rights to free blacks, but that "a tribunal derived from a government common to both parties" existed to resolve such "controversies."[41]

Blair argued that "as free negroes are permitted to hold property in all the States, to carry on commerce under the laws of the United States, are entitled to bounties . . . they must be embraced in a class of citizens." Blair's most convincing argument came toward the end of the brief when he quoted directly from the Missouri law that provided "for the residence of 'free negroes or mulattoes who produce a certificate of citizenship from some one of the United States.'" This quote from the Missouri law, Blair said, "is a recognition, both by Congress and by Missouri, which precludes the courts of both governments from holding . . . that such persons could under no circumstances become citizens of that state."[42]

On February 11, 1856, three days after Blair filed the brief, the Supreme Court commenced hearing oral arguments on the Dred Scott case.

Following custom, the court convened at 11 A.M. on that day; also according to custom, the justices entered the courtroom through a door behind the bench,

40. Blair brief in Dred Scott case.
41. Ibid.
42. Ibid.

preceded by the Marshal of the Court, who, walking backward with his face toward the door and the entering justices, announced in a loud voice, "The Honorable, the Judges of the Supreme Court of the United States."[43]

The room itself, with its stone-vaulted ceiling resting on Doric columns, was located directly below the chamber of the United States Senate, and was part of the old Capitol building. Intended originally to serve as a crypt for the remains of the nation's first president, George Washington, it was never used for that purpose, but it still retained the appearance and feel of a mausoleum, its dark and windowless interior lit only by the faint yellow light from flickering gas lamps along the walls.[44]

Dressed in a black silk robe, Chief Justice Roger Taney led the eight associate justices into the chamber. At age seventy-nine, Taney was a tall, "flat-chested and stooped man" with "homely features and tobacco-stained teeth." Already in bad health when he was sworn in as chief justice twenty years earlier, Taney had outlived several administrations and would outlive still more. Soft-spoken, he "presided gently but firmly over the Court" and his judicial opinions, "written in a plain, dry style, were much praised for their lucidity and pointedness."[45]

Filing in behind Taney were the eight justices of the court, among whom the stern and swarthy Peter V. Daniel of Virginia and dour, ruddy-faced Robert Grier of Pennsylvania stood out from the others: James M. Wayne of Georgia, John Catron of Tennessee, John McLean of Ohio, John A. Campbell of Alabama, Samuel Nelson of New York, John McLean of Ohio, and Benjamin Curtis of Massachusetts. Seated together and peering over the high bench at the spectators seated below, the faces of the justices, as one author noted, would have delighted Charles Dickens. Seven of these associate justices were Democrats and one was a Whig. More importantly, four were "unreserved defenders of slavery"—Daniel, Wayne, Catron, and Campbell—who along with Chief Justice Taney, gave the court a decidedly proslavery cast.[46]

According to the record book of the proceedings of the court, the arguments before the justices commenced on Monday, February 11 with Montgomery Blair, who was followed on Tuesday by Henry Geyer. On Wednesday, February 13, Reverdy Johnson spoke, followed again by Montgomery Blair, who, unable to finish his remarks, was allowed to continue the following day, Thursday, February 14.[47] Unfortunately, no transcripts were made at that time of arguments before the court. Historians, therefore, writing on the Dred Scott case before the United

---

43. John B. Ellis, *The Sights and Secrets of the National Capitol*, 258.

44. Even though Mrs. Washington gave her consent, the Virginia legislature protested moving the president's body to the new Capitol, and Washington's grave remained at Mount Vernon. Ibid., 65.

45. Fehrenbacher, *Dred Scott*, 227.

46. James MacGregor Burns, *The Vineyard of Liberty*, 575; Fehrenbacher, *Dred Scott*, 234.

47. Record book of proceedings of the Supreme Court, 8263, 8269, 8271, 8273, archives, USSC.

States Supreme Court, have been required to rely on newspaper reports and comments from participants to recreate, as best they could, what transpired in the court's chamber during those four days. Out of this mountain of speculation, several overall observations emerge.

First, based on comments by observers, Montgomery Blair's presentation before the court was said not to have been very impressive. It could have been Blair's awkward manner or his high-pitched voice, or perhaps his tendency toward windy oratory. Whatever the reason, he seemed "to be overmatched against the opposing counsel."[48]

On the other hand, there were indications that the court was extremely interested in the case and listened attentively to the arguments presented by the three lawyers. Indicative of this interest was the court's grant of a request by Reverdy Johnson that each attorney be allowed an unprecedented three hours for oral arguments instead of the customary two hours. Obviously, the court felt the additional time for arguments was needed and justified in the Dred Scott case.

By far the most significant observation, however, was that Henry Geyer and Reverdy Johnson, in their arguments before the justices, had challenged the constitutionality of the Missouri Compromise. The two attorneys probably argued that Congress, when it originally passed the act in 1820, had lacked the power to deny American citizens their right to slave property in the territories.[49] Geyer and Johnson probably told the court that Dred Scott was never made free by reason of residency in Wisconsin territory because Wisconsin itself had never been free. Whatever else might be speculated about what went on in the courtroom, it is almost certain that during that portion of the oral arguments by Geyer and Johnson, the two Sanford attorneys had the full and undivided attention of the court. Perhaps at that moment all nine justices leaned over the bench, just a little bit more than was customary, to make sure they heard every word. As historian Don E. Fehrenbacher observed, "the Dred Scott case and the major political issue of the day had finally converged."[50]

After the arguments had been completed, the Supreme Court justices met twice during the following two weeks to discuss the case. Then, on February 28, they adjourned for one month.

In St. Louis, Roswell Field had been following the developments in Washington. On March 12, Field wrote to Montgomery Blair.

> I rec'd your brief in the Dred Scott case and your two letters relating to it. I have delayed writing to you in the expectation that the case would soon be decided &

48. A quote attributed to Horace Greeley of the *New York Tribune,* who attended the proceedings. Fehrenbacher, *Dred Scott,* 282.

49. Based on several eastern newspaper reports on the arguments before the court. Ehrlich, *They Have No Rights,* 95.

50. Fehrenbacher, *Dred Scott,* 288.

that I should have the opportunity of congratulating you on the result. As the Court has taken its long recess without coming to a decision I will not delay longer the expression of my gratification at the able manner in which you have presented the questions to the court.[51]

Nowhere in his letter to Blair did Field mention the Missouri Compromise or his thoughts on the question raised by Geyer and Johnson as to its constitutionality. Neither did the letter mention Dred Scott, who was now working in Field's office.

Field also did not mention another matter, one that had nothing to do with Dred Scott or the Supreme Court, but one that nevertheless must have been much on Field's mind during those months in late 1855 when he and Blair worked on the points to be argued before the court. The preceding May his son Charles, only six months old, had died; now, just two weeks after the court's adjournment, death had claimed yet another son, two-year-old William Bradley Field, on February 21, 1856.[52]

51. Typescript copy of letter from Roswell Field to Montgomery Blair, March 12, 1856, Dred Scott Collection, MHS.

52. Charles James Field died on May 19, 1855, Field family record, Ludlow-Field-Maury Family Papers, MHS.

The Court Decision

Whatever optimism Roswell Field felt in the spring of 1856 that a favorable decision would be forthcoming from the United States Supreme Court, and that after ten years of litigation Dred and Harriet Scott would finally be granted freedom, was slowly but steadily eroded during the subsequent months. By the winter of 1856, Field's hopes were probably all but dashed.

What was even more disheartening, and likely brought Field to the point where he no longer cared what verdict the court reached as long as the Scotts got their freedom, was the grim turn of events within his family; after claiming his sons Bradley and Charles, death would by winter knock twice more on the door of the Field home on 135 South Fifth Street. The biting cold winds of that winter expunged forever those once-happy summer evenings when Roswell Field, with his violin in hand and his children about him, sat on the front steps and played the songs he remembered from his youth on Newfane Hill.

About two months after Field wrote to Montgomery Blair expressing his anticipation of a favorable decision by the high tribunal, the justices announced they wanted the attorneys for both sides to return to the court once again for further arguments. The date set for these new arguments was the next court term in December—some nine months distant.[1]

In announcing the delay, Chief Justice Taney stated as the reason that the court wanted to re-argue two legal issues: one on the plea of abatement, and the other on black citizenship. Some Washington observers, however, hinted the

1. Order "that this cause" be re-argued, May 12, 1856, Proceedings of the Court, 8413, Archives, USSC.

court had another reason, this one political rather than judicial.[2] The Southern-dominated court, they said, wanted to delay the Dred Scott decision until after the upcoming 1856 presidential election. Such a delay would deprive the newly formed Republican Party of a major issue in the campaign, and would also prevent Justice John McLean of Ohio, who was seeking the presidential nomination as a Republican, from writing "a ringing dissent with a denunciation of the Kansas-Nebraska Act."[3]

For the court to delay its decision until after the election indicated that the justices were leaning toward a controversial decision and one that the new Republican Party and the North would view as politically unfavorable. If true, the rumors confirmed Roswell Field's worst fears, for both he and Montgomery Blair agreed that the injection of politics into the deliberations of the court presented the biggest obstacle Dred Scott faced in obtaining a favorable decision. Field believed, as he told Blair, that Dred Scott had a strong case for freedom and "that there could be no doubt about the issue if factious politicks did not mingle in the counsels of the court."[4] During the spring and summer of 1856, Field had ample cause for concern.

When Reverdy Johnson and Henry Geyer questioned the constitutionality of the Missouri Compromise in their arguments before the court in February 1856, they brought the Dred Scott case into the very center of the political controversy that most divided the North and the South. That controversy centered on the extension of slavery into territories that antislavery forces felt should be free. The Kansas-Nebraska Act had opened both the Kansas and Nebraska territories to slaves; in challenging the Missouri Compromise, the proslavery advocates were now seeking to bring slaves into areas north of Missouri where, for more than thirty-five years, slavery had been prohibited by an act of Congress. If, indeed, as Southern politicians argued, slave property was protected by the U.S. Constitution, some Northerners feared it would permit slave-owners to take their slaves anywhere within the country without fear of loss.

Thus, the Dred Scott case, largely unnoticed by the press until Sanford's attorneys introduced the issue of the Missouri Compromise, quickly became the focus of national attention in 1856, and by the end of the year, Dred Scott's name was known to most Americans who followed national events. Dred and Harriet Scott were stripped of their personal identities as human beings, and converted into "an abstract constitutional issue."[5]

Further adding to the likelihood that politics would enter into the court's deliberations in this case was a growing feeling, especially among some Southern

2. Hill, *Decisive Battles,* 127.

3. Carl B. Swisher, *History of the Supreme Court of the United States,* 608.

4. Typescript copy of letter from Roswell Field to Montgomery Blair, March 12, 1856, Dred Scott Collection, MHS.

5. Fehrenbacher, *Dred Scott,* 305; Stampp, *America in 1857,* 82.

politicians, that a judicial resolution by the Supreme Court offered the only hope of resolving the territorial question, since neither Congress nor the White House seemed capable of doing so.[6] If the court decided to bow to this pressure and enter the fray, the court already had on its docket the Dred Scott case involving exactly the issues in question.

During 1856, as Roswell Field and Montgomery Blair planned the strategy for the re-arguments Blair was to present to the court in December, the territorial question continued to heat up. On the national level, the issue was at the very center of the political debates in the presidential election. Three candidates were in the race, and each was forced to take a position on the expansion of slavery in the territories. In the end James Buchanan, a Democrat with Southern support, triumphed over John C. Fremont, Republican, and Millard Fillmore of the American Party. Buchanan, running on a platform that supported the right of voters in the territories to decide the slavery issue, was viewed by some perhaps as representing the middle ground between two extremes: the "black Republicanism" of Fremont and the Know-Nothing nativism of Fillmore.[7]

In Missouri, the slavery issue was kept in the news by the emergence in 1856 of a Free Labor movement in St. Louis, championed by Frank Blair and others. Playing on the mounting fear that the Southern slaveocracy was seeking to turn white labor into slave labor throughout the country, the *Missouri Democrat* asked, "Shall white men—workingmen—laboring men, be made slaves, and reviled as slaves, and be placed on the same level with the negro?" The answer was a definite no, and on the eve of state election day in August 1856, according to a newspaper report, "thousands upon thousands and thousands thrice" met in the rotunda of the St. Louis Courthouse and on the streets surrounding the building to show support for the movement and its leaders. The following day, Frank Blair was elected to Congress, an achievement by the Free Labor movement that was much heralded in the East. For Southerners, on the other hand, the results in St. Louis caused alarm; a large Southern city had fallen into the hands of antislavery forces.[8]

In the South, antislavery successes during 1856 only added to mounting fears of slave uprisings. The *St. Louis Intelligencer,* citing reports of recent slave rebellions in Texas and near Memphis, noted that "talk of negro insurrections has become rather

6. Swisher, *History of Supreme Court,* 590.

7. Fremont was Thomas H. Benton's son-in-law, but Benton, who was running for governor of Missouri in 1856, supported Buchanan, believing Buchanan would "restore Jacksonian principles" and that Fremont would cause "sectional parties." Trusten Polk won the governor's seat. Benton, ill with cancer, died within two years. Scharf, *History of St. Louis City and County,* vol. 1, 593.

8. Merkel, *Anti-Slavery Controversy,* 24; *Missouri Daily Democrat,* August 3, 1856; Stampp, *America in 1857,* 141; In 1850, among the larger Southern cities—Baltimore, Charleston, Savannah, Mobile, Louisville, New Orleans, Norfolk, Richmond, and Washington—St. Louis with a population of 77,860 ranked third behind Baltimore and New Orleans in size. Wade, *Slavery in Cities,* 32.

frequent." The paper reported that in New Madrid County, Missouri, blacks "are joining with negroes from Albion County [Tennessee]" who have "concocted a general insurrection to take place about December 25."[9]

But the events that did most during 1856 to keep the issue of slavery in the territories before the American public were those on the Kansas-Missouri border. Hardly a day went by in which there was not some new violence to report, as more and more settlers from both the North and the South poured into eastern Kansas. Typical of the violence was that described in a St. Louis newspaper and headlined, "Great Excitement along the Borders."

> A gentleman who arrived yesterday afternoon from Weston, on [board] the *David Tatum,* reports that the most intense excitement prevails along the borders of Missouri and Kansas. Of the Free State party, men, women and children were flying in all directions. While the *David Tatum* was lying at Leavenworth, upwards of one hundred of these fugitives went on board. These persons had left behind them all their property, which had been taken possession of by those who ordered them to leave. The greatest and most shocking excesses had been committed a few days ago within five miles of Leavenworth. A party of men called at a house, and inquired for the head of the family. They were told he was absent . . . . "D—n your souls, then come out here yourselves—we want you." A mother and daughter were then taken out into the bushes, where they were kept all night, being subjected to the most foul indignities. In the morning they were allowed to crawl back home, more dead than alive. At Kansas City robbery of horses and valuables continued to be of common occurrence, and murders were almost equally frequent. A resident of Clay county had boasted that he would have the scalp of an abolitionist. Crossing the river to Leavenworth, he went a few miles back into the country, and shortly returned with a reeking scalp which he exhibited. His victim was a mechanic, just arrived in the territory. He had just returned from Lawrence, where he had left his wife, and was seeking employment at the time he was shot and scalped. Gov. Price had been in the disturbed districts, but was hurrying home, hourly expecting a dispatch from the President, ordering out the militia of the State. In this event, he would command them in person. Atchinson was also on the borders fanning the movements against Kansas. Lexington [a town in Missouri] has five hundred men under arms. Jackson, Clay and Platte counties were each to furnish the same number. Three thousand men from Missouri are expected to arrive in the territory in a few days.[10]

Given such reports, and the inability of a cautious president or a deadlocked Congress to contain the mounting sectional hostility, a vacuum was created, as one historian put it, that "some force was bound to fill." Since the issue, as many perceived it, involved the constitutional question of whether Congress had the power to regulate slavery in the territories, the vacuum seemed to invite "a judicial settlement" of the question. As Justice Wayne was later to state in his court opinion,

9. *St. Louis Intelligencer,* November 20, 1856.
10. *Missouri Republican,* August 25, 1856.

"The peace and harmony of the country required the settlement . . . by judicial decision."[11]

Southerners appeared to be more "willing to entrust the question to the Supreme Court" than were Northerners, for the proslavery makeup of the court gave Southerners a greater degree of confidence in the outcome. On the other hand, the Republican viewpoint on Supreme Court involvement in the issue was typified by the comment of Horace Greeley of the *New York Tribune,* who said, "For one, I may say, with every respect for those Judicial dignitaries, that I would rather trust a dog with my dinner." Also, some slavery opponents watching slave-owners pour into Kansas, where the land was suited for neither cotton nor tobacco, worried that a Supreme Court dominated by Southerners "might force slavery into the free states," a concern that only a few years earlier would have seemed "a paranoid illusion."[12] Such worries were not entirely without foundation perhaps, for there were Southerners who believed that the expansion of slavery was necessary for Southern survival and constitutional government. Judge Napton of Missouri wrote:

> The duration of this government depends upon our capacity peacefully and consti-tutionally to have these questions adjusted. . . . These questions must be settled. Will the South acquiesce in a virtual exclusion of her slaves from all new territory? Ought she to do so? Can she do so with safety? . . . If we cannot carry slavery into Kansas, it is quite obvious that we cannot succeed anywhere else. The result will be that no more slave states will be created. The majority of the North over the South will in a few years become overwhelming, in both houses of Congress. This majority can mold the Constitution to their own purposes. What will Constitutional guarantees be worth under such circumstances?[13]

As interest in the Dred Scott case mounted, and as the date approached for re-arguments, the justices of the Supreme Court came under increasing pressure to resolve judicially the issue of slavery in the northern territories. The *New York Courier* declared that it was "the most important [question] that has ever been brought before that tribunal."[14]

Rumors of this mounting pressure on the court did not escape Montgomery Blair, and during the months preceding the December term of the court, Blair set about finding an attorney with qualifications equal to those of Reverdy Johnson to

11. Burns, *Vineyard of Liberty,* 87; Stampp, *America in 1857,* 87; Edward S. Corwin, *The Doctrine of Judicial Review,* 132.

12. Swisher, *History of Supreme Court,* 599; *New York Tribune,* December 19, 1855, in Swisher, 591; William M. Wiecek, "Slavery and Abolition before the United States Supreme Court, 1820–1860," in *Law, Constitution and Slavery,* edited by Paul Finkelman, 34.

13. Undated entry for the year 1857, Napton journal, 201, William B. Napton Papers, MHS.

14. Stampp, *America in 1857,* 90; *New York Courier,* December 18, 1856, quoted in William Smith, 390.

assist him in arguing the constitutional questions. Blair stated, "As I perceived that the cause involved important issues, which might possibly be engulfed in the great political controversy then just emerging in relation to the power of Congress over the territory of the United States, I felt it my duty to seek assistance . . . to call to its support all the aid I could command."[15] Blair found the task a difficult one, and it was not until a few days before the re-arguments began that Blair acquired the assistance of George Ticknor Curtis, a prominent Boston attorney.

Whether Roswell Field had a voice in the selection of Curtis is not known. In fact, it is not even clear whether Field was at this time actively participating in the Dred Scott case.

Sometime in October 1856, Field, like Blair, also found himself in need of "assistance" and "help," and for the first time in his law career brought another attorney into his office to assist him. Field's caseload may have grown to the point where additional help was needed, or perhaps—and this seems more likely—there were more pressing needs other than his law practice during the last months of 1856.

The attorney who went to work in Field's law office in the fall of 1856 was a new arrival in the city named Arba N. Crane. Like Field, he was a Vermont native. Only twenty-two years old, Crane came from an old Vermont family and had attended Harvard Law School before coming to St. Louis. His major interest was railway law, and he had prepared an impressive treatise on railway cases while living in New England.[16]

Like Roswell Field, Crane probably had little experience in Southern slave law, but after his arrival in St. Louis, and while working in Field's law office, Crane met Dred Scott. As Crane later recalled, he became acquainted with Scott, and soon took on his shoulders the slave's cause. Crane related that as a bachelor, having no need to hurry home in the evenings to a wife and family, he frequently worked late in Field's law office, and during those evening hours talked to Scott about the slave's freedom suit, and soon became involved in the litigation.[17]

15. *National Intelligencer,* December 24, 1856, Dred Scott Collection, MHS.

16. Typed manuscript, T. K. Skinker, "Arba Nelson Crane, A Memorial," Dred Scott Collection, MHS.

17. John W. Burgess, *The Middle Period, 1817–1858,* 29; Crane claimed he was responsible for initiating Dred Scott's suit for freedom, incorrect since Crane was not in St. Louis when the litigation commenced, nor when Field filed the federal suit. A letter written by John F. Lee relates, "Mr. Crane told me that one night when he was sitting in Field's office (he was then a bachelor and had no home ties) Dred Scott, who had charge of cleaning the office, came into it to perform his duties. Crane having nothing to do entered into conversation with Dred Scott, and learning Scott's history, came to the conclusion that Scott was entitled to his freedom, and informed Scott of this. Scott accepted his conclusions without displaying much interest in the result, and Crane went to work on the case." Letter of February 15, 1907, Dred Scott Collection, MHS.

Whether Roswell Field turned over full responsibility for the Dred Scott case to the young attorney—or for that matter even permitted him to work on the suit—is uncertain. What seems likely, however, is that Crane, almost from his first day in Field's law office, assisted on the Scott case, and even though Roswell Field remained as Dred and Harriet's legal counsel, Crane was very much involved.[18] Such an arrangement would have been a logical step for Field to make, and one that was probably at that time in the Scotts' best interests as clients, for in those weeks preceding the re-argument of the case before the Supreme Court, Field's attention was directed elsewhere. On November 18, three weeks before the Supreme Court reconvened, Roswell Field's wife, Frances, died.[19]

Field has left behind no notes or correspondence that tell of his wife's death, or of his thoughts and feelings about it. On a family record sheet that Field later prepared for his children, Field simply wrote her name, Frances Maria Field, and death date, November 18, 1856, nothing more.[20]

Frances was thirty years old when she died, and her death followed by two months the birth of the Field's only daughter, Frances Victoria. Years later, a son would attribute his mother's death to cholera, but this seems very unlikely.[21] Frances Field may have been ill for some time and her death may have been anticipated. This would have required Field to spend more time away from the office, and would have prompted his decision to hire the young Arba Crane as an assistant.

Frances's death left Roswell Field with two young sons, one six years of age and another five, and a two-month-old infant daughter. The critical needs of these young children upon their mother's death were probably what prompted Field, when he wired back home to New England with the news of his wife's death, to ask also for help from his sister Mary in Massachusetts.[22] Mary, recently widowed, responded immediately by dispatching her unmarried, thirty-one-year-

18. Crane was active in the Scott case in June 1857, when a New York reporter visited. Crane was identified as "Dred's lawyer" and Dred Scott is quoted as saying he would do anything Crane asked, for "he was his friend, and knew best what he should do." *Frank Leslie's Illustrated Newspaper*, June 27, 1857.

19. "Died - On Tuesday, Nov. 18, 1856, Mrs. Frances M. Field, wife of R. M. Field, Esq., aged 30 years. Funeral on Thursday afternoon, 9 o'clock from No. 135 So. Fifth St." *Missouri Republican*, November 18, 1856.

20. Family record, Ludlow-Field-Maury Family Papers, MHS.

21. Cholera was not active then in St. Louis. Fifty-seven deaths were reported that week in the newspaper, none from cholera. Leading causes of death were croup, dysentery, and inflammation of the bowels. *St. Louis Intelligencer*, November 18, 1856.

22. Roswell Field's older sister, Mary, was twice widowed. After graduating from the Emma Willard Seminary in Troy, New York, she married in 1824 a merchant named Theodore F. French by whom she had three children, one of them Mary Field French, born in 1825. After French's death in 1828, she married Thomas Jones of Massachusetts and by him had three children before his death in 1853. Charles Kellogg Field III, *Field Family*, 50; Typed biography of Samuel M. Jones by John W. Burgess, Field Collection, JL.

old daughter, Mary Field French, to St. Louis to assist her brother and help care for his three young children.

As was customary in St. Louis, the doorway of the Field home on South Fifth was draped in black cloth, and on the day after Frances's death, Roswell Field accepted calls in the front parlor of the home from friends and relatives of his wife who came to offer condolences. Two days later, on a crisp and sunny fall afternoon, as families throughout St. Louis observed the Thanksgiving Day holiday, Roswell Field followed by carriage behind a hearse as it bore the body of his wife through the largely deserted streets of the city to Bellefontaine Cemetery. Here, on a wooded hillside near the confluence of the Missouri and Mississippi Rivers, some two hours by carriage from the city, Field buried his wife.[23] Field had personally selected the grave site, and it would serve as the Field family burial plot. Later, he had the remains of his three children who had died previously moved to Bellefontaine and reburied alongside the new grave of their mother.

On December 15, some three weeks after Frances Field's death, and probably about the time Mary Field French arrived in St. Louis from Amherst, a new brief in the Dred Scott case was filed by Montgomery Blair with the Supreme Court in Washington. On the same day, re-arguments in the case commenced before the court.

During the ten months since the first brief for Dred Scott was filed with the court, Blair's arguments had significantly changed, and the length of the brief had grown fourfold, from ten printed pages to forty. The two questions on which Field wanted a court ruling—citizenship and slave residence on free soil—were still covered in detail, but a whole new section totaling some fifteen pages was added on the question of slavery in the territories, the issue introduced by Sanford's attorneys. This territorial question was also again the primary focus in Henry Geyer's arguments, and the issue dominated his twelve-page brief, which he filed with the court several days earlier.[24]

While Blair added this new section on the issue of slavery in the territories, the portion on slave freedom that Field most wanted before the court still dominated the opening section of the brief. In the arguments on slave freedom Field and Blair did not waver, and, if anything, the arguments were strengthened. Their purpose

23. Field purchased the burial plot at Bellefontaine Cemetery following his wife's death. Measuring twenty feet square, the lot number is 611 on block 73. The cemetery was established in 1849, and many early St. Louis residents are buried there, including Senator Thomas Benton and members of the Blow and Charless families. Adjacent is Calvary Cemetery, where Dred Scott is buried, established by the Catholic Church several years later.

24. Arguments of Montgomery Blair, counsel for the Plaintiff in Error. Printed by Gibbons Printer, 511 Ninth Street, Washington, D.C., Blair Collection, Library of Congress, Washington, D.C.; Case for the Defendant in Error, December Term 1856, vol. 1, file copies of briefs, archives, USSC.

was to discredit the majority opinion of Missouri Supreme Court Justice Scott in which the court had discarded years of legal precedent in denying freedom to Dred Scott, a decision later used against Scott by Judge Wells in the federal court. Quite clearly, this was an issue that Field and Blair thought was important to Scott's freedom, although strangely the issue was completely ignored by Henry Geyer, who does not even mention it in his brief. The goal of Field and Blair was obviously to have the United States Supreme Court overrule Judge Scott's opinion in Missouri's highest court and accept instead the minority opinion of Judge Gamble, which supported the Scotts' claim to freedom. In Blair's brief, Justice Scott was depicted as supporting "the overthrow of the established law" when, as a Supreme Court justice, he was part of a "tribunal sworn to uphold" the law. Judge Gamble, on the other hand, was described as a "venerable jurist" and the "universal voice of the profession." He was proclaimed as the "chief" of the Missouri bar, having "no superior."[25]

The Supreme Court allowed the attorneys a total of twelve hours for oral arguments, three hours each day for four consecutive days. Montgomery Blair, Henry Geyer, and Reverdy Johnson each took one day; and on the fourth day, December 18, each of these attorneys briefly addressed the court, as did Scott's new legal counsel on constitutional law, George Curtis. Curtis spoke for one hour, and his remarks were universally described as scholarly.[26]

As might have been expected, most of the press interest centered on the arguments that involved the issue of slavery in the territories, the major controversy then before the nation. Within a day the reports from Washington began trickling in to St. Louis newspapers, and many residents were first made aware of the Missouri slave, living in their midst, who had now become the focus of national attention.[27] Amid reports from Washington, accounts of violence on the Kansas-Missouri border, and new rumors of slave uprisings in the South, almost hidden away in one of the news columns of the *Missouri Republican* on December 23 was this death notice:

> December 21st. Frances Victoria, only daughter of R. M. Field, aged 3 months and 8 days. The funeral will take place this (Tuesday) morning at 11 o'clock at No. 135 South Fifth.[28]

Once again the front doorway of the Field residence on South Fifth Street was draped in black cloth, and once again Roswell Field stood in the parlor of his home

25. Arguments of Montgomery Blair, 23.
26. Ehrlich, *They Have No Rights,* 121.
27. The *Missouri Democrat* published Blair's brief in full on page 1 of four issues, calling it "a very able argument" that "will well repay perusal" by readers. *Missouri Democrat,* January 27 through February 3, 1857.
28. *Missouri Republican,* December 23, 1856.

greeting visitors as they came to offer their sympathy and words of condolence. And once again, as he had done a month earlier, Field followed in a carriage, for some two hours, as the hearse, pulled by horses, and bearing his three-month-old daughter's body, slowly made its way out Bellefontaine Road to the cemetery.

On this rather cold December day, there were now five fresh graves on the Field family grave site, five rectangular mounds of earth, each newly turned and piled high with clumps of Missouri clay. In the center was the grave of Frances Field, and surrounding it four smaller graves for the Fields' children: Theodore, Bradley, Charles, and now baby Frances.

Perhaps sometime during the next week, Roswell Field decided to vacate the house at 135 South Fifth Street and to send his two young sons east to live with his sister and niece in Amherst. Just what prompted this decision is uncertain. Field may have bowed, as one family member said, to the urging of his sister Mary, who felt that it was not good for two boys, so very young, to be raised in a home without a woman to nurture and look after them. Another family member related that the idea came solely from Field, who, foreseeing the oncoming civil war, felt it would be better for his two sons to be raised in New England rather than St. Louis.[29] Whatever the reason for the decision, and regardless of whose prompting brought it about, when Mary Field French returned to Massachusetts several weeks later, she did so with her two wards, Eugene and Roswell. The father was left behind and alone in a silent and empty house.

Within the next few weeks, Field vacated the house at 135 South Fifth and took up once again the life of a single man, living alone in a single room and taking his meals in a public house.

Historians, politicians, and legalists for several generations have devoted much study to the deliberations of the United States Supreme Court justices during the weeks prior to their decision in the Dred Scott case. Numerous books and articles have been written on these deliberations as authors have sought—and continue to seek—explanations as to why the justices decided as they did. Throughout these years the Dred Scott case, even with ongoing study, remains preeminent as "the most controversial decision of the century and perhaps in the history of the Supreme Court."[30]

29. Kathryn Kilby Borland, *Eugene Field, Young Poet*, 6; Slason Thompson, *Study in Heredity*, 52. In the St. Louis Directory for 1857, Field's office and residence are listed at 58½ South Fourth Street. Field's quarters remain at that address until the 1867 directory, in which his office and residence are listed at 318 Market Street.

30. "The facts of *Dred Scott* have all the complexity of a well-constructed question on a law school examination." Earl M. Maltz, "Slavery, Federalism, and the Structure of the Constitution," 466; Finkelman, *Slavery in the Courtroom*, 45; In 1974 the *American Bar Association Journal* conducted a survey among lawyers, judges, and law professors on milestones in legal history. Of twenty milestones chosen, fourteen were Supreme Court decisions, and only *Dred Scott v. Sandford* "was drawn from the 115 years between 1819 and 1935." Fehrenbacher, *Dred Scott*, 594.

However, it was not the uniqueness of the legal issues contained in the Dred Scott case that gave it historic stature, but rather the court's departure from what previously had been clear and well-settled principles of law, and its almost blind willingness to permit itself to be dragged into the vortex of a national political tempest. The court could very easily have avoided the political fury it was about to unleash, had it limited its decision and narrowly decided the case "on well-established and non-controversial principles." It seems that until a month before the decision was announced, this was the intent of the court. According to what facts have been uncovered, Justice Nelson was to have prepared the opinion of the court and in doing so was given instructions by the justices "not to touch upon either the citizenship of Negroes" nor "on the power of Congress over slavery in the territories." The decision would have related solely to Scott's freedom upon return to Missouri, and here, as the court had done earlier in the Kentucky case of *Strader v. Graham,* the state law—in this case that of Missouri—would have been upheld. Dred Scott, of course, would have been denied freedom, but on the national stage that would have been of little consequence.[31]

Such a decision, had it been made, would have been a disappointment to Roswell Field, not only because it would have denied the Scotts their freedom, but also because it would have failed to address the question of African American citizenship, the one issue upon which Field felt it was "very desirable" to obtain a Supreme Court opinion.[32] And likewise, such a decision would have disappointed Henry Geyer, for while it would have been a victory for his client, John Sanford, it would have avoided addressing the South's urgent question of congressional power over slavery in the territories.

Therefore, the Supreme Court, had it issued such a narrow decision, would have disappointed the opposing counsels in the suit and very likely other unnamed parties who supported either Dred Scott or John Sanford. Both Field and Geyer, as each had clearly set forth in the briefs before the court, were seeking opinions on issues that the court—for obvious reasons—was reluctant to touch.

In addition to Roswell Field and Henry Geyer, there were others who would also have been disappointed had the court held to a narrow opinion and not ruled on the question of African American citizenship or on the issue of slavery in the territories. The American public itself probably would have been disappointed, as would President-elect James Buchanan.

By 1857, the American public had become fully involved in the Dred Scott case, and it was Justice Campbell who alerted the court to the public's interest, pointing out to his fellow justices that the case had been twice argued and that the public had been led to expect a decision on the issues. The court, he said, would

---

31. Ambrose Dockow, *Historic Opinions of the United States Supreme Court,* 118; Ehrlich, *They Have No Rights,* 127; Fehrenbacher, *Dred Scott,* 307; Finkelman, *Slavery in the Courtroom,* 46.

32. Typescript letter from Roswell Field to Montgomery Blair, January 7, 1856, Dred Scott Collection, MHS.

be condemned as failing to do its duty if it avoided ruling on the issues. The *New York Herald* commented that while the case involved "the freedom of a nigger of the name of Dred Scott," it was the United States Supreme Court that was on trial before the people.[33]

But probably the strongest pressure on the court to rule on the controversial issues in the case came from the president-elect. Buchanan, arriving in Washington on January 27, 1857, prior to his inauguration, almost immediately made contact with one of the justices to find out when the court was going to rule. Buchanan was not concerned about Dred Scott's fate, but he was interested in what the court might say on the constitutionality of the Missouri Compromise. Buchanan saw himself as the country's peacemaker, and believed his election constituted a mandate "to save the Union by repression of the abolitionist movement." A ruling on the territorial question in the Dred Scott case would "show that the three branches of the government were solidly together in their efforts to suppress abolitionist agitation." In the following weeks, during the court's deliberations, "direct but characteristically subtle" correspondence flowed back and forth between Buchanan and Justices Catron and Grier on the Dred Scott case.[34]

At this point the court made what some historians have called a "momentous change" in direction. The justices decided not to issue a narrow opinion as originally planned, and instead instructed Chief Justice Taney to write an opinion that covered all the major issues in the case. Also, word was leaked to Buchanan that a decision in the Dred Scott case would soon be forthcoming, and it would fulfill the need "he so desperately desired."[35]

On Wednesday, March 4, Chief Justice Taney gave the oath of office to James Buchanan on the east portico of the nation's capitol. Before a large audience assembled for the occasion, President Buchanan, in his inaugural address, said:

> A difference of opinion has arisen in regard to the point of time when the people of a Territory shall decide this question [of slavery] for themselves. This is, happily, a matter of but little importance. Besides, it is a judicial question, which legitimately belongs to the Supreme Court of the United States, before whom it is now pending, and will, it is understood, be speedily and finally settled.[36]

Then President Buchanan, aware privately of what the court had decided, assured his audience that "in common with all good citizens" he would "cheerfully submit" to whatever decision the court finally rendered.[37]

33. Swisher, *History of Supreme Court,* 619; *New York Herald,* December 25, 1856, in Swisher, *History of Supreme Court,* 614; Hopkins, *Dred Scott's Case,* vi.

34. Swisher, *History of Supreme Court,* 610, 615, 618; Fehrenbacher, *Dred Scott,* 307; Buchanan urged Justice Grier, who was from Pennsylvania, to join "the majority" so that the court's decision would not be seen as solely the decision of Southern justices. Corwin, *Judicial Review,* 132.

35. Ehrlich, *They Have No Rights,* 129; Fehrenbacher, *Dred Scott,* 312.

36. *St. Louis Leader,* March 9, 1857.

37. Ibid.

Oliver Wendell Holmes, a later justice of the Supreme Court, would say that "great cases are called great not by reason of their real importance in shaping the law of the future but because of some accident of immediate overwhelming interest which appeals to the feelings and distorts the judgment." In the Dred Scott case, the immediate interests "were so great that they led the Court to go out of its way to create a great case for the purpose of settling a pressing political issue."[38]

On the morning of Friday, March 6, 1857, two days after President Buchanan's inauguration, the United States Supreme Court handed down its opinion in the Dred Scott case. It was probably on the following day, Saturday, that Roswell Field first learned of the decision when he read wire dispatches from Washington carried on the pages of several of the St. Louis newspapers.[39]

The *Saint Louis Leader,* under a headline reading "U.S. Supreme Court on Negro Status," reported what it claimed was "a full and elaborate statement of the news of the Court" contained in a majority opinion read by Chief Justice Roger Taney. Taney's delivery of the opinion, according to the newspaper, took about three hours, and "it was listened to with profound attention in a crowded courtroom."[40]

According to the news dispatch, Chief Justice Taney's opinion covered three "important points" that the dispatch listed in this order:

First, "negroes, either slave or free, as men of the race, are not citizens of the United States by the Constitution."

Second, the Ordinance of 1787, after the adoption of the Constitution, could "not confer freedom or citizenship within the Northwest Territory" to Negroes.

And third, the "Missouri Compromise in so far as it undertook to exclude negro slavery . . . was a legislative act exceeding the powers of Congress, and void and of no legal effect."[41]

Listed in the dispatch as one of the "incidental points" in the opinion was the court's ruling that Dred Scott was not free, and that "a slave in the State of Missouri is not affected by the temporary sojourn" in another state and that upon "his return his condition still depends upon the laws of Missouri."[42]

The majority opinion of the United States Supreme Court could not have been clearer: after eleven years of litigation Dred and Harriet Scott were still slaves. Their case had been taken to the nation's highest court, and they had lost.

38. Quoted in Dockow, *Historic Opinions,* 118.

39. In the case of *Dred Scott v. Sandford,* "It is now ordered and adjudged by this court that the judgement of the said Circuit Court in this cause be and the same is hereby reversed for want of jurisdiction in that court and that this cause be and the same is hereby remanded to the said Circuit Court with directions to dismiss the case for want of jurisdiction in that court. Mr. Ch. Jus. Taney." March 6, 1857, proceedings of the United States Supreme Court, 8764, archives, USSC.

40. *St. Louis Leader,* March 7, 1857.

41. Ibid.

42. Ibid.

It is not known how the Scotts were told of the decision, or what their reaction was when they learned of it. Since they could not read, it is likely that the news was conveyed by Roswell Field, or perhaps by Field's assistant, Arba Crane. Field was undoubtedly disappointed by the decision, although probably not surprised, and in all likelihood Dred probably took the announcement better than Field. A St. Louis newspaper reported:

> Dred does not appear to be at all discouraged by the issue of the celebrated case, although it dooms him to slavery. He talks about the affair with the ease of a veteran litigant, though not exactly in technical language and is hugely tickled at the idea of finding himself a personage of such importance. He does not take on airs, however, but laughs heartily when talking of "de fuss dey made dar in Washington bout de ole nigger."[43]

Dred Scott's rather casual and unruffled response to the decision seems to reflect the reaction of St. Louis as well. A Democratic rally in the courthouse that same Saturday night went on as usual, and "every man who is neither a proscriptive Know-Nothing or a fanatical nigger worshipper" was urged to be present. At the St. Louis Theatre the "well-known drama" called "The Old Plantation, or Uncle Tom's Cabin As It Is" was presented as scheduled to an "enthusiastic" audience. Even St. Louis newspaper editors, unlike some of their contemporaries in the East, were unusually restrained in their comments. The Free-Soil *Daily Missouri Democrat* saw the decision as a marked departure from the government "laid down by its founders," and the editor observed that "in the judgment of the Court, slavery is national, and the time-honored immunities of personal liberty are done away." The proslavery *St. Louis Daily Evening News,* on the other hand, called the opinion "able and lucid," and prophetically predicted that a Northern political party would develop in opposition to the decision, but added that such a party would not have "permanent existence" because Judge Taney's decision "can no more be altered than the Constitution changed." The opinion, the paper said, will "have to be obeyed and observed because the refusal to regard it would be actual revolution."[44]

It was probably not until the fuller texts of Justice Taney's opinion found their way into the columns of the St. Louis newspapers a week or so later, that the ire of Roswell Field and other antislavery proponents was fully aroused.[45] Only by

43. *St. Louis Daily Evening News,* April 3, 1857.
44. *St. Louis Leader,* March 7, 1857; *Daily Missouri Democrat,* March 13, 1857; *St. Louis Daily Evening News,* March 12, 1857.
45. The full text of the Taney's opinion appeared on March 13, 1857, in the *Daily Missouri Republican* and the *Missouri Democrat.* Even after copies of the so-called full text reached newspapers, there were reports that the justices were revising their opinions. On March 16, the *Missouri Democrat* informed its readers that the *New York Tribune* reported that the justices were having their opinions privately printed and that Judges Curtis and McLean were making

reading the full decision, and the detailed, reasoned arguments of Taney, was it possible to detect the intensity of the chief justice's racial bigotry, and his clear bias and partiality in support of Southern slavery.

Justice Taney's opinion comprised fifty-five printed pages in Howard's *Reports,* and of these, twenty-one pages were devoted to the issue of slavery in the territories and the court's ruling nullifying the Missouri Compromise.[46] The remaining pages covered primarily the two questions that Roswell Field most wanted the court to rule upon: African American citizenship and slave freedom. Justice Taney devoted only passing attention to the matter of slave freedom, but on Negro citizenship he gave full vent to his deeply held beliefs that African Americans were of an inferior order and excluded from sharing in any of the rights guaranteed white Americans by the Constitution. The Chief Justice stated:

> It is difficult at this day to realize the state of public opinion in relation to that unfortunate race, which prevailed in the civilized and enlightened portions of the world at the time of the Declaration of Independence and when the Constitution of the United States was framed and adopted. But the public history of every European nation displays it in a manner too plain to be mistaken. They had for more than a century before been regarded as beings of an inferior order, and altogether unfit to associate with the white race, either in social or political relations; and so far inferior, that they had no rights which the white man was bound to respect; and that the negro might justly and lawfully be reduced to slavery for his benefit.[47]

The question before the court, Taney pointed out, was whether a black person, whose ancestors were imported into the country as slaves, could become a member of the "political community" that created the Constitution.

> We think they are not, and that they are not included, and were not intended to be included, under the word 'citizens' in the Constitution, and can, therefore, claim none of the rights and privileges which that instrument provides for and secures to citizens of the United States. On the contrary, they were at that time considered as a subordinate and inferior class of beings, who had been subjugated by the dominant race, and whether emancipated or not, yet remained subject to their authority, and had no rights or privileges but such as those who held the power and the government might choose to grant them.[48]

Taney then held that "upon a full and careful consideration of the subject, the court is of the opinion" that "Dred Scott was not a citizen of Missouri within the

revisions. Judge Taney was said to be "altering his materially" and that Judge Catron had "suppressed some portions clearly announced in the court." *Missouri Democrat,* March 16, 1857.

46. 19 Howard, *United States Reports,* 399–454, USSC.

47. Ibid., 407.

48. Ibid., 404.

meaning of the Constitution of the United States, and not entitled to sue in the courts." The lower court, he added, had no jurisdiction in the case.[49]

The issue to which both Field and Blair gave most attention in the briefs—slave residence on free soil—was given but passing mention by Justice Taney. The chief justice said the court had already decided that issue in the Kentucky case of *Strader v. Graham*. Based on that case, Dred Scott's "status, as free or slave, depended on the laws of Missouri, and not of Illinois." In reply to Roswell Field's argument that the Missouri Supreme Court disregarded all legal precedent in making its decision against Scott, Taney simply replied that the court was "satisfied, upon a careful examination of all the cases decided in the State courts of Missouri referred to, that it is now firmly settled by the decisions of the highest court in the State, that Scott and his family upon their return were not free."[50]

What may have most angered Roswell Field about the court's opinion was the criticism directed against him as Dred Scott's counsel for the procedures employed in getting the case before the United States Supreme Court. In the opinion, Taney charged that Field "did not pursue the mode prescribed by law for bringing the judgment of a State court before this court for judgment."[51] Noting that the original case "is yet open and pending in the lower state court," Taney said of Field that he goes to:

> the Circuit Court of the United States, upon the same case and the same evidence, and then against the same party, and proceeds to judgment, and then brings here the same case from the Circuit Court which the law would not have permitted him to bring directly from the State court.[52]

The chief justice added that:

> It would ill become this court to sanction such an attempt to evade the law, or to exercise an appellate power in this circuitous way, which it is forbidden to exercise in the direct and regular and invariable forms of judicial proceedings.[53]

Taney said that Roswell Field, as Scott's attorney, should have brought the case by writ of error from the Supreme Court of Missouri to the United States Supreme Court. Had this been done, the chief justice noted, perhaps with some effort at humor, the case would "have been dismissed for want of jurisdiction."[54] Either way, Dred Scott would have lost. What the chief justice did not mention was that if Roswell Field had followed the legal route Taney recommended, there would

49. Ibid., 452.
50. Ibid., 453.
51. Ibid., 454.
52. Ibid.
53. Ibid.
54. Ibid.

have been no *Dred Scott v. John F. A. Sandford,* and Roger Taney would have been denied his one great opportunity to "save" slavery and the South.

Chief Justice Taney's opinion was labeled the "Opinion of the Court," but it by no means represented a consensus. Each of the other eight justices issued his own opinion, prompting many to wonder during the months and years that followed just what exactly the Supreme Court did decide in the Dred Scott case.[55]

But there was little question about where the justices stood on the issue of Dred Scott's freedom. Of the nine justices on the court, seven explicitly held that Missouri law determined Dred Scott's status and that he, his wife Harriet, and his two daughters were not free, but slaves of John Sanford.[56]

The decision should have come as good news to John Sanford, but it is not certain that he was ever told about it. When the Supreme Court issued its opinion on March 6, 1857, Dred Scott's master was an inmate in an insane asylum in New York City, and before two months passed he would be dead.[57]

The decision by the nation's highest tribunal that ended Dred Scott's eleven-year pilgrimage through the courts in search of freedom did not end Roswell Field's role as legal counsel for the slave and his family.

The four-year relationship between Field as the lawyer and Scott as the client should have ended after Field informed Dred Scott that he had been denied freedom by the Supreme Court of the United States. Instead, Dred continued to show up as usual to clean Field's law office on Chestnut Street, and Field continued as legal counsel to the slave. Just why is unclear.

Perhaps Field formed an attachment for the slave during his years on the case. This would not have been at all unusual. Dred Scott seems to have had a way of making friends in the white community—Francis Murdoch, Charlotte Blow, Edmund LaBeaume, Taylor Blow, Arba Crane, and Joseph Charless, among others. Even seasoned court judges like Alexander Hamilton and Robert Wells seem to have felt a sympathy for him.

A more likely reason, however, is that Roswell Field, even after the Supreme Court's adverse decision, still had hopes that a way might yet be found to free Dred Scott and his family from slavery. When Field agreed in 1852 to take on Dred Scott's case, he had but one goal—the freedom of Dred Scott. Field had recommended a suit in the federal courts based on Scott's residence on free soil. This effort by Field had failed. Yet, according to Missouri law, there were other ways a slave might be freed. One was by manumission.

That manumission might offer the Scotts the chance they so desperately wanted may have occurred to Roswell Field about a week after the Supreme Court's

55. "Chief Justice Taney had the support of the majority of the Court for each point" in his opinion. John S. Vishneski III, "What the Court Decided in *Dred Scott v. Sandford,*" 390.
56. Ibid.
57. John Sanford died in New York City on May 5, 1857, Ehrlich, *They Have No Rights,* 180.

decision. On March 18, as Scott's attorney, Field was summoned before the St. Louis Circuit Court. Judge Alexander Hamilton was ready to close out the case of *Dred Scott v. Irene Emerson* that had been pending in Hamilton's court for five years "awaiting decision of the Supreme Court of the United States."[58] On March 18, 1857, the court clerk noted:

> Now at this day come the parties aforesaid by their respective attorneys and waiving a jury submit the issues joined between the parties to the court, and the court doth find that the defendant is not guilty in manner and form as in the plaintiff's declaration alleged.[59]

Judge Hamilton, in ruling against the Scotts, simply followed the decision of the United States Supreme Court; Irene Emerson Chaffee was still the master of Dred and Harriet Scott and their daughters. Logically, Irene Chaffee, as victor in the suit, should now have filed a motion by her attorney to reclaim her slaves from the sheriff in whose custody they were being held, and also to claim the slaves' wages for their seven years under court custody. This is what she did so promptly in 1852 after she won victory in the Missouri Supreme Court. The day after that decision, her attorney appeared in Judge Hamilton's court asking for the slaves.[60] Now, in March 1857, no such motion was filed.

The reason for not doing so was obvious. On March 17, 1857, the day when the court met in St. Louis, Irene Emerson Chaffee was probably in seclusion at the home of her husband, U.S. Congressman Calvin Chaffee, in Springfield, Massachusetts. The national spotlight of public attention that had been centered for a week on Judge Roger Taney's electrifying decision had suddenly and unexpectedly focused on the Chaffees also. To the shock of almost everyone, they had been exposed as the real owners of America's most famous slave—Dred Scott. Dr. Calvin Chaffee, a Massachusetts congressman, Republican, and avowed abolitionist, suddenly found himself the owner of slaves and the focus of public outrage. Proclaimed the *Springfield Argus,* "All the long years of servitude through which this [Scott] family has been doomed to labor . . . has this hypocrite kept their ownership by his family from the public, while he had profited, not only by their labor, but on the other hand by his extraordinary professions of love for the poor Negro." The *Cleveland Plain Dealer* described Chaffee as a "free soil hypocrite" who by the Supreme Court's decision and "by right of his wife" had been given "the body and blood of Dred Scott and his family."[61] Similar disparaging commentary appeared in newspapers throughout the country.

58. Record book 24, November term 1853, SLCC.
59. Record book 88, 163, SLCC.
60. The court records do not mention the name of Mrs. Chaffee's attorney. Typescript copy of notice to the circuit court dated March 23, 1852, Irene Emerson by her attorneys, Dred Scott Collection, MHS.
61. Chaffee was a member of the 34th Congress and for twenty years "had held an Honorable record as an anti-slavery man." Biography of Calvin Chaffee. Springfield vertical file.

The only thing that might further have outraged the public and added to the Chaffees' disgrace would have been the appearance of an attorney in court in St. Louis to lay claim to Irene Chaffee's slaves and their wages. Had this occurred, the press—and the congressman's Democratic opponents—would have had a field day. Quite clearly, Congressman Chaffee had to do something with the slaves he owned in St. Louis.[62]

To Roswell Field, it was probably evident why Irene Chaffee's attorney did not file a motion to claim her slaves. It was also clear to Field that there was only one option open to the Chaffees, and that was to get rid of their slaves as quickly and humanely as possible, thus sparing themselves further public embarrassment.

Throughout the whole ruckus, Irene Chaffee remained silent, leaving it to her husband to defend himself as best he could. Congressman Chaffee wrote the *Springfield Republican,* claiming that John Sanford, his wife's brother, was the only person who had any power in the matter and that "neither myself nor any member of my family were consulted in relation to, or even knew of the existence of the suit till after it was noticed for trial, when we learned it in an accidental way."[63] The explanation had a rather weak ring to it.

In the weeks that followed, as the press continued its attacks upon Congressman Chaffee, deliberations took place in Massachusetts and St. Louis concerning the fate of the slaves. John Sanford, confined in an asylum, was incapable of making any decisions, but negotiations probably took place between Roswell Field in St. Louis and the Chaffee attorneys in Massachusetts, along with the members of the Blow family, the Scotts, and, without doubt, Dr. Chaffee and his wife, Irene. Mrs. Chaffee, it seems, was probably not as willing as her husband to bow to public pressure and give up her slaves, but in the end she apparently consented as long as she could keep the wages the slaves had earned for her during their years of custody under the sheriff.[64]

Since Dr. Chaffee was a Massachusetts resident he could not manumit the Scotts under Missouri law, but two months later in mid-May he signed a quitclaim deed

Connecticut Valley Historical Museum, Springfield, Mass.; In an undated clipping from the *Springfield Republican,* the Chaffees, following the disclosure, said that Dred Scott was not their property. Springfield vertical file, Connecticut Valley Historical Museum, Springfield, Mass., 683; Dr. Chaffee "was denounced from one end of the country to the other, and on the floor of Congress." Springfield vertical file. Connecticut Valley Historical Museum.

62. The episode further underscores the likelihood that John Sanford never actually had title to Dred Scott, and that throughout the entire litigation the slaves remained the property of Irene Emerson. An article in the *St. Louis Daily Evening News* on April 3, 1857, reported that Dred "is anxious to know who owns him, being ignorant whether he is the property of Mrs. Chaffee or Mr. Sanford, though we presume there is no doubt that the former is his real legal owner."

63. *Springfield Daily Republican,* March 16, 1857; Calvin Chaffee claimed that he was totally unaware that the Scotts even existed.

64. Irene Chaffee, in view of the criticism that her husband was living off the labor of slaves, could have allowed the Scotts to retain the wages. Instead, she claimed her legal right to their wages, an action that reveals much about her feelings concerning slavery and the Scotts.

in Massachusetts conveying the slaves to Taylor Blow in St. Louis. Arba Crane in Field's law office drew up the emancipation papers manumitting the slaves, and on May 26, 1857, Dred and Harriet Scott, along with Taylor Blow, appeared before Judge Alexander Hamilton in the St. Louis Circuit Court, where Judge Hamilton declared Dred and Harriet Scott and their two daughters free. The court record read:

> Taylor Blow, who is personally Known to the Court, and acknowledges the execution by him of a Deed of Emancipation to his slaves, Dred Scott, aged about forty eight years, of full negro blood and color, and Harriet Scott wife of said Dred, aged thirty nine years, also of full negro blood and color, and Eliza Scott a daughter of said Dred and Harriet, aged nineteen years of full negro color, and Lizzy Scott, also a daughter of said Dred and Harriet, aged ten years likewise of full negro blood and color.[65]

Quietly, on the following day, as press attention focused on Dred Scott's freedom, Irene Chaffee's attorney appeared in court to claim the wages the Scotts had earned during the seven years they had been held in custody of the sheriff. The clerk noted:

> On motion of defendant's attorney it is ordered that the Sheriff of St. Louis County so render his account to the court of the wages that have come to his hands of the earnings of the above named plaintiff and that said Sheriff do pay to the defendant all such wages that now remain in his hands, excepting all commissions and expenses to which the said Sheriff may be legally entitled.[66]

Since Dred Scott's wages were about five dollars a month, and Harriet's perhaps four dollars, the amount received by Irene Chaffee from the sheriff for the seven years of labor by her slaves probably totaled about $750. Since Dred and Harriet were worth about $350 each on the slave market, their wages equaled or exceeded what Mrs. Chaffee would have received had she sold Dred and Harriet to Bernard Lynch, operator of the slave pen, or auctioned them off. Irene Chaffee later claimed that "she was always in sympathy with the cause of the negro" and that it was she, and not her husband, who had made the decision to free the slaves.[67]

65. Record book 26, 263, SLCC; Taylor Blow also signed bond for one thousand dollars each for Dred and Harriet Scott so that the former slaves could obtain a license from the county to live in Missouri as free blacks. The license was conditioned on their continued "good behavior." Copies of bonds dated May 4, 1858, Dexter P. Tiffany Collection, MHS.

66. Record book 26, 267, SLCC; The St. Louis newspapers did not mention this motion in their daily reporting of happenings in the St. Louis Circuit Court, which probably explains why newspapers in Massachusetts were not aware that the Chaffees were awarded the wages of the slaves.

67. *Springfield Daily Republican,* February 12, 1903. Irene Chaffee apparently believed that the only reason attorneys in St. Louis were assisting Dred Scott was to get his money. By her calculations, the Scotts earned seventeen hundred dollars during their court custody, and Dred also had "between $200 and $300" saved. Her fear apparently was that the Scotts' money would go to Roswell Field and the other attorneys.

The emancipation of Dred Scott on May 26, 1857, made the pages of newspapers throughout the country. In St. Louis, under a headline, "Dred Scott Free At Last, Himself and His Family Emancipated," the *St. Louis Daily Evening News* reported:

This morning Taylor Blow, Esq., appeared in the Circuit Court and entered the emancipation of Dred Scott, his wife Harriet, and his two daughters, Eliza and Jane [*sic*]. The persons thus liberated were conveyed to Mr. Blow by their owner, the Hon. Mr. Chaffee of Massachusetts, for the purpose, as the law of this state on the subject, requires that the emancipation shall be performed by a citizen of Missouri. Dred Scott was originally the slave of Capt. Peter Blow who brought him to this state from Virginia, and the act of liberation was therefore appropriately performed in the names of and of his first master's family. Taylor Blow is one of "them boys" whom Dred says he was "raised" with. So the famous old darkey is free at last. After battling in vain for his freedom for ten years, and at a heavy expense, in the courts of Missouri, and the Supreme Court of the Republic, he has received it as a gift at the hands of his master. His daughters Eliza and Jane [*sic*] were virtually free before, having achieved by their heels what the more conscientious Dred could not secure by ten years of litigation. Their whereabouts have been kept a secret, though no effort has been, and none probably would have been, made to recover them. Their father knew where they were and could bring them back at any moment. He will doubtless recall them now. He might have run away himself, if he had desired, without the slightest apprehension of any attempt being made to re-capture him, but he staked his fate on the result of the famous suit of Scott vs. Sanford, and was determined to abide by that decision, whatever it might be. He is getting to be pretty well advanced in years, and, as a slave, would be estimated at about $350. He can now, if he feels inclined, indulge the desire he formerly expressed to us, of traveling over the North and make a "right smart chance of money" by telling who he is. If he should start out on such a pilgrimage, we bespeak for him the kindest attention from all.[68]

As legal counsel for Dred Scott, there was a final service that Roswell Field performed for his client. He probably got Dred his first real job as a free man. For Dred Scott, it was very likely the first employment he had ever had that allowed him to pocket the money he earned by his own labor.

This job was that of porter at Barnum's Hotel, one of the "widely known hotels of the West," which was located at Second and Walnut Streets. Field had taken his board at this hotel since moving out of the house on South Fifth Street. Field was probably also a good friend of Theron Barnum, the proprietor, who was from Vermont and had arrived in St. Louis in 1840, a year after Field.[69]

Working in the hotel, Dred Scott quickly became a sort of celebrity, pointed out to hotel guests who were eager to know and meet the famous former slave. Scott made friends with not only the guests but also the other workers at the

68. *St. Louis Daily Evening News,* May 26, 1857.
69. Hyde and Conard, *Encyclopedia of the History of St. Louis,* vol. 1, 101; St. Louis city directories for 1859, 1860, 1864, and 1865; Hyde and Conard, *Encyclopedia of the History of St. Louis,* vol. 1, 101.

hotel. Even Theron Barnum's wife took a liking to Scott. When a New York newspaper had photographs of Dred and his family taken by one of the city's finest photographers, J. H. Fitzgibbons, Mrs. Barnum had a copy made for herself. Later the photograph was made into an oil portrait by artist Louis Schultze. It shows Dred Scott as an African American man of small stature, sporting a mustache, red vest, and matching bow tie, with a sort of quizzical look on his face.[70]

After freedom Dred and Harriet Scott lived in a small wooden house protected by a balcony in an alley somewhere off Carr Street: its location, according to one visitor, was "more clearly defined in the plan of the city than on mother earth." Here Harriet supplemented her husband's wages by laundering and ironing clothes, which Dred, when not working at the hotel, delivered to customers in the neighborhood.[71]

Dred Scott lived only a little more than a year after gaining freedom. On September 17, 1858, fifteen months after his emancipation, Scott died of consumption in the little alley house that he and his wife shared. He was buried in the Wesleyan Cemetery on the western fringes of the city. Harriet died shortly thereafter.[72]

70. One biographer, based on unknown sources, says Dred Scott was a "curiosity" at the hotel, and a "lazy porter." Malone, *Dictionary of American Biography,* vol. 16, 489; "To travelers stopping at the hotel he was an object of interest, and he reaped a golden harvest from their generosity." Dred Scott manuscript, T. W. Chamberlain Collection, MHS; *Leslie's Illustrated Newspaper,* June 27, 1857; The portrait was commissioned by African American citizens of St. Louis in 1881 and presented to the Missouri Historical Society. It has been reproduced over the years in countless school textbooks and histories.

71. *Leslie's Illustrated Newspaper,* June 27, 1857.

72. The Methodist cemetery was located on the south side of Laclede Avenue at Grand Avenue. Later, as the city expanded, the cemetery was abandoned; Of Harriet's life after the death of her husband nothing is known. An account says that Harriet died "a few years" after Dred and before the Scott's eldest daughter, Eliza, who died in about 1862 at age twenty-five. Eliza had no children, but Lizzy, the younger of the Scotts' daughters, married Henry Madison and had seven children, several of whose descendants lived in St. Louis a century later. T. W. Chamberlain Collection, MHS.

Epilogue

Friends following Dred Scott's coffin to the grave site on the wooded, gently sloping hillside of the Wesleyan Cemetery in the fall of 1858, and watching as his body was lowered into the brown Missouri clay, could not have envisioned that within three years the same quiet landscape on the western edge of the city would thunder to the tramp of boots as thousands of young men in uniform met there to decide the fate of St. Louis in the Civil War. On May 10, 1861, seven hundred soldiers of the Missouri Volunteer Militia, encamped in a grove of trees adjacent to the cemetery, were captured by federal troops.[1]

By May 1861, Fort Sumter in the harbor of Charleston had fallen to the Confederacy, and eleven states in the South had by then seceded from the Union. The sectional controversy had only worsened, and the court's effort at judicial statesmanship, instead of preventing war, had helped bring it about. The Dred Scott decision demonstrated to Northerners the fixed determination of the South to expand slavery, and solidified their opposition to it. In politics, the Dred Scott decision created division within the old Democratic Party, strengthened the Republican Party, and in the presidential election of 1860, helped bring victory to Abraham Lincoln, who would not defy the Dred Scott decision but committed himself to having it reversed. With Lincoln's election, South Carolina immediately seceded from the Union, unable to abide a president "whose opinions and purposes" were "hostile to slavery."[2]

1. Camp map and surrounding areas, Camp Jackson Collection, MHS; William C. Winter, *The Civil War in St. Louis,* 34; Christopher Phillips, *Damned Yankee: The Life Of Nathaniel Lyon,* 187–90.
2. Hans Christian Adamson, *Rebellion in Missouri,* 2; Hill, *Decisive Battles,* 133; Smith, *Blair Family,* 396; Richard B. Morris, ed., *Encyclopedia of American History,* 228.

In the presidential election in Missouri, Lincoln had but meager support, running last among four candidates, and carrying only two of Missouri's counties, one of them St. Louis County.[3] But in St. Louis, the state's largest city, Lincoln had strong voter support, mainly from German immigrants. He also had allies among many of the city's leaders, who, if not publicly identified as Republicans, were willing to work with the president toward preserving the Union. One of these allies was Roswell M. Field.

By 1861, Field had probably made the transition from the Democratic Party to the Republican. It was probably an evolutionary process. A Union supporter and pro-Benton Democrat in the late 1840s, Field over the next decade probably supported Frank Blair's Free Soil movement and from there became involved in the late 1850s with the Free Democratic Party, along with his friends Congressman Frank Blair, Mayor O. D. Filley, and attorneys Edward Bates and Samuel T. Glover. In the winter of 1860 and 1861, the Free Democratic Party in Missouri became the Republican Party.[4]

When war between the states broke out in 1861, it probably came as no surprise to Field. As attorney in the Dred Scott case, Field was well aware that the judicial bonds that had united the states since the nation's founding, had, in the years before the Civil War, greatly deteriorated.[5] When the Missouri Supreme Court in its decision in the Dred Scott case in 1852, nine years before the outbreak of war, ruled that the states were "possessed with a dark and fell spirit" and that Missouri as a sovereign state had "the right" to determine "how far, in the spirit of comity, it will respect the laws of other states," the United States of America, according to one historian, was "well on its way to dissolving the judicial and legal bonds" that held the nation together. The secession of states in 1861 simply "completed that process."[6] Preservation of the Union—along with comity—was not a *new* battle for Roswell Field, but a continuation of one he had waged for years on behalf of his client Dred Scott.

Field's commitment to the Union was strong, as clearly evidenced by the attorneys with whom he chose to be most closely associated in his law practice. After his arrival in St. Louis, Roswell Field allied himself with attorneys who supported the Union, most notably Senator Thomas H. Benton, Hamilton Gamble, Edward Bates, Alexander Hamilton, and Montgomery Blair. Many of these men were Southerners by birth, and some were slave-owners, but all had taken a public stand for the Union. Another ardent pro-Union group in St. Louis were the German immigrants, and Field probably had friendships with many of them. When Field first arrived in St. Louis, he chose to live with a German family. He also spoke

3. Bonnie Murphy, "Missouri, A State Asunder," 29; Merkel, *Anti-Slavery Controversy,* 29.
4. James Peckham, *Gen. Nathaniel Lyon and Missouri In 1861,* x.
5. Finkelman, *Imperfect Union,* 182.
6. 15 *Missouri Reports,* 368, MSC; Finkelman, *Imperfect Union,* 190.

the language fluently, and often frequented, it was said, the many German beer gardens in the city.[7]

However, in the winter of 1860 and 1861 most Missourians were neither pro-Union Republicans nor secessionist Democrats. These two parties represented political extremes, and in 1861 Missourians were seeking ways to compromise and avoid war. In the presidential election, John C. Breckinridge, the pro-Southern candidate, fared little better than Lincoln. The majority of Missouri voters favored the middle-of-the-road candidates, Stephen Douglas and John Bell, who together reaped more than 70 percent of the state vote.[8] Most of all, Missourians in 1861 wanted to stay out of the sectional conflict, which perhaps explains why so many applauded the action of the state's pro-Southern governor, Claiborne Fox Jackson, when he denied President Lincoln's request for Missouri troops to help put down the "insurrection" following the fall of Fort Sumter. Jackson termed Lincoln's request "illegal, unconstitutional and revolutionary" and furthermore, "inhuman and diabolical."[9]

The President's request, however, did not go unfulfilled. In St. Louis, Republican Congressman Frank Blair, whose brother Montgomery was now serving as postmaster-general in the president's cabinet, offered ten thousand troops made up of Union loyalists he had been slowly, and secretly, organizing. Obviously pleased by the offer, the War Department in Washington immediately issued orders to U.S. Captain Nathaniel Lyon, stationed at the federal arsenal in St. Louis, to enroll the men, and commissioned Frank Blair as colonel of the volunteers. Within days, more than ten thousand troops, mostly Germans from St. Louis, were recruited.[10]

In these events, Roswell Field played an active role. According to Melvin L. Gray, Field's good friend and fellow attorney, Field, "on the outbreak of the Civil War . . . was a loyal supporter of the government and an active co-laborer with Lyon, Blair, Glover and others, in retaining Missouri in the Union." Gray was certainly in a position to know. As early as May 1860, a year before the war, Gray was secretary of the executive committee of the Union Club, a secret organization of

7. An entry in Judge William B. Napton's journal for 1869 notes that Field spent his time "drinking lager beer" and "lounging at German beer houses." Journal, William B. Napton Papers, MHS.

8. John McElroy, *The Struggle for Missouri,* 21; "The vast majority of Missourians revealed a desire for compromise on the great issues facing the nation. They had overwhelmingly rejected the candidates of the sectional parties." William E. Parrish, *A History of Missouri, Volume III, 1860–1875,* 3.

9. Robert Rombauer, *The Union Cause in St. Louis in 1861,* 180.

10. Arthur Roy Kirkpatrick, "Missouri on the Eve of the Civil War," 238; "The President of the United States directs you to enroll in the military service of the United States the loyal citizens of St. Louis and vicinity, not exceeding with those heretofore enlisted, ten thousand in number." Copy of letter dated April 30, 1861, from L. Thomas, Adjutant General, Washington, to Captain Nathaniel Lyon, St. Louis. James D. Broadhead Papers, MHS; Kirkpatrick, "Missouri on the Eve," 138.

Union loyalists with chapters throughout the city. As secretary, Gray was responsible for the organization's membership roles, secret ritual, passwords, and the "cypher system" for the club's correspondence. Meeting secretly in Gray's law office at 26 North Fifth Street, the executive committee established networks of supporters and recruited members in St. Louis and rural Missouri. Providing protection from pro-Southern rowdies who often congregated outside Gray's office, a semi-military group known as the "Wide Awakes" stood guard at the entrances, armed with lanterns on the end of strong sticks. The group was created by Frank Blair, who also organized more highly trained military units called the "Union Guards," consisting predominantly of Germans. The Union Guards met regularly throughout the city at such locations as Washington Hall, Winkelmeyer's Brewery, Filley's foundry, and Yaeger's Garden where the men secretly drilled and received instructions on arms. When Lincoln's call for troops came, most of the members of the Union Guard responded.[11]

While the secessionists in St. Louis were not as numerous as the Union loyalists, they also had their military units. Called the "Minute Men," these units were chartered by the State of Missouri and operated under state militia laws. For that reason they did not have to meet in secret as did the Union groups, and from the Minute Men's headquarters in the Berthold mansion on the northwest corner of Fifth and Pine, the flag of the Confederacy was prominently flown; young Southern men often stood at the entrance leading cheers for Jefferson Davis and General Beauregard.[12]

While Field, as Gray states, was a "co-laborer" with Blair, Lyon and Glover, he was certainly not as prominent in the Union movement as they were, nor as well known to the public. Field's distaste for positions of leadership, and his avoidance of any elected or appointed office, perhaps helps to explain this obscurity. Another

11. Gray, "Recollections," 128; An embellished version was published in Vermont in 1877, and read, "In the dark days of the rebellion, during the years 1861 and 1862, when friends of the Union in St. Louis and Missouri felt they were in imminent danger of being driven from their homes and estates confiscated by rebels and traitors, Gen. Lyon, Gen. Blair and R. M. Field were among the calm, loyal and patriotic men who influenced public action and saved the city and state." *Newfane's First Century*, 48; Records of the Executive Committee, State Union Club of Missouri Minute Book, MHS; Civil War Collection, MHS; "At the first two meetings which the *Wide Awakes* thus attended, the enemy, not understanding the purposes of the club, began their usual serenade of yells and cheers, but they were speedily initiated into the mysteries of the new order; which initiation consisted in being besmeared with burning camphene, and vigorously beaten with leaded sticks." Peckham, *Lyon and Missouri*, xiii; March, *History of Missouri*, vol. 2, 864; Rombauer, *Union Cause*, 189.

12. The Minute Men "regretted the determination of the Cotton States to secede. They would rather have had them remain within the Union, and fight within it for their constitutional rights. But they believed nevertheless that these States had the right to secede and to establish a separate Government if they chose to do so." The God-given right of revolution, they held, was the same natural right to which "the Republic owes its existence." Thomas L. Snead, *The Fight for Missouri*, 107; Peckham, *Lyon and Missouri*, 30.

explanation may lie in the secrecy surrounding most of the pro-Union activities, and the absence of written records and public notices. Unionist meetings, as one observer noted, "were always held in secrecy."[13]

The top decision-making body within the Union loyalists was the "Committee of Safety," which comprised six prominent men: Mayor O. D. Filley, John How, Samuel T. Glover, James O. Broadhead, and J. J. Witzig, along with Frank Blair as leader. These men directed Unionist activities in St. Louis and developed plans and strategy for keeping Missouri in the Union fold—all "prosecuted with the utmost secrecy." Furthermore, the Union Committee of Safety had authority to issue directives to Captain Nathaniel Lyon at the St. Louis Arsenal. Lyon had been told by President Lincoln to work with the committee in "maintaining the authority of the United States and for the protection of the peaceable inhabitants of Missouri." The Committee of Safety was probably the group with which Roswell Field worked as a "co-laborer," perhaps in some legal capacity. Given Field's fluency in the German language, the committee may also have looked to Field to work with leaders in the German community, for the Germans constituted not only the majority of pro-Union men in the city but also most of the military volunteers, and also, as Congressman Blair and President Lincoln were no doubt aware, the bulk of Missouri's Republicans.[14]

In the spring of 1861, of major concern to President Lincoln and the Department of the Army, and certainly to Captain Lyon and Frank Blair, was the St. Louis

---

13. Peckham, *Lyon and Missouri,* 31.

14. Ibid., 32; "Blair's strong convictions, fearless utterance and oratorical power brought him to the front among a number of able men in his party, and his family connections in Washington and the East gave him a far reaching influence in shaping the Union movement in St. Louis, although the very great majority of Republicans in St. Louis were naturalized citizens, chiefly Germans, who lifted him on their shoulders in the commencement of his political career." Rombauer, *Union Cause,* 105; Blair also had the support of the city's free blacks. Notes Clamorgan, "The colored men of St. Louis have no votes themselves, but they control a large number of votes at every election. Many of them own houses which are rented to white voters, and others trade extensively with white dealers. It is an easy matter for them to say to their tenants, 'Mr. Blair and Mr. Brown are our friends—vote this ticket or seek another place of abode.' It is no less easy for them to tell the merchant that, unless he votes for certain men, he will lose a large custom." Christensen, "Cyprian Clamorgan," 13; Peckham, *Lyon and Missouri,* 33; A letter dated June 4, 1861, addressed to Simon Cameron, Secretary of War, and signed by the six members of the Committee of Safety, begins, "The undersigned, a Committee of Safety appointed by the Union men of St. Louis, to look after their interests in the present contest, deem it proper to make a suggestion to you." James O. Broadhead Papers, MHS; Winfield Scott in Washington to Captain Lyon in St. Louis, April 30, 1861, James O. Broadhead Papers, MHS; President Lincoln in this order also authorized Captain Lyon to "proclaim martial law in St. Louis" if Lyon deemed it necessary. Lincoln Collection, MHS; If Field's role was that of influencing public action, the German Americans certainly would have been a key constituency. Field may have been looked upon by St. Louis leaders as an authority on the Germans. An 1869 entry by Judge Napton in his journal quotes Field's opinion of Carl Schurz, Missouri senator, as a "German Revolutionist." Journal, William B. Napton Papers, MHS.

Arsenal, located on the banks of the Mississippi on the southern edge of the city. Stored here were 30,000 rifles, carbines, and muskets; 150,000 ball cartridges; scores of field pieces; 50 tons of gunpowder; and $400,000 in gold bullion in the vaults.[15] With pro-Southerners in control of the Missouri statehouse, President Lincoln, after what had happened at Fort Sumter, had grounds for concern.

Governor Jackson's Southern sympathies were well known, and in the early months of 1861 he had been corresponding with Confederate leaders in the South. He also requested military supplies from Virginia and the Confederate government at Montgomery, and both of them responded with guns and field pieces. In April 1861, Governor Jackson wrote, "Missouri should act in concert with Tennessee and Kentucky. They are all bound to go out and should go together if possible. My judgment is that N. Carolina, Tennessee and Arkansas will all be out in a few days, and when they go, Missouri and Kentucky must follow. Let us then prepare to make our exit."[16]

Therefore, in May 1861, when General Daniel M. Frost set up the annual encampment of the Missouri State Militia in a grove of trees on the western edge of St. Louis and named it Camp Jackson in honor of the governor, Captain Lyon and Frank Blair's Committee of Safety viewed the presence of the state militia troops as a threat to the St. Louis Arsenal. After a hurried night meeting of the Committee on May 9, 1861, ten thousand U.S. troops under Captain Lyon marched the next morning through the streets of St. Louis to Camp Jackson, where the seven hundred state militia troops, totally outnumbered, surrendered without firing a shot. The incident did not end without bloodshed, however. As Captain Lyon's troops marched back into the city with their prisoners along the Olive Street Plank Road, thousands of curious spectators lined the route. Gunshots rang out, a federal soldier was wounded, and several federal soldiers opened fire into the crowd. By the time order was restored, twenty-eight were dead, including several women and children. As the troops entered the center of the city, the sidewalks were deserted, doors were closed and windows shuttered, and not until the troops reached the German section of South St. Louis were flags seen flying. Throughout the remainder of the day violence, including shootings, continued throughout the city, and the next day, amid rumors that the German soldiers had revolted and were about to sack the city, a frenzied exodus began with people seeking every available boat and wagon they could find, many in such panic that they left the windows and doors of their houses open in their rush to escape.[17] It was days before some semblance of calm returned.

15. Snead, *Fight for Missouri*, 101.

16. March, *History of Missouri*, vol. 2, 12; "Virginia authorized the sending of twenty-two guns. Jefferson Davis ordered two 12-pound howitzers and two 32-pound guns sent to Frost." Parrish, *History of Missouri*, 12; Copy of letter dated April 28, 1861, from Governor Jackson to J. W. Tucker, James O. Broadhead Papers, MHS.

17. *The Last Political Writings of Gen. Nathaniel Lyon*, 42; March, *History of Missouri*, vol. 2, 873; Van Ravenswaay, *Informal History*, 487–89.

Captain Lyon's action was not a popular one with some St. Louis citizens. Many directed their anger at the Unionists, denouncing "the ambition, self-will and dominating spirit of Francis P. Blair, Jr., and his political confederates." Wrote one Southerner from St. Louis, "Frank Blair is a dictator. My blood boils when I think of the position of Missouri—held in the Union at the point of Dutchmen's bayonets."[18]

One last effort was made to achieve peace in Missouri. A month after the capture of the state troops at Camp Jackson, Governor Jackson came to St. Louis to meet with Captain Lyon. After a four-hour meeting between the two men and their staffs in a hotel room at the Planter's House, no agreement was reached. Abruptly Captain Lyon ended the meeting with these words:

> Rather than concede to the State of Missouri the right to demand that my government shall not enlist troops within her limits, or bring troops into the state wherever it pleases, or move its troops at its own will into, out of, or through the state, rather than concede to the State of Missouri for one single instant the right to dictate to my government in any matter, however unimportant, I would (rising as he said this, and pointing in turn to everyone in the room) see you, and you, and you, and you, and you, and every man, woman, and child in the state, dead and buried.[19]

The governor and his staff left immediately, and boarding a train that was waiting at the Pacific Railroad Station, raced for the state capital at Jefferson City, a hundred miles west, stopping twice along the way: once at the Osage River and again at the Gasconade River, where they set fire to the railroad trestles to prevent pursuit by Union troops. Arriving in Jefferson City at 2 A.M., they packed public records and papers in crates, emptied the state treasury of $635,081.37, abandoned the capital, and fled south.[20]

The Union loyalists, with Missouri for the most part safely under the control of U.S. troops and the state no longer likely to secede, turned their interests to another issue of great importance to their cause—the matter of the emancipation of Missouri's slaves. On this controversial issue, however, a division of opinion among the Unionists very quickly developed. One observer commented:

> In our hot fight for Missouri and the Union we unhappily split into factions. We not only contended against secession but against each other. And the warring factions were significantly named Charcoals and Claybanks. The Charcoals taken as a whole were uncompromising radicals, while the Claybanks were the conservatives.[21]

18. *Missouri Republican,* May 14, 1861; Letter of Mrs. Charles Parsons to sister in Keokuk, May 20, 1861, Civil War Collection, MHS.

19. Quote of Thomas L. Snead, aide-de-camp to the governor, in Kirkpatrick, "Missouri on the Eve," 243.

20. Ibid., 244; State Treasurer's Report, July 27, 1861, Capitol Fire Collection, Missouri State Information Center, Jefferson City, Mo.

21. Galusha Anderson, *The Story of a Border City during the Civil War,* 276.

In this controversy Roswell Field gave his allegiance and support to the Radi-cals.[22] While both groups supported the Union, they differed on when and how slaves in Missouri should be emancipated. The Radicals contended that, since slavery was the cause of the rebellion, it should therefore be abolished as quickly as possible. Conservatives, on the other hand, favored gradual emancipation over a period of years, with some urging compensation to masters who willingly freed their slaves. The issue was complicated by the fact that some loyal Unionists were also slave-owners, and some were even proslavery. The controversy was not to be easily resolved, and it dominated Missouri politics throughout the war. Only in the later months of the conflict was the issue finally resolved. In January 1865, a state convention meeting at the Mercantile Library in St. Louis reached an agreement, and on January 11, Governor Thomas C. Fletcher, a Radical like Field, issued a proclamation granting freedom to every Missouri slave.[23]

> It having pleased Divine Providence to inspire to righteous action, the sovereign people of Missouri, who, through their delegates in convention assembled, with proper legal authority and solemnity, have this day *Ordained,* That hereafter, in this State, there shall be neither slavery nor involuntary servitude, except in punishment of crime, whereof the party shall have been duly convicted; and all persons held to service or labor as slaves are hereby declared free.[24]

Roswell Field's activities in support of the Radical movement during the war years, like his earlier activities with the Union loyalists, are unknown. Whatever he did, however, must have pleased the Radicals and Governor Fletcher. Shortly after the emancipation proclamation was issued, the governor offered Roswell Field the position of justice on the Missouri Supreme Court. As might be expected, Field declined the appointment. His friend Melvin Gray gave as the reason Field's preference for "the freedom and independence of private citizenship to official station."[25]

22. Judge William Napton describes Field as a "leading radical." Journal, William B. Napton Papers, MHS.

23. Merkel, *Anti-Slavery Controversy,* 31–36, 46.

24. Ibid., 47.

25. Gray, "Recollections," 128; Field may have foreseen the problems ahead. Governor Fletcher, acting on the authority of a state act (February 13, 1864) passed by the Radicals, ousted from office the entire judiciary in the state. Three new supreme court justices were appointed, but the former justices refused to give up their positions, claiming they were still legally in office. With two sets of justices meeting at two different locations on the same day (June 14, 1865), the governor called upon the state militia and local St. Louis police to remove bodily the old justices from the courtroom, and they were arrested and jailed. The incident is covered in 35 *Missouri Reports* (Preface), and 36 *Missouri Reports,* 144–59 (*James S. Thomas v. Andrew W. Mead and James C. Moodey*). Field participated as one of several attorneys in the resulting litigation. The incident is discussed in Dunne's *Missouri Supreme Court,* 59–63.

A little later, Roswell Field was considered as a candidate for the United States Senate, a post in which he also had no interest. Commented a St. Louis newspaper correspondent:

> [Roswell M. Field] is the Nestor of the Missouri bar, and the legal adviser of the radical party, if it has one. The Democrats sometimes call him the 'head devil of radicalism.' His enunciations, however, in favor of radicalism have all been in the form of legal opinions which have so frustrated Democratic designs that they give him probably more credit than he deserves, and hence the epithet. He never appears at the hustings, and in fact is a sort of old Diogenes that sticks to his tub till it is time to be in the supreme court, when he comes forth and delivers his profound legal philosophy. He is devoid of ambition—cares not a fig for popular applause, and as for any desire to go to Congress, he would about as soon go to the devil.[26]

The Civil War in St. Louis and Missouri was marked by four years of deprivation and guerrilla warfare, as neighbor was pitted against neighbor, friend against friend, and brother against brother. For the fortunate, the war opened new opportunities for success, prosperity, and public acclaim; for others less fortunate, it brought financial ruin and sometimes death.

After the abortive effort to achieve peace in Missouri in June 1861, General Nathaniel Lyon and his troops pursued the fleeing governor of Missouri, and within a few months Lyon met his death on the battlefield at Wilson's Creek near Springfield. Governor Jackson, with some members of the state government, continued fleeing south to Little Rock, where he died in December 1862. At a stop along the way, he took a vote among the fleeing members of the government and declared the state out of the Union; for his efforts, the South awarded him a star for Missouri in the Confederate flag.[27]

After Governor Jackson's departure, a state convention elected Field's friend, Hamilton Gamble, as provisional governor of Missouri. He held the post until his death in January 1864, when he was mourned as "one of the purest minded, most unselfish and wisest of men."[28]

Frank Blair, leader of the Union cause, resigned his seat in Congress in 1863. Commissioned a major general, he joined the army of General Ulysses S. Grant in the siege of Vicksburg and ultimately followed General William T. Sherman on his march through Georgia. Blair left the Republican Party in 1868, repulsed by what he saw as the party's harsh measures against the defeated Southern states. He later ran unsuccessfully for vice president of the United States on the Democratic ticket

---

26. *Vermont Phoenix,* December 26, 1868, reporting on a news item in the *Springfield Republican.*

27. Murphy, "State Asunder," 112–13; More than forty thousand men from Missouri fought in the Confederate Army during the war.

28. Philips, "Hamilton Gamble," 13; Jackson, *Missouri Democracy,* vol. 1, 153.

with Horatio Seymour; he died in 1873. Blair's brother, Montgomery, remained in Lincoln's cabinet as postmaster-general until he resigned in 1864. He died at his father's estate at Silver Springs, Maryland, in 1883.[29]

As for Dred Scott's friends, Joseph Charless, who posted bond for Scott in 1846, was shot and killed in 1859 on a St. Louis street. His widow, Charlotte Blow Charless, lived to be ninety-five, dying in Louisiana in 1905. Charles Drake, who served as Dred Scott's attorney early in the litigation, became a Republican Radical and the much-despised author of Missouri's oaths of loyalty, which he said were designed to crush the spirit of the "Southern Aristocrats." He died in Washington, D.C., in 1892.[30] Henry Blow, the only one of Peter Blow's sons to support the Union during the Civil War, made a fortune in business, became a strong supporter of President Lincoln, and went off to South America in 1869 as the United States Minister to Brazil. Taylor Blow, considered Dred Scott's strongest supporter and who, in 1857, gave freedom to Dred Scott, remained loyal to the South throughout the war. His once-thriving business came under close military scrutiny during the war and later closed; he filed for bankruptcy in 1867. Taylor Blow died in August 1869, after a long illness.[31]

Two years before he died, however, Taylor Blow, bankrupt and in failing health, moved the body of Dred Scott to a new grave site in Calvary Cemetery. In a beautiful parklike setting, he gave his father's old slave a final resting place among the graves of some of the city's most prominent citizens. The Wesleyan Cemetery, overlooking Camp Jackson, was being abandoned to make way for the westward expansion of St. Louis.[32]

When the Civil War ended in the spring of 1865, Roswell Field was fifty-eight years old. Twenty-six years had passed since he had first arrived on the levee at St. Louis as a young lawyer. During those years he had achieved recognition among his peers at the bar as one of the ablest attorneys in the state. In the crises that faced his country during those same years, he had taken the side of those who favored the Union, and giving his support to that cause, he had witnessed its triumph over the secessionists. Slavery, which Field abhorred and which along with other Radical

29. Hyde and Conard, *Encyclopedia of the History of St. Louis,* vol. 1, 173.

30. Bryan, "Blow Family," pt. 2, 26; Hyde and Conard, *Encyclopedia of the History of St. Louis,* vol. 1, 313; Bryan, "Blow Family," pt. 2, 27; Jackson, *Missouri Democracy,* vol. 1, 153.

31. Hyde and Conard, *Encyclopedia of the History of St. Louis,* vol. 1, 183; *Missouri Republican,* July 16, 1869; Bryan, "Blow Family," pt. 2, 28; *Missouri Republican,* August 21, 1869.

32. Taylor Blow moved Dred Scott's grave to Calvary Cemetery on November 27, 1867. The cemetery, like the adjacent Bellefontaine Cemetery, did not allow burials of African Americans, but did allow families to bury their personal servants. Scott's grave on lot number 177, section 1, remained unmarked and unnoticed for ninety years. In 1957 the grave was found by the Rev. Edward J. Dowling, S.J., of St. Louis while searching cemetery records. That same year a stone was placed on the grave by a granddaughter of Taylor Blow, along with a bronze grave plaque by St. Louis African Americans.

Republicans he had fought to erase, had now ended and those held in bondage had been freed. During those years he had met a woman whom he loved, and by her had fathered six children. Yet, with all these accomplishments and successes, Roswell Field retreated behind a veil of his own making in the years following the Civil War, and separated himself socially from friends and fellow attorneys. Acquaintances said of Field that he "mingled but little in general society," and became "reserved and distrustful."[33]

Whatever the nature of his condition, Field probably brought it upon himself. It was Field's decision to live alone. When Frances died in 1856, he could have sought out another wife and provided a new mother for his children. Second marriages, in view of the high mortality rate among young women of child-bearing age, were often seen as a necessity for widowed men with young children. Field chose not to follow such a course. Furthermore, he decided to send his two sons to the East to live with his sister. Had he so chosen, Field could have kept them in St. Louis with him, or followed after them and practiced law once again in New England. He could have practiced with his brother Charles or his friend Jonathan Bradley in Brattleboro. For whatever reasons, he did not do so.

There may have also been some other reasons for Field's melancholy. For one thing, Field may have found his practice of the law less challenging than it had been. The large land cases in which Field specialized, and by which he had achieved his reputation as a lawyer, had all but disappeared by 1865. Also, St. Louis was rapidly expanding, and Field, who cherished the rural life lauded by the Latin poet Horace, may have felt less at home in the city. The population of St. Louis, which was fifteen thousand in 1839 when Field arrived, had increased twentyfold by 1865 to almost three hundred thousand, and the stately mansions that reflected the city's more leisurely Southern heritage were "giving way to warehouses and railroad yards."[34]

During those years, if anything gave meaning to Field's life and enriched his later years, it was the affection he had for his two sons, Eugene and Roswell, and his interest as a father in stimulating and guiding their intellectual growth, particularly in literature and the classics. Throughout their twelve years of separation, as the two boys grew to maturity, Field made frequent trips to visit them in Amherst,

33. Pierce, *Field Genealogy,* vol. 1, 510; In 1901, a historical novel set in St. Louis during the Civil War entitled *The Crisis* was published. The author was a St. Louis novelist named Winston Churchill. While the author claimed that the characters were fictional, newspapers in St. Louis and Vermont (*St. Louis Globe Democrat,* January 7, 1917, and *Vermont Phoenix,* May 15, 1903) reported that the main character in the novel, Judge Silas Whipple, was patterned after Roswell Field. The book was very popular, selling 320,000 copies the first year, and was made into a silent motion picture in 1917. The similarity of events in the novel to actual situations in Roswell Field's life are too exact to be pure coincidence. Since Churchill was born in 1871 after Field's death, the *Globe-Democrat* speculated that Churchill "probably obtained his impressions" from an aunt who raised him. Another source might have been Arba Crane, who worked in Field's law office and died in 1904. Winston Churchill, *The Crisis.*

34. Van Ravenswaay, *Informal History,* 556.

and he brought them to St. Louis for visits at every opportunity. In between, he maintained a steady correspondence with both.

The departure of his sons in 1857 was undoubtedly a sad moment in Field's life, which may help explain why, of all the letters received from his sons, he treasured one letter that Eugene wrote to him shortly after the boys left St. Louis for Massachusetts with their cousin Mary. The letter, written from Chicago and folded and refolded so frequently that it eventually fell to pieces, read:

> Dear Papa—We got here safely at 5 o'clock this morning. I was so tired then that I had to go right to bed so I could not write to you Papa until this afternoon. We were delayed more than 4 hours between Gerard & Springfield by an accident on the train from Chicago to St. Louis . . . . We ate all our basket of fodder . . . . Mr. Everett who was in the same car with us gave us some sandwiches when we were too noisy. Cousin Mary says that she guesses he thinks that the seat of our affections is in our stomach . . . . This is a nice hotel and we have a large room with two beds and we have taken a nap today. Papa, I miss you very much. Please write to me very soon. Say Goodbye to Mr. Crane. . . . I would send you a lock of my hair Papa but I am afraid of cutting any of it off I shall catch cold. Goodbye Papa, Your son Geny. Rosy sends love, and so does Cousin Mary.[35]

As heartsick as Field likely felt when his sons departed, and as lonely as he probably was without them, he was probably buoyed by his certainty that sending his sons to live with his sister was in the long run best for them. In Amherst, Eugene and Roswell's needs would be lovingly met by Field's sister and niece, and their education enhanced in an environment where intellectual curiosity was encouraged.

Two years earlier, in 1855, Field's sister, Mary, after her second husband died, had moved to the college town of Amherst. Here, in a large colonial house on Amity Street overlooking the Hadley meadows and the hills of Berkshire, Mary quickly achieved a leading position in Amherst society, and established her home as a meeting place for the brightest minds of the college and community. Described as a "lady of rare intellectual ability, beautiful character, generous heart and charming courtesy," Mary Jones was also "a good business woman" like her mother, Esther Field. Mary kept current with the commercial and financial news of the day, and managed her estate with "shrewdness and success." She also was considered "a voracious reader of books," and well versed in Ralph Waldo Emerson's philosophy and Samuel Bowles's political essays.[36]

In Amherst at the time, there were six chief social rendezvous where young men of the college congregated. Foremost in prestige was that of Mrs. Austin

35. Undated letter from Eugene Field to his father Roswell Field, Collections, Eugene Field House and Toy Museum, St. Louis, Mo.
36. Undated letter from John W. Burgess to the Jones Library in Amherst, Mass., Field Collection, JL; Martin Field's will left all of his books to his daughter, with the exception of his law books and his books on science.

Dickinson, but second in rank among the students was the home of Roswell's sister, Mary Jones. Her home was well known for its hospitality to students and professors, and was also frequently visited by distinguished alumni of the college, such as Henry Ward Beecher and Frederick D. Huntington. One Amherst student later recalled:

> Mrs. Jones was an exceedingly interesting conversationalist. . . . In this house one also met the most distinguished alumni of Amherst, and there seemed to be no limit to the hospitality dispensed by Mrs. Jones and her two daughters. They conducted a veritable salon and exerted a great and beneficial influence on the education of the students in manners and behavior.[37]

Until Roswell Field's sons left for college in the late 1860s, and except for visits to St. Louis and to see their grandmother in Newfane, Mary Jones's house in Amherst was home to the Field boys. For more than a decade they spent their youth and grew to maturity there, raised as wards of their unmarried cousin, Mary Field French, who looked after them as if they were her children. Years later, Eugene Field, in a volume of poetry called *A Little Book Of Western Verse,* wrote a dedicatory poem to his cousin, to whose home he was taken as a young child.

> A dying mother gave to you
> Her child a many years ago;
> How in your gracious love he grew,
> You know, dear, patient heart, you know.
>
> The mother's child you fostered then
> Salutes you now and bids you take
> These little children of his pen
> And love them for the author's sake.
>
> To you I dedicate this book,
> And, as you read it line by line,
> Upon its faults as kindly look
> As you have always looked on mine.
>
> Tardy the offering is and weak;
> Yet were I happy if I knew
> These children had the power to speak
> My love and gratitude to you.[38]

During the long periods in between the visits of the father to Amherst and the sons' visits to St. Louis, letters helped shorten the distance between them. Most, if not all, of these letters were written in Latin, a language Roswell Field early

---

37. John W. Burgess, *Reminiscences Of An American Scholar,* 62–63.

38. First published in 1889, the poem was reprinted in 1896 in *The Collected Works of Eugene Field,* vol. 1, v.

on established as the one they would use in their correspondence. The intent quite clearly was to make his sons proficient in Latin, although this practice also harkens back to Roswell Field's youth when he sometimes corresponded with his brother Charles or his friend Jonathan Bradley in Latin or Greek, usually when discussing young ladies of common acquaintance. Field's strategy to make his sons proficient in Latin apparently was successful, for years later Eugene and Roswell coauthored a translation into English of odes by the Latin poet Horace in a book they called *Echoes of the Sabine Farm.* Eugene felt a great personal loss when all of his father's letters, which he had saved, were destroyed in a fire while he was attending college.[39]

Field also seems to have been successful in cultivating within his sons his own personal—almost passionate—affection for books, which had no doubt been passed on to Field by his own father Martin Field. Eugene would later write, "Books, books, books—give me ever more books for they are the caskets wherein we find the immortal expressions of humanity—words, the only thing that live forever."[40] One book that Eugene most treasured was a copy of *Pilgrim's Progress,* of which he later wrote:

> About my favorite copy of the *Pilgrim's Progress* many a pleasant reminiscence lingers, for it was one of the books my grandmother gave my father when he left home to engage in the great battle of life; when my father died this thick, dumpy little volume, with its crude cuts and poorly printed pages, came into my possession. I do not know what part this book played in my father's life, but I can say for myself that it brought me solace and cheer a many a time.[41]

Melvin Gray, who knew Roswell Field and his sons well, years later observed:

> If I had never believed in the influence of heredity before, I would now, after having known Eugene Field and his father before him. The father was a lawyer of wonderful ability, but he was particularly distinguished by his keen wit, his intense appreciation of the humorous side of life, and his fondness for rare first editions of literary works. He was a profound student, and found much time to cultivate the fairer qualities that some lawyers neglect in the busy round of their profession. Eugene is not a lawyer, but he had his father's tastes, his father's wit, and much of the same fineness of character and literary ability.[42]

39. *Vermont Reformer,* April 10, 1891; Roswell Field to Jonathan Bradley, October 2, 1826, Bradley Collection, The Arthur and Elizabeth Schlesinger Library on the History of Women in America, Cambridge, Mass.; Charles H. Dennis, *Eugene Field's Creative Years,* 17.

40. Eugene Field, *The Love Affairs of a Bibliomaniac,* 61.

41. Ibid., 194; A copy of *Pilgrim's Progress,* published in 1819, is one of Roswell Field's books in the Field Collection, Windham County Historical Society Museum, and may be the same volume referred to by Eugene Field.

42. Slason Thompson, *Study in Heredity,* 47.

Melvin Gray was the executor of Roswell Field's estate, but when Roswell Field drew up his will, he apparently was not quite ready to abdicate his paternal responsibility for properly educating his two sons, or of abandoning, even in death, his role in guiding their educational development. Therefore, though an executor alone would have been sufficient since both sons were by then adults, Field provided each son with an educational guardian. For Roswell, the younger of the two, Field selected his good friend Judge Alexander Hamilton, whose interests in literature so closely paralleled those of his own. For Eugene, the father appointed a young Amherst student, John W. Burgess, whom Field had probably met during one of his visits to see his sons. Burgess graduated, then taught at Knox College in Illinois, and later achieved distinction as Professor of History at Columbia University.[43]

After the Civil War, the number of legal cases Field handled significantly decreased, and by 1868 they were a mere trickle of what he had handled a decade or two earlier. To his friends, Field seemed to be withdrawing even more from social life, rarely venturing out onto the sidewalks of the city except to take infrequent meals at Barnum's Hotel. His visits to Amherst also became less frequent; one of the last trips he made to New England was in 1867, after he received word that his mother had died on June 6 at age eighty-seven. It was Field's last visit to Newfane and the family homestead. Esther Field had occupied the house alone ever since Roswell had left for St. Louis twenty-eight years earlier, and now, after her death, it was to be sold. For Roswell Field this final visit to his family home was clearly a sentimental one. Before leaving and locking the door for the last time, Field asked several neighbor women to prepare his favorite meal for him, cooking it as his mother had done and following her recipes. He also asked that they use the family china and the hand-painted tea service with its little green leaves and pink heart-shaped flowers that his mother had received as a wedding present in 1802. When the meal was ready, Field sat down by himself at the family dining table in the place where he had usually sat as a young man, and slowly ate the food the women had prepared. After finishing, he thanked them and left.[44]

Alexander Hamilton, who probably knew Field as well as anyone, described Field's last two years as ones of "studious seclusion."[45] This observation was very likely an accurate one, for while Field avoided almost all social visits and professional contacts, he surrounded himself with what to him were undoubtedly his most treasured friends—his books.

During the last two years of his life, Field lived on the second or third floor of a brick business building at 318 Market Street near the courthouse. His quarters

43. Field estate papers, SLPC; H. Hale Bellot, *American History and American Historians,* 12.

44. Remarks of Alexander Hamilton, *Missouri Democrat,* July 15, 1869; Charles Kellogg Field III, *Field Family,* 45; Fish, "Roswell Field," 246.

45. *Centennial Proceedings,* 49.

consisted of two rooms: the front, which was a law office; and the rear, which was his bedchamber. All of Roswell Field's books—some two thousand volumes—were located in these two rooms, divided into two main collections as had been the books in his father's library in Newfane—law books in one, and so-called miscellaneous books in the other.[46]

His law books, one of the largest collections in the city, were contained in two large bookcases along the wall of the office, which in addition to a stove, sofa, and light stand, contained a large table and chair, where Field did his legal work.[47]

From the office, a door led to Field's bedchamber in the rear, which contained a walnut bed, three large bookcases, and a secretary desk containing more than one thousand of Field's miscellaneous books. This room also had two lamps and a small stove for warmth in winter.[48]

The miscellaneous books covered a variety of subjects: literature, science, religion, philosophy, politics, history, opera, travel, and poetry. Most were in English, but some were in Spanish, French, German, Italian, Greek, and Latin. Many of the books formed collections, and among these volumes were four of Rousseau's confessions and two on his politics, seventeen of Schiller's works, four on the history of France, four of Don Quixote, ten of Campbell's *Lives of the Chancellors,* nineteen of Swift's works, four of Macaulay's *History of England,* four of Gibbon's Rome, and four of Jefferson's writings. There were also three Bibles—one in English and two in Italian.[49]

By early 1869, Field's friends began to notice a pronounced deterioration in his physical condition, which, given his once-impressive six-foot stature, struck many as alarming. Field appeared to be almost withering away before their eyes. Judge Hamilton urged him to follow the lessons of philosophy that taught the need to look after the health of the body. Melvin Gray encouraged him to get more exercise, and to take walks about the city as he once had. But Field would have none of it. He remained in his rooms for days, alone with his books and relying on his housekeeper, Mary Beatty, to bring in most of his meals.[50] By the spring of 1869, Field had become so weak that he could only get about his two rooms in a wheelchair.

46. St. Louis directories for 1867, 1868, and 1869; Inventory of Field's furnishings, Field estate, SLPC.

47. Ibid.; "The undersigned executor will sell at public auction on Saturday, June 16, 1875, beginning at 11 o'clock a.m. at 517½ Chestnut Street, second floor, the large and valuable law library of the late R. M. Field, Esq., consisting of U.S. Reports and Statutes, Standard American and English Reports, and a large number of valuable treatises on all branches of the law including rare collections of Spanish and civil law." *Missouri Republican,* June 16, 1875.

48. Inventory, Field estate, SLPC.

49. Ibid.

50. Hyde and Conard, *Encyclopedia of the History of St. Louis,* vol. 2, 741; *Centennial Proceedings,* 49; Roswell Field estate papers, SLPC.

Both Hamilton and Gray believed that Field was suffering from "physical exhaustion"—"a wearing out," as Hamilton observed, "of the machine before the end of the term for which its duration was designed." However, unknown to either Hamilton or Gray, Field had a cancer at the lower end of his esophagus that was obstructing the intake of nourishment. Field was suffering from inanition—and was slowly but steadily starving to death.[51]

By the end of June 1869, Field's physical condition had deteriorated so much that he was moved to Sisters' Hospital at Fourth and Spruce Streets, and his sons and brother Charles were summoned from New England.[52]

Judge William Napton, who called on him at the hospital, found Field in bed "nearly blind" and unable to recognize him except by voice. To another friend who visited him, Field confided that he knew he was dying. "I know I shall soon go," Field told him. "The flesh goes first, and then the muscles, and then the vital forces. My flesh is gone, my muscles are going, and my vital forces will soon give way. My friends call here and say to me that I look better, but I know how it is. I am prepared."[53]

On a very hot and humid July 12, Roswell Field, with his sons and his brother Charles at his bedside, died at six o'clock in the evening. Three days later, on July 15, following services at the First Trinitarian Congregational Church, Roswell Field was buried in a grave next to that of his wife Frances in Bellefontaine Cemetery.[54]

For a man who shunned public acclaim throughout his life, the eulogies that followed Roswell Field's death would have been disconcerting. Under bold headlines, the newspapers ran obituaries and biographical sketches terming his death "a great loss" and one that the "community and the members of the bar throughout the Union will read with regret." The *Missouri Republican* observed, "There is no one who will be more widely missed or whose usefulness has been more extensively recognized in our city."[55]

51. *Centennial Proceedings*, 49; Autopsy report on cause of death of R. M. Field, *Missouri Republican*, July 16, 1869. The autopsy was done at the request of Field's brother Charles and conducted by "a well known physician of high standing" to meet the "desire amongst several friends of the late Roswell M. Field to know the exact nature of the disease which proved fatal to him."

52. Scharf, *History of St. Louis City and County*, vol. 2, 1548; Roswell Field estate papers, SLPC.

53. Entry for 1869, Journal, William B. Napton Papers, MHS; *Missouri Democrat*, July 13, 1869.

54. *Missouri Democrat*, July 13, 1869; "The funeral of Roswell M. Field will take place today, July 15, at 2 o'clock p.m., at the Congregational Church, corner Tenth and Locust streets. Friends and acquaintances of the deceased are invited to attend. The pall-bearers are requested to meet at the Sisters' Hospital, southwest corner, Fourth and Spruce at 1 o'clock p.m." *Missouri Democrat*, July 15, 1869; Cemetery records, Bellefontaine Cemetery, St. Louis; The pallbearers were Samuel Treat, S. T. Glover, Albert Todd, M. L. Gray, Alexander Hamilton, T. T. Gantt, Samuel Knox, and L. G. Picot.

55. *Missouri Republican*, July 13, 1869.

Yet almost without exception, the tributes and eulogies also lamented Field's lack of ambition, and his pronounced dislike for honors and recognition. In a resolution presented before the St. Louis bar the day following his death, Colonel T. T. Gantt said, "It is not a paradox to say that if he had been more covetous of gain and of credit, more susceptible to the spur of emulation and less firmly persuaded of the emptiness of the things ordinarily proposed as the rewards of ambition, his life would have been at once happier and useful to mankind." Another attorney said, "If he had possessed more ambition, his reputation would have been national, and he would have ranked among the most distinguished lawyers of the country."[56]

Now after almost a century and a half, what was said of Roswell Field in the days immediately following his death has been forgotten. He, like most of his contemporaries—even those of great ambition and achievement—has become a mere name filed away on index cards and on yellowing scraps of paper in the archives of libraries and museums. Even the laudatory resolutions made before the courts, including the Missouri Supreme Court, have long ago been filed away in musty record books and forgotten.[57] Yet Roswell Field has not been totally lost to posterity.

In Newfane where he was born, and where he lived for half of his life, an oil portrait of Field hangs on the wall behind the judge's bench in the Windham County Courthouse. Here it looks down on the bar before which Roswell Field, then only eighteen years old, stood with his brother and his friend Jonathan Bradley in 1825, seeking authority to practice law.

A thousand miles to the west in St. Louis, where Field spent the other half of his life, a similar portrait hangs over the mantle in the front parlor of the house on South Fifth Street where Field, with his wife and children, enjoyed their happiest years. The house, now a museum, pays tribute to Field's son Eugene, to whom the father passed along his love of children and poetry, and whose verses about Wynken, Blynken, and Nod and the gingham dog and the calico cat have brought smiles to generations of children.

Finally, the memory of Roswell Field lives on in the Old Courthouse in St. Louis, now a National Historic Site, where thousands of visitors daily wander through its historic hallways seeking the place where the famous American slave began his long legal journey in search of freedom and justice. Most have never heard of Roswell Field, but all know the name of Dred Scott. Given Field's dislike for public acclaim, this is probably the way he would have liked it.

---

56. *Missouri Democrat,* July 15, 1869; Pierce, *Field Genealogy,* vol. 1, 510.

57. Resolutions were presented to the Missouri Supreme Court by Samuel Knox, to the U.S. Circuit Court by L. V. Bogy, the U.S. District Court by C. Harding, the St. Louis Circuit Court by J. R. Shepley, and the St. Louis Criminal Court by Charles P. Johnson. *Missouri Democrat,* July 15, 1869.

Bibliography

Primary Sources

Collections

Schlesinger Library, Radcliffe College, Cambridge, Mass.
    Bradley Family Papers
Chicago Historical Society, Chicago, Ill.
    Zebina Eastman Scrapbook of 1878
    Zebina Eastman Collection
Connecticut Valley Historical Museum, Springfield, Mass.
    Springfield Vertical File
Eugene Field House and Toy Museum, St. Louis, Mo.
Jones Library, Amherst, Mass.
    Field Family Collection
Library of Congress, Washington, D.C.
    Blair Family Papers
Missouri Historical Society, St. Louis, Mo.
    Bates Family Papers
    St. Louis (Mo.) Board of Education Records
    James O. Broadhead Papers
    Carondelet (Mo.) Collection
    T. W. Chamberlain Collection
    Chouteau Family Papers
    Civil War Collection
    First Trinitarian Congregational Church of St. Louis Minute Book
    John F. Darby Papers

Dred Scott Collection
Hamilton R. Gamble Papers
William Carr Lane Papers
John B. C. Lucas Family Papers
Ludlow–Field–Maury Family Papers
Mullanphy Family Papers
William B. Napton Papers
Slaves and Slavery Collection
Dexter P. Tiffany Collection
State Union Club of Missouri Minute Book
Wills Collection
Missouri State Information Center, Jefferson City, Mo.
Capitol Fire Collection
Starr Library, Middlebury, Vt.
Executive Government Proceedings of Middlebury College
Vermont Historical Society, Montpelier, Vt.
Kellogg Family Collection
Phelps Collection
Windham County Historical Society, Newfane, Vt.
Field Family Collection
General Newfane Collection

Court Cases and Documents

Marlboro District Probate Court, Brattleboro, Vt.
Field, Martin, will and estate (1834)
Missouri Supreme Court, Jefferson City, Mo.
Beaupied v. Jennings, 28 Missouri Reports
Cutter v. Waddington, 22 Missouri Reports
Scott v. Emerson, 11 Missouri Reports
Scott v. Emerson, 15 Missouri Reports
Winny v. Whitesides, 1 Missouri Reports
St. Louis Circuit Court, Mo.
Diana, woman of color v. McConnell (1840)
Dred Scott v. Emerson (1846)
Harriet, woman of color v. Emerson (1846)
James of color v. Cordell (1844)
Josiah Cephas v. McConnell (1840)
Martha Ann, woman of color v. Cordell (1844)
St. Louis Probate Court, Mo.
Blow, Peter, estate (1832)
Emerson, John, estate (1844)
Field, R. M., estate (1869)

Field, R. M., guardianship (1869)

Sanford, Alexander, estate (1848)

United States District Court, Eastern Missouri Division, St. Louis, Mo.

 Dred Scott v. John F. A. Sanford (1853)

 Dred Scott file, court archives.

United States Supreme Court, Washington, D.C.

 Dred Scott v. John F. A. Sandford, case 3230, docket G.

 Proceedings of the Court, library archives

Vermont Supreme Court, Montpelier, Vt.

 Clark et al. v. Field, 6 *Vermont Reports*

 Easterbrook v. Low, 3 *Vermont Reports.*

 Field et al. v. Torrey, 4 *Vermont Reports.*

 Kimball v. Lamson, 3 *Vermont Reports.*

 Torrey v. Field, 5 *Vermont Reports.*

Windham County Court, Vt.

 Burnham v. Nursel, book 11, 315.

 Higgins v. Taggart, book 10, 465.

 State v. Curtis, book 12, 505.

 State v. Scott, book 12, 506.

 Thayer v. Chase, book 10, 386.

 Transfer of Courthouse, book 10, 235.

 Ward v. Briggs, book 10, 401.

 White v. Gillet, book 11, 64.

Other

Bellefontaine Cemetery Records, St. Louis, Mo.

Calvary Cemetery Records, St. Louis, Mo.

Newfane Village Hall, Newfane, Vt.

 Records of deeds.

St. Louis City Hall, St. Louis, Mo.

 Recorder of Deeds.

Secretary of State Archives, Montpelier, Vt.

 A List of the Members of the General Assembly for the Year 1835, ms. Vol. 76.

 Acts and Resolves Passed by the General Assembly of the State of Vermont at the October Session, 1851. Montpelier: E. P. Walton and Son, 1851.

 Directory and Rules of the House of Representatives. Montpelier: Knapp and Jewett, 1835.

 Journal of the General Assembly of the State of Vermont. Middlebury: Knapp and Jewett, 1835.

 Vermont Special Proceedings, vols. 43 and 60.

 Walton's Vermont Register [Legislative]. Montpelier: E. P. Walton, 1836.

United States 1850 Census for Missouri, St. Louis, third ward, slave schedule.

Secondary Sources

Books

A New Fane in the Second Century. Newfane, Vt.: Published for the Village Bi-
   Centennial, 1974.
Adams, James T. *Dictionary of American History.* New York: Charles Scribner's Sons,
   1949.
Adamson, Hans Christian. *Rebellion in Missouri.* Philadelphia: Chilton, 1961.
Anderson, Galusha. *The Story of a Border City during the Civil War.* Boston: Little, Brown,
   1908.
*An Account Of The Life, Trials and Perils of Rev. Elijah P. Lovejoy Who Was Killed By A
   Pro-Slavery Mob At Alton, Illinois The Night Of November 7, 1837.* Reprint, New
   York: August M. Kelley, 1971.
Bay, P. Orman. *The Repeal of the Missouri Compromise, Its Origins and Authorship.*
   Cleveland: Arthur H. Clark, 1909.
Bay, W. V. N. *Reminiscences of the Bench and Bar of Missouri.* St. Louis: F. H. Thomas,
   1878.
Beckley, Rev. Hosea. *The History of Vermont.* Brattleboro, Vt.: George Salisbury, 1846.
Beckwith, Paul. *Creoles of St. Louis.* St. Louis: Nixon-Jones, 1893.
Bellot, H. Hale. *American History and American Historians.* Norman: University of
   Oklahoma Press, 1952.
[Benton, Thomas Hart]. *Historical and Legal Examinations of that Part of the Decision
   of the Supreme Court of the United States in the Dred Scott Case which Declares
   the Unconstitutionality of the Missouri Compromise Act and the Self-Extension of the
   Constitution to Territories, carrying Slavery Along With It.* New York: Appleton and
   Company, 1857.
Borland, Kathryn Kilby. *Eugene Field, Young Poet.* New York: Bobbs-Merrill, 1964.
Bryan, Frank M. *Yankee Politics in Rural Vermont.* Hanover: University Press of New
   England, 1974.
Burnham, Henry. *Brattleboro, Windham County, Vermont.* Brattleboro, Vt.: D. Leonard,
   1880.
Burgess, John W. *The Middle Period, 1817–1858.* New York: Charles Scribner's Sons,
   1897.
————. *Reminiscences of an American Scholar.* New York: Columbia University Press,
   1934.
Burns, James MacGregor. *The Vineyard of Liberty.* New York: Alfred A. Knopf, 1982.
Cabot, Mary Roger. *Annals of Brattleboro.* Brattleboro, Vt.: E. L. Hildreth, 1921.
Catalogue of the Officers and Students of Middlebury College, October, 1821. Middlebury,
   Vt.: Copeland and Allen, 1821.
Catalogue of the Officers and Students of Middlebury College, 1901. College of Middlebury
   Publishers, 1901.
Centennial Proceedings and Other Historical Facts and Incidents Relating to Newfane.
   Brattleboro, Vt.: D. Leonard Steam Job Printer, 1877.

Chambers, William Nisbet. *Old Bullion Benton, Senator from the New West*. Boston: Little, Brown, 1956.

Christensen, Lawrence O. "Black St. Louis: A Study in Race Relations, 1865–1916." Ph.D. diss., University of Missouri, 1972.

Churchill, Winston. *The Crisis*. New York: Grosset & Dunlap, 1901.

Collet, Oscar W. *Index to St. Louis Cathedral and Carondelet Church Records,* vol. 1, typed ms. St. Louis: Missouri Historical Society, 1918.

Collected Works of Eugene Field. New York: Charles Scribner's Sons, 1896.

Conard, Howard L., ed. *Encyclopedia of the History of Missouri*. 4 vols. St. Louis: The Southern History Company, 1901.

Corwin, Edward S. *The Doctrine of Judicial Review.* Gloucester, Mass.: Peter Smith, 1963.

Crowell, Robert L. *Historic Newfane Village*. Newfane: Moore Free Library, 1989.

Cunningham, Mary B., and Jeanne C. Blythe. *The Founding Family of St. Louis*. St. Louis: Midwest Technical Publications, 1977.

Darby, John F. *Personal Recollections*. St. Louis: G. I. Jones, 1880.

Davis, Henry. *Inaugural Oration*. Boston: Farrand, Mallory, 1810.

Dennis, Charles H., *Eugene Field's Creative Years*. New York: Doubleday, Page, 1924.

Dickens, Charles. *American Notes and Pictures From Italy*. London: Macmillan, 1893.

Directory of Windham County Vermont, 1724–1884. Syracuse, N.Y.: Gazeteer and Business Journal, 1885.

Dockow, Ambrose. *Historic Opinions of the United States Supreme Court*. New York: Vanguard Press, 1935.

Dunne, Gerald T. *The Missouri Supreme Court*. Columbia: University of Missouri Press, 1993.

Ehrlich, Walter. *They Have No Rights*. Westport, Conn.: Greenwood Press, 1979.

Ellis, John B. *The Sights and Secrets of the National Capitol*. Chicago: Jones, Junkin and Company, 1869.

Fehrenbacher, Don E. *The Dred Scott Case*. New York: Oxford University Press, 1978.

Field, Charles Kellogg III. *A Genealogical and Biographical History of the Field Family of Massachusetts and Vermont and the French-Henry Families of Virginia and Texas*. Baltimore: Gateway Press, 1985.

Field, Eugene. *The Love Affairs of a Bibliomaniac*. New York: Charles Scribner's Sons, 1896.

Field, Eugene, and Roswell Martin Field. *Echoes from a Sabine Farm*. New York: Charles Scribner's Sons, 1895.

Finkelman, Paul. *An Imperfect Union, Slavery, Federalism and Comity*. Chapel Hill: University of North Carolina Press, 1981.

———. *Slavery in the Courtroom, An Annotated Bibliography of American Cases*. Washington: Library of Congress, 1985.

Finkelman, Paul, ed. *Law, the Constitution and Slavery*. Vol. 2. New York: Garland, 1989.

Foley, William E. *A History of Missouri, Volume I, 1673–1820*. Columbia: University of Missouri Press, 1971.

———. *The Genesis of Missouri from Wilderness Outpost to Statehood*. Columbia: University of Missouri Press, 1989.

Foley, William E., and C. David Rice. *The First Chouteaus, River Barons of Early St. Louis*. Urbana: University of Illinois Press, 1983.

Furnas, J. C. *The Americans, A Social History of the United States*. New York: G. P. Putnam's Sons, 1969.

Genovese, Eugene D. *Slavery in the Legal History of the South and Nation*. In *Law, the Constitution and Slavery*, edited by Paul Finkelman. Vol. 2. New York: Garland, 1989.

Gill, McCune. *The St. Louis Story*. St. Louis: Historical Record Association, 1952.

Gilman, M. D., ed. *The Biography Of Vermont Or A List Of Books And Pamphlets Relating In Any Way To The State*. Burlington, Vt.: Free Press Association, 1897.

Glasman, Paula. "Zebina Eastman, Chicago Abolitionist." Master's thesis, University of Chicago, 1969.

Glimpses of the Past. 10 vols. St. Louis: Missouri Historical Society, 1933–1943.

Greene, Lorenzo, Gary R. Kremer, and Antonio F. Holland. *Missouri's Black Heritage*. Columbia: University of Missouri Press, 1993.

Hall, Kermit L., William M. Wiecek, and Paul Finkelman. *American Legal History*. New York: Oxford University Press, 1991.

Harris, NiNi. *History of Carondelet*. St. Louis: Patrice Press, 1991.

Hemenway, Abby Maria, collator, *Vermont Historical Gazetteer*. Vol. 5. Brandon, Vt.: Mrs. Carrie E. H. Page, 1891.

Hill, Frederick Trevor. *Decisive Battles of the Law*. New York: Harper and Brothers, 1907.

Historic Fort Snelling Chronicles. No. 2. Minnesota Historical Society, 1975.

History of Madison County, Illinois. Edwardsville, Ill.: W. R. Brink Company, 1882.

Holbrook, Stewart H. *Lost Men of American History*. New York: Macmillan, 1946.

Hopkins, Vincent C., S. J. *Dred Scott's Case*. New York: Atheneum, 1967.

Hurt, R. Douglas. *Agriculture and Slavery in Missouri's Little Dixie*. Columbia: University of Missouri Press, 1992.

Hyde, William, and Howard L. Conard. *Encyclopedia of the History of St. Louis*. 4 vols. St. Louis: Southern History Company, 1899.

Jackson, William Rufus. *Missouri Democracy*. Vol. 1. St. Louis: S. J. Clarke, 1935.

Jordan, Winthrop D. *White over Black*. New York: W. W. Norton, 1968.

The Last Political Writings of Gen. Nathaniel Lyon. New York: Rudd and Carlton, 1861.

Lawson, John D., ed. *American State Trials*. Vol. 13. St. Louis: Thomas Law Book Company, 1921.

Longhead, Flora H., ed. *Life, Diary and Letters of Oscar Lovell Shafter*. San Francisco: Blair-Murdoch, 1915.

Lovejoy, Joseph C., and Owen Lovejoy. *Memoir Of The Rev. Elijah P. Lovejoy*. Reprint, New York: Arno Press and The New York Times, 1969.

Ludlum, David M. *Social Ferment in Vermont 1791–1850*. New York: AMSA Press, 1966.

Malone, Dumas, ed. *Dictionary of American Biography,* Vol. 16. New York: Charles Scribner's Sons, 1935.

March, David D. *The History of Missouri.* Vol. 1. New York: Lewis Historical Publishing, 1979.

Mather, Cotton. *Magnalia Christi Americana.* Vol. 2. Hartford: Silas Andrus & Son, 1852.

Maximilian, Prince of Wied. *Travels in the Interior of North America 1832–1834.* In *Early Western Travels 1748–1846,* edited by Reuben Gold Thwaites. Vol. 22. Cleveland: Arthur H. Clark, 1906.

McCandless, Perry. *A History of Missouri, Volume II: 1820 to 1860.* Columbia: University of Missouri Press, 1972.

McCorison, Marcus A. *Vermont Imprints.* Worcester: American Antiquarian Society, 1963.

McElroy, John. *The Struggle for Missouri.* Washington: National Tribune Company, 1909.

McManus, Edgar J. *Black Bondage in the North.* Syracuse, N.Y.: Syracuse University Press, 1973.

Merkel, Benjamin. *The Anti-Slavery Controversy in Missouri, 1819–1865.* St. Louis: Washington University, 1942.

Morris, Richard B., ed. *Encyclopedia of American History.* New York: Harper and Row, 1961.

Neely, Mark E. Jr. *The Last Best Hope of Earth.* Cambridge: Harvard University Press, 1993.

Newfane's First Century. Brattleboro, Vt.: D. Leonard Steam Job Printer, 1877.

Norton, E. T., ed. *Centennial History of Madison County, Illinois and Its People 1812–1912.* Chicago: Lewis Publishing, 1912.

Oberholzer, Emil. "The Legal Aspects of Slavery In Missouri." Master's thesis, Columbia University, 1949.

Parramore, Thomas C. *Southampton County, Virginia.* Charlottesville: University Press of Virginia, 1978.

Parrish, William E. *A History of Missouri, Volume III, 1860–1875.* Columbia: University of Missouri Press, 1973.

Peckham, James. *Gen. Nathaniel Lyon and Missouri in 1861.* New York: American News Company, 1866.

Phelps, James H. *Collections Relating to the History and Inhabitants of the Town of Townshend, Vermont.* Brattleboro, Vt.: Geo. E. Selleck, 1877.

Phillips, Christopher. *Damned Yankee: The Life of Nathaniel Lyon.* Columbia: University of Missouri Press, 1990.

Pierce, Frederick Clifton. *Field Genealogy.* Vol. 1. Chicago: Hammon Press, 1901.

Post, T. A. *Truman Marcellus Post, D.D., A Biography.* Boston: Congregational Sunday School and Publishing Society, 1891.

Primm, James Neal. *Lion of the Valley, St. Louis, Missouri.* Boulder, Colo.: Pruett, 1981.

Rombauer, Robert. *The Union Cause in St. Louis in 1861*. St. Louis: Municipal Centennial Year, 1909.

Rowan, Steven, trans. *Germans For A Free Missouri: Translations From The St. Louis Radical Press*. Columbia: University of Missouri Press, 1983.

St. Louis Directory for the Years 1838–39. St. Louis: Charles Keemle, 1839.

St. Louis Directory for the Years 1840–41. St. Louis: Charles Keemle, 1841.

St. Louis Directory for 1845. St. Louis: James Green, 1844.

St. Louis Directory for the Years 1854–5. St. Louis: Chambers & Knapp, 1854.

Scharf, J. Thomas. *History of St. Louis City and County*. Vols. 1 and 2. Philadelphia: Louis H. Everts, 1882.

Schlesinger, Arthur M. Jr. *History of U.S. Political Parties*. Vol. 1. New York: Chelsea House, 1980.

Siebert, Wilbert H. *Vermont's Anti-Slavery and Underground Railroad Record*. New York: Greenwood, 1969.

Sloss, J. H. *St. Louis Directory for the Year 1848*. St. Louis: Charles and Hammond, 1848.

Smith, Elbert B. *Francis Preston Blair*. New York: The Free Press, 1980.

Smith, William Earnest. *The Francis Preston Blair Family in Politics*. New York: Macmillan, 1933.

Snead, Thomas L. *The Fight for Missouri*. New York: Charles Scribner's Sons, 1886.

Stameshkin, David M. *The Town's College: Middlebury College, 1800–1915*. Middlebury, Vt.: Middlebury College Press, 1985.

Stampp, Kenneth M. *America in 1857, a Nation on the Brink*. New York: Oxford University Press, 1990.

———. *The Imperiled Union*. New York: Oxford University Press, 1980.

Stevens, George E. *A History of Central Baptist Church*. St. Louis: King Publishing, 1927.

Stevens, Walter B., ed. *St. Louis, the Fourth City*. St. Louis: S. J. Clarke, 1909.

Stewart, A. J. D., ed. *History of the Bench and Bar of Missouri*. St. Louis: Legal Publishing, 1898.

Stilwell, Lewis D. *Migration from Vermont*. Rutland, Vt.: Academy Book, 1948.

Story, Joseph. *Commentaries on the conflict of laws, foreign and domestic, in regard to contracts, rights, and remedies, and especially in regard to marriages, divorces, wills, successions, and judgments*. Boston: Little, Brown, 1857.

Story, William W., ed., *The Miscellaneous Writings of Joseph Story*. Reprint, New York: DeCapo Press, 1972.

Swisher, Carl B. *History of the Supreme Court of the United States*. New York: Macmillan, 1974.

Thompson, Slason. *Eugene Field, A Study in Heredity and Contradictions*. New York: Charles Scribner's Sons, 1901.

———. *Life of Eugene Field*. New York: S. Appleton, 1927.

Thompson, Zadock. *History of Vermont*. Pt. 2. Burlington, Vt.: Chauncey Goodrich, 1842.

[Trow, John Towler]. *Alton Trials: Of Winthrop S. Gilman, Enoch Long, Amos B. Roff,*

George H. Walworth, George H. Whitney, William Harned, John S. Noble, James Morris Jr., Henry Tanner, Royal Weller, Reuben Gerry, and Thaddeus B. Hurlbutt; For The Crime Of Riot. New York: Published by John T. Throw, University Press, 1838.

Trexler, Harrison Anthony. *Slavery in Missouri, 1804–1865.* Baltimore: Johns Hopkins Press, 1914.

Tushnet, Mark V. *The American Law of Slavery.* Princeton: Princeton University Press, 1986.

Van Ravenswaay, Charles. *Saint Louis: An Informal History of the City and Its People, 1764–1865.* St. Louis: Missouri Historical Society Press, 1991.

Wade, Richard C. *Slavery in the Cities, The South 1820–1860.* New York: Oxford University Press, 1964.

Walton, E. P., ed. *Records of the Governor and Council of the State of Vermont.* Montpelier, Vt.: Steam Press of Joseph Poland, 1880.

Winter, William C. *The Civil War in St. Louis.* St. Louis: Missouri Historical Society Press, 1994.

Articles

Bryan, John A. "The Blow Family and Their Slave Dred Scott." 2 pts. *Missouri Historical Society Bulletin* 6, no. 5 (July/August 1948).

Christensen, Lawrence O. "Cyprian Clamorgan, The Colored Aristocracy of St. Louis (1858)," *Bulletin of the Missouri Historical Society* 31, no. 1 (October 1974).

Drumm, Stella M. "The Year of the Cholera—1849." In *Glimpses of the Past,* vol. 3. Missouri Historical Society (1936).

Drumm, Stella M., and Charles Van Ravenswaay. "The Old Courthouse." In *Glimpses of the Past,* vol. 8. Missouri Historical Society (January–June 1940).

Ehrlich, Walter. "Dred Scott In History." *Westward* 1, no. 1. St. Louis: Jefferson National Expansion Memorial Historical Association, n.d.

Field, Eugene. "The Woman Who Most Influenced Me." *Ladies Home Journal* 12 (January 1895).

Fish, Judge Frank L. "Roswell M. Field." *Proceedings of the Vermont Historical Society,* 1923.

Foley, William E. "The Lewis and Clark Expedition's Silent Partners: The Chouteau Brothers." *Missouri Historical Review* 77, no. 2 (January 1983).

———. "Slave Freedom Suits before Dred Scott: The Case of Marie Jean Scypion's Descendants." *Missouri Historical Review* 79, no. 1 (October 1984).

Foley, William E., and Charles David Rice. "Pierre Chouteau, Entrepreneur as Indian Agent." *Missouri Historical Review* 72, no. 4 (July 1978).

Forster, Henry A. "Did the Decision in the Dred Scott Case Lead to the Civil War?" *American Law Review* 52, no. 3 (November–December 1918).

Frank, John P. "Edward Bates, Lincoln's Attorney General." *American Journal of Legal History* 10 (1966).

Gray, Melvin L. "Recollections of Judge Roswell M. Field." In *History of the Bench and Bar of Missouri,* edited by A. J. D. Stewart. St. Louis: Legal Publishing, 1898.

Grissom, David M. "Personal Recollections of Distinguished Missourians." *Missouri Historical Review* 14, no. 4 (July 1925).

Hier, Marshall D. "A Hero's Death for a Lawyer, Hamilton Rowan Gamble." *St. Louis Bar Journal* (winter 1989).

———. "Henry S. Geyer's 'Sale of Indulgences,' The 1840 Darmes Case." Pts. 1 and 2. *St. Louis Bar Journal* (summer, fall 1994).

———. "Jackson Resolutions of 1849, Extracts from the Diary of the Author." *Bulletin of the Missouri Historical Society* 5, no. 1 (October 1948).

Holt, Michael F. "The Democratic Party 1828–1860." In Arthur M. Schlesinger Jr., *History of U.S. Political Parties,* vol. 1. New York: Chelsea House Publishers, 1980.

Kirkpatrick, Arthur Roy. "Missouri on the Eve of the Civil War." *Missouri Historical Review* 55, no. 2 (January 1961).

Maltz, Earl M. "Slavery, Federalism, and the Structure of the Constitution." *American Journal of Legal History* 36 (1992).

McDermott, John Francis. "America Vespucci or Abroad In America." *Missouri Historical Society Bulletin* 11, no. 4 (July 1955).

"Memorial Sketch of Mr. Melvin L. Gray." *Missouri Historical Society Collections* 1, no. 7 (October 1906).

Mendelson, Wallace. "Dred Scott Case—Reconsidered." *Minnesota Bar Journal* 38 (1954).

Moore, Robert Jr. "A Ray Of Hope Extinguished." *Gateway Heritage* 14, no. 3 (winter 1993–1994).

Murphy, Bonnie. "Missouri, A State Asunder." *Journal of the West* 14, no. 1 (January 1975).

Philips, Jno. F. "Hamilton Rowan Gamble and the Provisional Government of Missouri." *Missouri Historical Review* 5 (October 1910–July 1911).

Richter, Tom. "If Walls Could Talk: A Courtroom's Story." *Westward* 1, no. 1. St. Louis: Jefferson National Expansion Memorial Historical Association, n.d.

Saunders, A. M. "Newfane, the Beautiful." *The Vermonter* 42, no. 10 (October 1937).

Strickner, Charles P. "Brookline." *Vermont Historical Gazetteer* 5 (1891).

Vishneski, John S. III. "What the Court Decided in *Dred Scott v. Sandford.*" *American Journal of Legal History* 32 (1988).

Wiecek, William M. "Slavery and Abolition before the United States Supreme Court, 1820–1860." In *Law, Constitution and Slavery,* edited by Paul Finkelman. New York: Garland, 1989.

Other

Conley, Melvina. Manuscript, compilation of slave suits for freedom in the St. Louis Circuit Court.

Moore, Robert Jr. Manuscript, research and tabulation of freedom suits, emancipations, and manumissions in the St. Louis Circuit Court.

Index